SPIRAL GUIDES

Travel With Someone You Trust

W9-BLY-888

Contents

the magazine 5

Finding Your Feet 33

Eiffel Tower to St-Germain 45

The Latin Quarter and the Islands 69

Written by Teresa Fisher
"Where to" sections by Mario Wyn-Jones

Updated by Elisabeth Morris

American editor Tracy Larson

Edited, designed and produced by AA Publishing.
© Automobile Association Developments Limited 2006, 2008
Maps © Automobile Association Developments Limited 2006, 2008

Published in the United States by AAA Publishing,
1000 AAA Drive, Heathrow, Florida 32746-5063
Published in the United Kingdom by AA Publishing

ISBN-13: 978-1-59508-242-8

Cover design and binding style by permission of AA Publishing
Color separation by Keenes, Andover
Printed and bound in China by Leo Paper Products

10 9 8 7 6 5 4 3 2

A03138

Paris
the magazine

LIBERTÉ

1789

AND ALL THAT

"Is it a revolt?" the incompetent, indecisive King Louis XVI is said to have enquired on hearing of the fall of the Bastille in 1789. "No, sire," responded a duke, "It's a revolution!"

Times were tough in the late 1780s. Since the reign of Louis XIV, the expensive cult of absolute monarchy had glorified France abroad and enriched its aristocrats and courtiers at home. But for the poor and the middle classes – heavily over-taxed and under-represented – the story was dramatically different. Things came to a head when a bad harvest in 1788

Previous page: The Eiffel Tower – Pride of Paris

sent bread prices soaring while wages sagged to a new low. As an out-of-touch king dithered about how best to regain control of a palpably disaffected populace, and his unpopular queen, Marie-Antoinette, depleted the coffers, the masses took to the streets. On 14 July, 1789 they raided Les Invalides (▶ 60) for weapons and stormed the fortress-prison of the Bastille, the ultimate symbol of royal repression, massacring its defenders and releasing its prisoners – all seven of them! Later that year, a mob forcibly removed the despised king and queen from their seclusion at Versailles (▶ 165), to keep them as virtual prisoners in the Tuileries palace (▶ 102). Little did they both realise that the building of the magnificent palace at Versailles was to be one of the last grand gestures of the French monarchy as, following the events of the 1780s – apart from the brief and luckless reigns of Louis XVIII and Charles X – France has to this day remained a republic.

At first the Revolution was led by relative moderates called Girondins, and France was declared a constitutional monarchy. Following external threats to their new government by Austria, Prussia and exiled French nobles, the masses rallied patriotically together, and soon the conservative Girondins had lost power to the extremist Jacobins, the most famous anti-royalist political group of the Revolution. They abolished the monarchy, revoked religious freedom and deconsecrated churches, established a "Revolutionary Convention" and, in September 1792, declared the First People's Republic of France.

This marked the start of the dreaded two-year "Reign of Terror", a period governed by the ruthless, power-crazed Jacobin leaders Robespierre and Danton, during which revolutionary ideals increasingly waned as more and more heroes were tried on unlikely charges of treason, and beheaded. The king was convicted of "conspiring against the liberty of the nation" and in January 1793 was guillotined on the newly named place de la Révolution (formerly place Louis XV, now place de la Concorde, ▶ 108–109), followed by Marie-Antoinette in October, and a further 1,343 "enemies of the Revolution". By mid-1794 some 17,000 people throughout France had been beheaded and the Revolution had reached such a frenzy of blood-lust that it turned on itself, even executing its leaders Danton and Robespierre.

A leading protagonist in this last stage of the revolution was Paul Barras, a moderate Republican who, with four others, established the "Directoire" as the Republic's ruling body. And waiting in the wings was a young Napoléon Bonaparte, who, within a decade, was to work his way up to eventually become "Emperor of the French".

The Taking of the Bastille *by Jean-Pierre Houel*

A Hungry King

Even in the face of death, poor King Louis XVI didn't lose his appetite. During his trial, he became hopelessly distracted by a plate of filled rolls. In tears, and unable to concentrate on the questions put to him, he eventually blurted out, "Please might I have one of those?" Just before having his head removed, he ate 16 pork chops!

THE GRAVE SIDE OF *GAI PARIS*

Step inside the three great cemeteries of Paris, where the seemingly endless celebrity guest list of illustrious dead are conveniently assembled, and you will begin to understand why they say "You haven't lived until you've died in Paris".

The largest cemetery, Père-Lachaise (➤ 136) boasts 43 hectares (106 acres; the size of the Vatican State) of higgledy-piggledy headstones and sepulchres, lined up like bathing huts along the tranquil, tree-shaded avenues. Since 1804, when it was first opened on the edge of the city to put an end to the overcrowding of inner-city graveyards, and the great French playwright Molière and lovers Abélard and Héloïse were reburied here, it rapidly became the place to be interred – the ultimate status symbol for the rich and famous. Once inside the walls of Père-Lachaise, scarcely a sound disturbs the other-worldly calm, except for the cawing of the black crows that swirl ominously overhead.

By no means all of the great who are buried here are French. Many, including Maria Callas, Gertrude Stein and Alice B Toklas, were foreigners who came to live and work in France. Others – Oscar Wilde, Rossini, Isadora Duncan – simply had the misfortune to die here. The most visited grave is also the most controversial – that of Jim Morrison, lead singer of The Doors, who died in Paris of a drug overdose while on holiday in 1971. His simple tomb, often surrounded by adoring fans (and protected by a security guard), is covered with cigarette stubs, magazines, dead flowers and beads – trinkets intended as homage here, but which elsewhere would be considered merely rubbish.

Many graves have tales to tell, such as the life-size statue of 19th-century journalist Victor Noir, shot for daring to criticise one of Napoléon's relatives (he lies flat on his back, fully clothed, his top hat fallen at his feet), or the grave of lion-tamer Jean Pezon, shown riding his pet lion, which later ate him.

Tribute to Diana

The underpass near Pont de l'Alma in the city centre became notorious as the location of the car crash and deaths of Dodi Al Fayed and Diana, Princess of Wales, in 1997, and is still occasionally adorned with flowers.

Artistic tomb of painter Théodore Géricault at Père-Lachaise cemetery

Perhaps the most powerful memorials are the vast monuments to violent, mass deaths – the grotesquely carved memorials to the victims of the Nazi concentration camps and to those never accounted for in World War II. Close by, the southeast corner of the cemetery was the site of the last battle of the Paris Commune in 1871, a bloody workers' revolt that lasted a mere 72 days, until 28 May when the remaining "Communards" (revolutionaries) were cornered, lined up and shot against the Mur des Fédérés (Federalists' Wall), today a simple shrine to socialism.

The cemetery at Montmartre (➤ 152) is full of writers – Alexandre "fils" Dumas, Stendhal and the German poet Heinrich Heine, while sombre Montparnasse boasts some more unusual memorials. Henri Langlois, founder of France's national cinematic collection, lies smothered in small stills from great films, while the great Romanian artist Brancusi has a primitive sculpture of an embracing couple atop his grave in response to Rodin's *The Kiss* (➤ 61).

The intriguing grave of inventor Charles Pigeon and his wife, lying fully clad in a bed of granite, Montparnasse cemetery

Chamber of Horrors

If it's real bones you want, visit Paris's eerie Catacombs – ancient Roman stone quarries filled in the 18th and 19th centuries with the overflow from the cemeteries. The sides of the underground route are constructed from the bones of some 6 million people, arranged from floor to ceiling, with spooky seams of skulls running through them. Not for those of a sensitive disposition or young children. It is advisable to wear practical shoes.

✉ avenue du Colonel Henri Rol-Tanguy, 75014 ☎ 01 43 22 47 63 🕐 Tue–Sun 10–4 🚇 Denfert-Rochereau 🎫 Moderate

Did You Know?

Paris is the world's perfume centre, so it should come as no surprise to learn that 90 per cent of Parisian women and 50 per cent of men regularly use perfume. But did you know the city uses a fragrance to mask the unpleasant odours of the Métro – a "woody musk base with a touch of vanilla, enhanced with citrus, lavender, jasmine, rose and lily", named Madeleine, after one of the smelliest underground stations?

The tiny vineyard of Montmartre (▶ 148), the only one left in Paris, produces a token 125 gallons (about 570 litres) of red wine (called Clos de Montmartre) per year. You can buy bottles at the Montmartre Tourist Office (▶ 149).

There are an estimated 250,000 dogs in Paris, who, according to the Mairie de Paris, together produce around 25 tonnes of poo daily. When Jacques Chirac was mayor, every resident received a leaflet listing the "Ten Commandments of the Tidy Parisian Dog", accompanied by a chart showing the quantities of *besoins liquides* (liquid necessities) and *besoins solides* (solid necessities) dogs are likely to produce daily. Should your dog do his *besoins* in the wrong place, you may now be fined up to €90 by a special dog poo squad.

The basilica of the Sacré-Coeur (▶ 150–151) is built from a local white stone that secretes calcite when wet, which means that the more it rains, the whiter it gleams. Another feature is that its belfry houses the mighty 19-tonne Savoyarde, one of the biggest bells in the world.

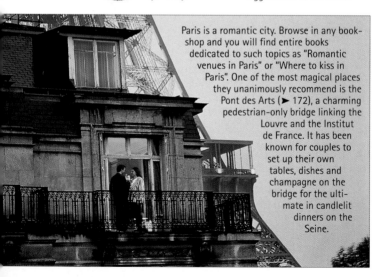

Paris is a romantic city. Browse in any bookshop and you will find entire books dedicated to such topics as "Romantic venues in Paris" or "Where to kiss in Paris". One of the most magical places they unanimously recommend is the Pont des Arts (▶ 172), a charming pedestrian-only bridge linking the Louvre and the Institut de France. It has been known for couples to set up their own tables, dishes and champagne on the bridge for the ultimate in candlelit dinners on the Seine.

Parisian waiters walk on average between 10 and 20km (6 and 12 miles) a day on their rounds from table to table.

Up to 6.2 million vehicles drive around the 35.5km (22-mile) *périphérique* (ring road) each hour.

Some 30,000 people visit the Louvre (► 96–101) daily. Of those, 36 per cent are French, 15 per cent are American and 5 per cent are Japanese; 6 per cent stay for less than half an hour, and about 1,000 visitors a year end up in the Louvre sick bay. If you spend just 10 seconds at each picture, it would still take nearly four days to see everything.

In summer 2002, imported sand and sunloungers transformed an area of the Right Bank into a beach for four weeks. "Paris Plage" was a hit and has since become an annual event.

Everything in Paris is a pleasure – even going to the lavatory, if you visit the beautiful *belle époque* lavatories dating from 1905, on the eastern side of place de la Madeleine (► 109).

Rollerblading is a popular mode of transport in Paris. Every Friday at 10pm, the "Pari-Roller" rally leaves the Gare Montparnasse, and follows a 25km (15-mile) circuit, drawing up to 30,000.

The famous breakfast croissant is surprisingly not French in origin but actually a *viennoiserie*, imported from Austria. The *brioche* (sweet bun), however, was invented in Paris in the late-17th century, giving rise to Marie Antoinette's celebrated and callous remark concerning the poor: "If they have no bread, let them eat cake *(brioche)*." Other Parisian inventions include the stick-like *baguette* (weighing 250g/9 ounces), which first appeared in 1920 and the larger *pain* (weighing 400g/14 ounces).

CATWALK PARIS
(Behind the Scenes)

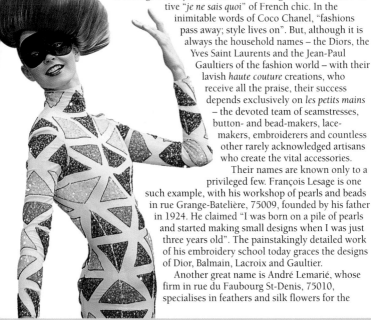

NO MATTER what each year's fashion fad is, whether frivolous or enduring, it always contains one vital ingredient – the distinctive "*je ne sais quoi*" of French chic. In the inimitable words of Coco Chanel, "fashions pass away; style lives on". But, although it is always the household names – the Diors, the Yves Saint Laurents and the Jean-Paul Gaultiers of the fashion world – with their lavish *haute couture* creations, who receive all the praise, their success depends exclusively on *les petits mains* – the devoted team of seamstresses, button- and bead-makers, lace-makers, embroiderers and countless other rarely acknowledged artisans who create the vital accessories.

Their names are known only to a privileged few. François Lesage is one such example, with his workshop of pearls and beads in rue Grange-Batelière, 75009, founded by his father in 1924. He claimed "I was born on a pile of pearls and started making small designs when I was just three years old". The painstakingly detailed work of his embroidery school today graces the designs of Dior, Balmain, Lacroix and Gaultier.

Another great name is André Lemarié, whose firm in rue du Faubourg St-Denis, 75010, specialises in feathers and silk flowers for the likes of Chanel, Mugler, Nina Ricci, Valentino and Dior. It was founded in the days of Charles Frédéric Worth (see below) and has played a major role in *haute couture* ever since.

Gérard Lognon's family business – the art of pleating – operates in an apartment in rue Danielle-Casanova, 75001; Patrice Wolfer at the renowned Michel in rue Ste-Anne, 75002, an ancient street of milliners, is the principal supplier of *haute couture* hats; while Raymond Massaro (2 rue de la Paix, 75002) is the most celebrated shoemaker in Paris. Creator of the famous Chanel-style shoe, he prides himself on his craftsmanship.

Perhaps the most extraordinary aspect of *haute couture* is that all these designers cater for a clientele of no more than 2,000 women, and that *haute couture* constitutes only 6 per cent of a fashion house's turnover. An average outfit requires at least 100 hours' work with three or four fittings and costs around €8,000, while an evening dress would cost four times as much!

These extravagant and prestigious creations, the result of months of work, are presented, together with the less exclusive ranges, at the fashion shows staged at the Carrousel du Louvre every January and July, before 2,000 journalists and celebrities and 800 buyers. The atmosphere is electric, and tickets virtually impossible to obtain. Some of the seats are reserved for *les petites mains* – who can watch their handiwork come alive in movement as the world's top models step out on to the catwalk to rapturous applause, in a pivoting swirl of silk, chiffon, brocade, organza and moiré.

The Inventor of *Haute Couture*

Ironically it was an Englishman, Charles Frederick Worth, who founded French *haute couture*. Having moved to Paris from London in 1845, aged 20, he worked in a draper's shop until he could afford a shop of his own, 13 years later, at 7 rue de la Paix. Specialising in well-cut clothes, he not only radically changed the female silhouette but also introduced the rhythm of the seasons to fashion by preparing his collections in advance. Another of his innovations was the use of live models for fashion shows.

Classic Couturier – Christian Dior (top left)

Flamboyant fashions of Givenchy (bottom left)

Linda Evangelista wears Dior

Les Deux Magots – still the place to see and be seen (above); belle époque décor at La Palette (below)

Café
culture

A Tour of the Best of Paris

Nothing is more Parisian than the café. From the famous, fashionable and exotic to the local neighbourhood haunt, Paris would not be Paris without its 10,000 or so cafés. There is one at virtually every crossroads, a place to meet friends and to people-watch. Dating back to the 17th century, cafés were an instant success as places where people could shed their social and class distinctions and talk freely about politics and affairs of the day. Café life is an essential part of everyday Paris, whether you choose a traditional zinc café (named after its metal counter) or a Left Bank philo-café (made famous by its "arty" patrons), a 1980s designer café or a 21st-century cybercafé.

This café crawl takes you round the city's most celebrated cafés.

Le Fouquet's
This chic café (► 113), in a prime Champs-Elysées location, was once frequented by writer James Joyce. These days, it is *the* place to spot local stars of French radio, TV and cinema. That is, if you can afford the coffee!

Head eastwards towards the Louvre.

Café Marly
In recent years, famous architects and designers have designed various cafés in Paris, giving them immediate *caché*. This one, by Olivier Gagnère, boasts a glamorous

Café Crawl

Le Fouquet's ✉ 99 avenue des Champs-Élysées, 75001 Ⓜ George V

Café Marly ✉ Le Louvre, 93 rue de Rivoli, 75001 Ⓜ Louvre-Rivoli

Café Beaubourg ✉ 43 rue St-Merri, 75004 Ⓜ Hôtel de Ville

Le Procope ✉ 13 rue de l'Ancienne Comédie, 75006 Ⓜ Odéon

Café de Flore ✉ 172 boulevard St-Germain, 75006 Ⓜ St-Germain-des-Prés

La Closerie des Lilas ✉ 171 boulevard du Montparnasse, 76006 Ⓜ Vavin

setting, I M Pei's glass pyramid, and provides a perfect balance between the monumental architecture of the Louvre, the need for privacy and the need to be seen.

Continue eastwards to the Centre Pompidou.

Café Beaubourg

This sleek, post-modern café, overlooking the Centre Pompidou, is the ultimate 1980s designer café. Its interior, by Christian de Portzamparc, is spacious, comfortable and unabashedly sophisticated (➤ 138–139). Look out, too, for the stylish lavatories.

Head due south, across the Seine and towards Odéon.

Le Procope

Paris's first, and therefore the world's first, café (today a restaurant), was opened in 1686. It was an instant success and, over the years, has attracted the local political and literary élite, including Rousseau, and Voltaire, who would drink 40 cups of mixed coffee and chocolate here a day. Oscar Wilde was also a regular.

Marat is said to have plotted the Revolution here; and Napoléon Bonaparte, as a penniless young artillery officer, was forced to leave his hat as a deposit while he went to get money for the bill.

Continue west along Boulevard St-Germain.

Les Deux Magots and Café de Flore

Parisian cafés are best known as a popular rendezvous for the literary élite, and none more so than these two neighbours. Les Deux Magots (➤ 62), made famous in the early

Café de Flore has long been a literary café

Le Zinc

To experience the traditional Parisian zinc café, with its zinc-lined counter top, and its dark, smoky, traditional atmosphere, head to the stylish **Café de l'Industrie**, on rue St-Sabin near the Bastille, **La Palette** on rue de Seine, frequented by art dealers and students of the nearby Academie des Beaux Arts, or **Le Cochon à l'Oreille** at 15 rue Montmartre. This tiny workers' café, in its heyday, was famous for its onion soup served at dawn – the end of the working day for the local prostitutes and the start of another for Les Halles' market workers.

Café de Flore – some things don't change

20th century by Picasso and poets Verlaine and Breton, has been the watering-hole of almost every Paris intellectual. The more cosmopolitan Café de Flore is famous for its existentialist clientele – notably writer-philosophers Camus, Simone de Beauvoir and Sartre. Both retain their literary atmosphere.

Head southwards to Montparnasse.

La Closerie des Lilas

The brass plaques on the tables of this dark, cosy café help you enjoy your pricey drink where poets Baudelaire, Apollinaire and writer Hemingway once sat. Picasso came here every week to poetry readings and it was frequented by Lenin and Trotsky in their time. Today, its sunny flower-filled terrace makes a pleasant spot for an early evening drink.

Oberkampf

The latest fashionable café district is the Ménilmontant end of rue Oberkampf, 75011. **Café Charbon** at No 109 (tel: 01 43 57 55 13) is a former music hall with a *belle époque* interior. Old dancehall murals evoke a traditional neighbourhood café of the 1920s. The clientele and atmosphere varies from hour to hour, from breakfast coffee to bistro lunch through to an evening pub then dance club in the early hours. Nearby **Le Cithéa** at No 112 (tel: 01 40 21 70 95) is popular for modern jazz while **Mercerie** at No 98 (tel: 01 56 98 14 10) is a favourite place for reggae.

City of Celebrities

Great cities are moulded as much by their citizens as by the skills of their architects and masons, and Paris has had more than its fair share of celebrated citizens – both native and adopted. Thomas Jefferson, who lived here for a short while before becoming president of the United States in 1801, declared the city "everyone's second home".

Its appeal can be traced back to the 13th century, when the Sorbonne University was founded. The French capital became one of the leading creative and academic centres of the Western world, attracting writers, poets, artists, philosophers and musicians, all under the spell of the city's style and distinctive charm. As Cardinal Eudes de Châteauroux remarked at that time: "France is the oven in which humanity's intellectual bread is baked."

In the 18th century, when it became fashionable for the wealthy to go on a one- or two-year "Grand Tour" of the Continent, taking in the most famous destinations and sights, Paris became labelled as the most romantic city in Europe and a popular place for foreigners to visit or to live in.

Paris in words

Paris has been the focus of countless literary masterpieces. "In Paris one can lose one's mind, but one can never lose one's way," claimed Oscar Wilde. He lost both, however, dying in a run-down, cheap hostel simply called **L'Hôtel**, now one of the few luxury hotels of the Left Bank (► 38). Today it is frequented by such celebrities as Robert de Niro, Barbra Streisand and Mick Jagger.

Other writers include 17th-century playwright, Molière, who helped create the **Comédie-Française** (► 118), France's national theatre, while Jean Racine (1639–99) premiered some of his plays at the **Théâtre de l'Odéon**. The 19th century saw the genius of novelists Balzac, Zola, Flaubert and Hugo. Hugo, a committed Republican, regularly fell out with the authorities and was forced to write many of his works, including Paris-based *Les Misérables*, in exile in the Channel Islands. Among the countless 20th-century writers, it is Marcel Proust who has captured Paris most completely. And, recently, Dan Brown has put the city on the literary map again with his best-selling *The Da Vinci Code*, set largely in Paris.

Painting Paris

Paris first attracted artists on a major scale during the reign of Louis XIV, and before long the capital became the main artistic centre in Europe. Over the centuries, virtually all the major French artists have at some point lived and worked in Paris. Paris was also the cradle of Impressionism, the founders of which, Monet, Renoir and Sisley, all met in a studio here in the mid-19th century. In 1907, Picasso broke through the boundaries of art once more, painting his first Cubist work, *Les Demoiselles d'Avignon*, at the Bateau-Lavoir (► 153) in Montmartre, where he shared a warren of tiny ateliers with other artists, including Georges Braque, Modigliani and Chagall. Dalí and Toulouse-Lautrec, perhaps the most popular of all artists associated with Paris, both lived and painted near by, while Rodin, Brancusi and others found niches for themselves on the Left Bank.

Musicians of Paris – Edith Piaf (left) and Pierre Boulez (right)

Paris in music

Musicians, too, have been attracted to the city: Rameau (1683–1764), pioneer of harmony, Berlioz (1803–69) and Liszt (1811–86) are all associated with **Église St-Eustache** (► 132), while the great organist family, the Couperins, gave frequent recitals in various churches, and Offenbach (1819–80) composed his famous cancan here. Mozart (1756–91) visited Paris often as a child. His final trip, however, was a disaster. He was no longer acknowledged as a prodigy, and his mother died during their stay. Mozart left in 1788, utterly contemptuous of Parisian society, never to return.

The **Opéra Garnier** (► 107), one of the most prestigious opera houses in the world, has staged such premieres as Wagner's *Tannhäuser*, Bizet's *Carmen* and Debussy's *Peléas et Mélisande*; and soprano Maria Callas gave numerous acclaimed performances here.

Jazz has thrived in Paris since its heyday in the 1920s when Cole Porter lived here and Gershwin composed his *American in Paris*. Today a host of clubs, including **Le Duc des Lombards** (21 boulevard de Sébastopol, 75001, tel: 01 42 33 22 88) and the **Lionel Hampton Jazz Club** (Hôtel

Café Society

For centuries, certain Parisian cafés have been a popular rendezvous for the literary élite – an inimitable forum of ideas discussed over a coffee. Le Procope (Paris's first café, ► 15) established in 1686 in rue de l'Ancienne Comédie, was an instant success with Voltaire, Diderot and Rousseau as regulars, and Racine is said to have written his plays here, cup of coffee in hand. During the 19th century, Tortoni became a popular meeting place for the intelligentsia of the grand boulevards, while in the 20th the Café de Flore was famous for its existentialist clientele, including such notables as Sartre, Camus and Simone de Beauvoir. Modigliani paid his bills at La Rotonde with paintings, and Trotsky was to be found at La Closerie des Lilas (► 16).

Le Méridien-Etoile, 81 boulevard Gouvion-St-Cyr, 75017, tel: 01 40 68 30 42), continue to attract top international performers. The city's most celebrated *chanteuse*, however, is Edith Piaf (▶ 136–137), famous for her sexy, husky voice and her nostalgic songs of street life, lost loves, drugs, death and whores, which are still performed in the bars and cafés of **Montmartre**.

Star-gazing

Today's city celebrities include film stars Gérard Depardieu, and Catherine Deneuve; fashion gurus Yves Saint Laurent and wacky Jean-Paul Gaultier, who brings life and colour to the Parisian fashion scene with his quirky clothing, perfume and accessories.

Both resident and visiting celebrities, from pop stars to foreign royalty, tend to keep a low profile in the city. Nevertheless, the best star-spotting venues are the top hotels, such as the **Crillon** (10 place de la Concorde, 75008, tel: 01 44 71 15 00), where Michael Jackson, Madonna and Tom Cruise all stay, and the **Ritz** (15 place Vendôme, 75001, tel: 01 43 16 30 30), where Princess Diana and Dodi Al Fayed spent their last hours together. American writer, Ernest Hemingway, who took up residence here in the 1920s, once hoped that heaven would be as good as the Ritz. His ghost is said to haunt the bar named after him here.

To mingle with supermodels, stay in the **Plaza Athénée** (25 avenue Montaigne, 75008, tel: 01 53 67 66 65) and **Hôtel Costes** (239 rue St-Honoré, 75001, tel: 01 42 44 50 00; book well in advance during fashion weeks). You could spot a celebrity or two at the trendy bar and restaurant **Man Ray** (32 rue Marbeuf, 75008, tel: 01 56 88 36 36, Métro: Franklin D. Roosevelt). And if you can't get a table, you can always just enjoy a coffee while reading the gossip rag, *Paris Match*.

Parisians of today – Gérard Depardieu (left) and Catherine Deneuve (right)

Open All Hours
24-hour Taste of Paris

8am
Skip breakfast at your hotel and slip into a local café for a more authentic start to the day, with coffee and a croissant, or a delicious *pain au chocolat* (eaten in true Parisian fashion, standing at the bar).

11am
In need of refreshment? Then find a seat on a sunny café terrace, order a *petit noir* (espresso), a *noisette* (espresso with a dash of milk), a *grand crème* (large white coffee), a *tisane* (herbal tea) or a *citron* or *orange pressé* (freshly squeezed juice), relax and watch the world go by. In winter, treat yourself to a *chocolat chaud* (hot chocolate). The best are served at Angélina (226 rue de Rivoli, 75001, tel: 01 42 60 82 00, Métro: Tuileries).

1pm
Not wishing to occupy too much valuable sightseeing time, grab a light lunch – an omelette, steak *frites*, crusty filled baguette or *croque-monsieur* – in one of the jolly bistros in the Marais (► 138–140) or St-Germain (► 64–66). Or put together a mouth-watering picnic to eat in a nearby park.

4pm
Enjoy a fine cup of tea and a pastry in the refined surroundings of one of Paris's many charming *salons de thé*.

7pm
Aperitif time! Typical pre-dinner café tipples include a glass of wine, *un demi* (small beer) or a *kir* (chilled white wine with *crème de cassis*), accompanied by a *tartine* (slice of bread and butter) topped with *pâté*, *rillettes* (potted meat) or cheese.

A Sweet Tooth
French *pâtisseries* are famous the world over, thanks to centuries-old recipes devised by the master pastry-makers employed at princely courts. In the 17th century, Vatel created *crème Chantilly*, and Ragueneau invented the almond tart called *amandine*. In the 1800s, Carême produced nougat and meringues, with candied chestnuts, and *mille-feuille* pastries first appearing in the 1830s. Anne of Austria introduced chocolate from Spain in the 17th century, and today Paris still boasts many exceptional *chocolatiers*.

"Lunch kills half of Paris, supper the other half."

MONTESQUIEU (SOCIAL AND POLITICAL PHILOSOPHER, 1689–1755)

Recommended...

Breakfast venue – Café Charbon, 109 rue Oberkampf, 75011 – popular weekend brunch venue in a stylish *belle époque* café in a modish *quartier* of Paris.

Tea salon – Mariage Frères, 30 rue du Bourg-Tibourg, 75004 – tea shop, tea museum and *salon de thé* (➤ 65–66).

Aperitif venue – Les Portes, 15 rue de Charonne, 75011 – ideal bar for an intimate *tête-à-tête*.

For additional recommendations, ➤ 42.

Joël Robuchon – one of France's top chefs

9pm

Dine at a "baby-bistro" – annexe restaurants where you can sample the cuisine of top chefs like Guy Savoy. His satellite restaurants include Les Bouquinistes (➤ 65), La Butte Chaillot (110 bis av Kléber, 75016, tel: 01 47 27 88 88) and Le Chiberta (3 rue Arsène Houssaye, 75008, tel: 01 53 53 42 00). Or splash out at Jacques Cagna's eponymous restaurant, where you can sample gourmet French cuisine (14 rue des Grands-Augustins, 75006, tel: 01 43 26 49 39).

After midnight

Quell after-party hunger pangs at an all-night eatery such as Le Grand Café des Capucines (4 boulevard des Capucines, 75009) or Café de l'Atelier (95 boulevard du Montparnasse, 75006), or at late-night cafés such as La Chaise au Plafond (10 rue du Trésor, 75004) and Café Beaubourg (➤ 138–139).

The Seine

It is no coincidence that the inscription on Paris's coat-of-arms reads: "She is buffeted by the waves but sinks not". The city's history has been inextricably linked with the Seine since its earliest origins as a Gaulish village on the Île de la Cité, an islet in the river. The river represents the very lifeblood of Paris, flowing through its heart, animating the city, defining the capital geographically and reflecting its history in its many fine buildings. Yet, as tourist boats peacefully ply the river today, it is easy to forget how, in the 9th century, the Seine was used by 700 Viking warships to invade Paris, or how thousands of dead bodies floated through the city in 1572, victims of the brutal Saint Bartholomew's Day Massacre of Protestants.

Just three centuries ago, the Seine served a multitude of purposes: it was both the city's sewer and the main source of drinking water; washerwomen did their washing in it, laying the clothing out to dry on the watersides; workshops churned their waste into it; horses drank from it; workers at the floating fish market near the Île de la Cité threw their fish heads into it, and Parisians bathed in it – a fashion introduced by the flamboyant Henri IV in the swelteringly hot summer of 1609, when he took to nude bathing. By mid-August of that year, as many as 4,000 of his male subjects could be counted frolicking naked in the river – much to the delight of onlooking ladies!

The Seine was also a major trading route. During the

CLEANING UP ITS ACT

Thanks to new techniques for water treatment and the numerous parks and green spaces along its flanks, the river is cleaner than before and is once more starting to attract a flourishing wildlife. Aquatic plants have been reintroduced along the walkways, and over 20 species of fish have been identified, including pike, bream, roach, gudgeon and dace.

Paris wakens slowly on the tranquil Île St-Louis, at the heart of the city

17th and 18th centuries a large port grew up near the Louvre, to supply the court with coal, wood, hay and food. Before the invention of engines powered by steam and gas, barges travelling upstream had to be towed by men or horses. The narrow arches of the bridges were particularly hard to navigate, so expert boat-handlers known as "bridge-swallowers" were employed to haul the barges through the bridges with the help of poles, ropes and rings, the remnants of which can still be seen under some bridges.

During the 18th century, as the port went from strength to strength, the construction of waterfronts (built to ward off the then-frequent danger of flooding), corbelled houses and mills started to encroach on the river. Near Châtelet, the river is 43m (141 feet) narrower than it was during the Middle Ages. Nowadays, the river is cleverly regulated by a number of locks upstream and the

RIVERSIDE READING

Lining the banks of the Seine, you will find *les bouquinistes* – row upon row of rickety old green booths, full of second-hand and antiquarian books, prints, postcards and other treasures which are very much a part of the Parisian riverscape. Most are concentrated on the Rive Gauche between quai de la Tournelle and quai Malaquais. Try quai des Grands-Augustins for ancient maps, cartoon strips and books on history, politics and romance; quai St-Michel for stamps and prints; quai de Montebello for literary texts, ancient engravings and postcards; and quai de la Tournelle for early paperbacks and cinema and theatre reviews.

Suresnes dam downstream. Paris remains the country's leading river port and its water is less polluted than it has been for years. But the "cross-Seine swim" is sadly a thing of the past – you would no doubt be decapitated by one of the many *bateaux-mouches* and other pleasure craft that ply the city-centre stretch of the river that includes some of the world's most photographed views.

In bygone days, bustling watersides lined the Seine

BRIDGES ANCIENT AND MODERN

The city's 37 bridges reflect the architectural history of Paris, representing every period and built in every style. The oldest and most famous, ironically called Pont Neuf (New Bridge), dates back to 1604, erected to ease Henri IV's journey between the Louvre Palace and the abbey of St-Germain-des-Prés. The newest, inaugurated in 1999, is the Passerelle de Solférino, a metal-arched footbridge joining the quai des Tuileries to the Left Bank near the Musée d'Orsay. But the most photogenic is Pont Alexandre III with its ornate candelabra-style lamps, its winged horses, lions, gilded nymphs and garlands.

A trip on one of the legendary bateaux-mouches *(► 172–174) is a must*

A Walk in the Park

Never before has Paris been greener. After a decade of monumental building in the city, in the 1990s Paris turned to the softer medium of the park and garden. Even derelict industrial sites blossomed into flower throughout the city as Parisians now, more than ever, seek respite from the congestion of urban life and a natural antidote to its noise, stress and pollution. More than 400 parks and gardens currently enliven the city. Each has its own character: some are à la française (with neat symmetrical rows of lawns, trees and pathways), some à l'anglaise (more freely landscaped), others are totally modern; some are ideal for kids, others for a riverside stroll, for romance or a game of boules.

Jardin des Tuileries and Jardin du Luxembourg

Many of the mature parks serve as reminders of the capital's illustrious past. The oldest – the **Jardin des Tuileries** (➤ 102–103) was created for Catherine de Médicis in the 16th century, with later modifications by the great master of the French-style garden, André Le Nôtre, designer of the gardens of Versailles (➤ 165–167). Marie de Médicis' **Jardin du Luxembourg** (➤ 63), originally a private garden like the Tuileries, has hardly changed in character since the early 1800s, apart from a later addition by Napoléon III – the now little-visited orchards of the **Verger du Luxembourg** (National Conservatory of Apples and Pears).

Bois de Vincennes and Bois de Boulogne

Gardens featured high on Napoléon's priorities during his transformation of Paris into a more resident-friendly city, including the development of the Bois de Boulogne and the Bois de Vincennes, both ancient royal hunting forests that encircled Paris in the Middle Ages. These wild, unkempt parks make you feel you've escaped Paris altogether. The **Bois de Vincennes** to the east also contains a magnificent

Few people associate Paris with parks and gardens, yet every district has its own green spaces for recreation and ornamentation

Green Fingers

The City of Paris gardeners take care of a staggering 3,075ha (7,600 acres) of parks and gardens, and 600,000 trees – one for every 3.5 Parisians! For each of the last ten years, they have planted on average 3,100 new trees, 215,000 perennials and climbing plants, and no fewer than 3 million green or flowering plants.

Say it with Flowers

As so few city-dwellers have their own gardens, shop-bought flowers play a vital role in daily life and, as a result, Paris boasts some eye-catching florists. For that beautiful bouquet, try **Monceau Fleurs** (84 boulevard Raspail, 75006), just one store of the city's most popular florist chain, **Christian Tortu** (6 Carrefour de l'Odéon, 75006, ➤ 67) or **Au Nom de la Rose** (4 rue de Tournon, 75006). For artificial flowers, it's hard to beat **Emilio Robba's** seasonal collections (➤ 67). For orchids try **Les Fées d'Herbe** (23 rue Faidherbe, 75011).

château and a zoo, while the **Bois de Boulogne** to the west, inspired by London's Hyde Park, is better known for its beautiful Bagatelle gardens with strutting peacocks, its **Jardin d'Acclimatation** (a children's amusement park) and, by night, when it can be dangerous, for its prostitutes.

Les Halles, La Villette, Parc André-Citroën and Parc de Bercy

President Mitterrand's architectural renaissance of the 1980s and 1990s (➤ 31) has revived interest in gardens, with new parks seemingly springing up everywhere. These include **Les Halles** (➤ 133–134), **La Villette** (➤ 156–157), the **Parc André-Citroën** and **Parc de Bercy**. Most ambitious is the futuristic Parc André-Citroën, built in 1992 on the site of the old Citroën car factories in southwestern Paris, with two juxtaposed gardens (**Jardin Blanc** and **Jardin Noir**) dominated by gigantic high-tech greenhouses, six sophisticated areas – *les Jardins Sériels* – each associated with the colour of a metal, fun, computerised water features for children and a striking river perspective. By contrast, the more classical Parc de Bercy, also on the Seine, was created in 1997 as part of a vast programme of urban renewal for eastern Paris, and comprises several themed gardens, including the **Jardin des Plantes Aromatiques** for the visually impaired.

Musée de la Sculpture en Plein Air and the "green trail"

Finally, for a pleasant (daytime) stroll away from it all, try the city's two new promenades: the **Musée de la Sculpture en Plein Air** (Open Air Sculpture Museum – ➤ 85), squeezed between the Seine and the Jardin des Plantes, and another along the Daumesnil Viaduct, dubbed the "green trail", stretching from the Bastille to the Bois de Vincennes.

You can often see the ancient game of boules *being played in shady corners of parks and gardens*

Secret Gardens

For a quick dose of greenery in the city centre, make for the square de la Tour St-Jacques near the Louvre, a small, grassy retreat surrounding an ornate Gothic tower, all that remains of an ancient church, or the river-lapped square du Vert-Galant at the western point of the Île de la Cité. This magical park bears the nickname of amorous King Henri IV and is one of the most romantic corners of Paris. The Jardin Sauvage de St-Vincent comes as a surprise in the heart of Montmartre – a totally wild patch of land, established to encourage natural flora and fauna – and don't overlook the gardens attached to many museums, most notably the extensive statue-studded grounds of the Musée Rodin (➤ 61–62).

GRANDS TRAVAUX

Over the centuries, French leaders have sought to glorify – and possibly even to immortalise – themselves by carrying out ambitious and monumental public building schemes in Paris, which have come to be known as *les grands travaux*. But are they self-promoting ego trips or inspired designs for the future?

Louis XIV, the Sun King, was the first to use architecture to aggrandise the institution of absolute monarchy through the construction of imposing squares, theatres, aristocratic *hôtels particuliers* (mansions), **Les Invalides** (► 60–61) and the grandiose château of Versailles (► 165–167). His breathtaking extravagance, combined with the ceaseless wars he waged against various neighbouring countries, eventually led to a decline in the monarchy.

The second major transformation of Paris, perhaps

High-tech architecture at La Défense

its most radical, took place in the mid-19th century under Napoléon III, when Baron Haussmann transformed it into the most magnificent city in Europe. In a massive and ruthless exercise of urban and social engineering, he demolished the narrow, crowded, insanitary streets of the medieval city and created a well-ordered capital within a geometrical grid of straight, broad boulevards, which linked such focal points as the new **Opéra Garnier** (► 107–108), the **Gare de l'Est** and the **Arc de Triomphe** (► 104–105). His uncompromising vision can best be appreciated from the top of the Arc de Triomphe, which looks out over 12 grand avenues radiating like the points of a star.

In the latter half of the 20th century, unlike anywhere else in the world, it was the turn of politicians to leave their stamp on the city. President Georges Pompidou constructed the once-reviled but now much-loved Centre Beaubourg, later called the **Centre Georges Pompidou** (► 124–127). His successor Giscard d'Estaing played a key part in transforming a derelict railway station into the glorious **Musée d'Orsay** (► 54–57).

A Musical Sensation

One of Paris's lower profile "Mitterrand" buildings is the dazzling white Cité de la Musique, designed by Christian de Portzamparc. Part of La Villette complex (► 156–157) it is home to the National Conservatory of Music and Dance. The odd man out in the current French trend towards straight-lined, rational modernism, de Portzamparc chose undulating and conic forms to translate the sensations of music into architecture. Inside, a multicultural music programme adds to the effect, with clever interior lighting that changes colour to suit the musical mood.

Previous page: The Louvre Pyramide – one of Paris's more recent landmarks

But the late François Mitterrand surpassed them both in his achievements of the 1980s and 1990s. His programme of *grands travaux* excited great controversy, as he was accused of seeking king-like immortality as he changed the face of Paris.

One of the greatest advocates of urban renewal, Mitterrand feared that Paris was becoming a "museum". He wanted to keep the city alive, to protect it from becoming a much-loved but mummified place, frozen in the past. To prove that France also looked to the future, he launched a series of architectural competitions to create "modern" monuments in the capital. But Parisians are apparently capricious by nature. Whenever something new arrives in their city, they often complain like fury and claim to hate it, but soon afterwards learn to love it. When the **Eiffel Tower** (▶ 50–53) was constructed more than 100 years ago, it was regarded as a hideous eyesore. Now it is the most universally beloved symbol of Paris.

Many of Mitterrand's projects were greeted with a similar initial horror, in particular his first and most daring construction – the Louvre **Pyramide** (▶ 96–101). From the outset, his buzzword for transforming the landscape of the city was "transparency": take a look at the **Fondation Cartier** (261 boulevard Raspail, 75014), with its clever glass slices, and the **Institut du Monde Arabe** (▶ 86), with its extraordinary aperture-effect glass panels. Other dramatic constructions included the glass-fronted **Opéra de Paris Bastille** (▶ 135) and **La Grande Arche** (▶ 111), a hollow cube of marble and glass symbolising a window, which gave the district of La Défense a badly needed monument and focal point. It also completed his Grand Axis, a line linking the Arc de Triomphe, the Champs-Elysées, his Pyramide and the Louvre (although there are plans to extend it out further into the western suburbs). Whether Mitterrand's *grands travaux* were aimed at self-aggrandisement or at bringing Paris into the 21st century, there is no denying he achieved both. The last of his projects – the new national library – was completed following his death in January 1996, and renamed the **Bibliothèque Nationale de France François-Mitterrand** (11 quai François-Mauriac, 75013) in his honour.

La Grande Arche at La Défense – one of President Mitterrand's most pointless yet most successful projects

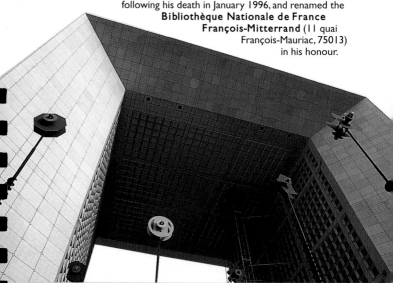

The Best of Paris

Best Experiences
• Take a boat trip along the Seine.
• Mingle with chic Parisians in the *haute couture* boutiques of the 1st *arrondissement*.
• Indulge yourself in a bistro in St-Germain-des-Prés.
• Take the funicular (► 151) up to the Sacré-Coeur.
• Watch the world go by over coffee on a café terrace.
• Stroll through the park beside Notre-Dame cathedral (► 82) when the blossom is out in springtime.
• Explore Père-Lachaise cemetery and pay your respects to the many great villains and heroes buried here (► 8 and 136).
• Relax by the Stravinsky fountain (► 127), the wacki-est waterworks in Paris.

Best Children's Activities
• Disneyland® Resort Paris (► 169).
• La Cité des Sciences et de l'Industrie (► 156).
• Grevin (► 111).
• The high-tech circus, Cirque Alexis Grüss, in the Bois de Boulogne (certain months only; tel: 01 45 01 71 26 for details).
• Jardin d'Acclimatation (► 28) with its mini-train, fairground, museum and zoo.

• Open-air puppet shows, held in the Champ de Mars, Luxembourg, Buttes-Chaumont and Montsouris parks.

Best Bird's-eye Viewpoints
• Eiffel Tower (► 50–53).
• Tour Montparnasse (33 avenue du Maine, 75015, tel: 01 45 38 52 56; Apr–Sep daily 9:30am–11pm; rest of year 9:30am–10pm (Fri, Sat 10:30pm); Métro: Montparnasse Bienvenue).
• Sacré-Coeur (► 150–151).
• Notre-Dame tower (► 80–83).
• Arc de Triomphe (► 104–105).

Best Modern Architecture
• La Grande Arche de la Défense (► 111).
• La Cité de la Musique (► 30).
• The Frank Gehry-designed former American Center's sculptural exterior (51 rue de Bercy, 75012, Métro: Bercy).
• Masayuki Yamanaka's Maison de la Culture du Japon (101 bis quai Branly, 75015, Métro: Bir-Hakeim) with its curvaceous jade-coloured glass façade.

Best Oases of Peace
• Square du Vert-Galant (► 28).
• Cimetière Père-Lachaise (► 8 and 136).

If You Go To Only One –
Museum: Surprise, surprise! Not the Louvre but the Musée d'Orsay (► 54–57).
Restaurant: Alain Ducasse – for some of France's finest cuisine (► 112).
Hotel: Pavillon de la Reine (28 place des Vosges, 75003, tel: 01 40 29 19 19, Métro: Chemin Vert) – possibly Paris's prettiest and most romantic hotel, with refined *grand siècle*-style rooms, each overlooking delightful private gardens.
Café: La Palette (► 15), a surviving Parisian classic in St-Germain.
Shop: Fauchon, the foodies' paradise, and a perfect one-stop source of gifts (► 116).

Opposite page: Atmospheric Montmartre, with its famous landmark, the Sacre-Coeur, is on everyone's must-see list

Finding
Your Feet

First Two Hours

Don't be daunted by the size of Paris. It's actually quite a small city and finding your way to the centre on arrival is surprisingly straightforward, thanks to the efficient and easy-to-use public transport systems.

Roissy Charles de Gaulle Airport

Roissy (www.adp.fr) is Paris's main airport, 23km (14 miles) northeast of the city centre. There are three terminals. Air France uses Terminal 2. You can get to the city in three ways:

- **By bus:** Air France operates a bus service between the airport and Montparnasse every half-hour 7am–9pm; and to the Arc de Triomphe every 15 minutes, 5:45am–11pm. (You needn't have flown on Air France to use this service.) Alternatively, the Roissybus runs every 15 minutes to Opéra from 5am to 11pm (every 20 minutes after 7pm), and takes 45 minutes to 1 hour.
- **By taxi:** The most expensive option. A taxi to the centre costs around €45 and takes 30 minutes to1 hour, depending on the traffic.
- **By train:** The RER (Réseau Express Régional – suburban express train network) line B takes around 35 minutes into central Paris. Trains leave every 4 to 15 minutes.

Orly Airport

Orly Airport (www.adp.fr), the older and smaller of Paris's two main international airports, lies 14km (8.5 miles) south of Paris, and is therefore much closer to the city centre than Roissy. There are two terminals: Orly-Sud for most international flights; and Orly-Ouest for domestic flights, Air France and some international carriers. Unfortunately, there are no direct public transport links to the city centre.

- **By bus:** Don't bother with the Orlybus, as it only goes as far as the Denfert-Rochereau Métro. Instead, Air France provides shuttle buses to Les Invalides and Gare Montparnasse every 15 minutes 6am–11:30pm. The trip takes about 30 minutes.
- **By taxi:** A taxi will cost around €35 to the city centre, and takes around 15 to 30 minutes.
- **By train:** The Orlyval train, which operates every 4 to 8 minutes daily 6am–11pm, will take you two stops to Antony where you can change on to the main Paris RER rail system (line B). From here it takes around 30 minutes to reach the city centre.

Gare du Nord – Arrival Point for Eurostar

This is probably the easiest way to arrive in Paris. The train (www.eurostar.com) takes you right into the heart of Paris, just 3km (2 miles) from the official centre, and, as all the customs and immigration formalities are completed before arrival, you can head straight into the city from the station.

- The **Eurostar terminal** is on the upper level of the Gare du Nord, and includes a currency exchange bureau, a newsagent, cafés and bars.
- The **Gare du Nord** station is on two Métro (underground) lines and three RER (overland) lines (► 36 for how to use the Métro, and inside back cover for a map of the system).
- **Taxi** queues are depressingly long when a Eurostar train arrives but they move fairly quickly. Be aware of extra charges for baggage.

Getting Around

The city can be divided into two halves; the Right Bank or Rive Droite and the Left Bank or Rive Gauche. Its official centre is Notre-Dame cathedral (► 80–83). Most of the top sights are within an 8km (5-mile) radius.

Arrondissements

For more than a century, Paris has been divided into 20 *arrondissements* (districts) which spiral out clockwise from the city centre like a snail's shell. The central *arrondissements* are logically numbered from 1 to 8:

1er (75001)	heart of the Right Bank, centred on the Louvre and part of the Île de la Cité.
2er (75002)	the commercial district to the east of the Opéra.
3er / 4er (75003/4)	Marais district, part of Île de la Cité, and Île St-Louis.
5er (75005)	Latin Quarter on the Left Bank.
6er (75006)	St-Germain district.
7er (75007)	residential Faubourg St-Germain and the Eiffel Tower.
8er (75008)	chic district of broad avenues radiating out from the Arc de Triomphe.

City Centre Tourist Offices

Paris's three tourist offices are good for maps and information on what's on. They will also help you to sort out accommodation. The department stores – Au Printemps, La Samaritaine and Galeries Lafayette – also offer free tourist maps.

Office du Tourisme (main office)
✉ 25 rue des Pyramides, 75001
☎ 08 92 68 30 00
🕐 Daily 9–7, Jun–Oct; Mon–Sat 10–7, Sun and public hols 11–7, rest of year
🚇 Pyramides

Île de France
✉ Carrousel du Louvre (lower level) 99 rue de Rivoli, 75001
☎ 08 92 68 30 00
🕐 Daily 10–6
🚇 Palais Royal-Musée du Louvre

Anvers Office
✉ boulevard de Rochechouart (opposite No 72), 75018
🕐 Daily 8–6. Closed public holidays
🚇 Anvers

Montmartre
✉ 21 place du Tertre, 75018
☎ 08 92 68 30 00
🕐 Daily 10–7. Closed 1 May
🚇 Abbesses

Gare de Lyon
✉ 20 boulevard Diderot, 75012
☎ 08 92 68 30 00
🕐 Mon–Sat 8–6. Closed public hols
🚇 Gare de Lyon

Gare du Nord
✉ 18 rue de Dunkerque, 75010
☎ 08 92 68 30 00
🕐 Daily 8–6. Closed public hols

Paris Expo Office
✉ 1 place de la Porte de Versailles, 75015 ☎ 08 92 68 30 00
🕐 Daily 11–9 during fairs and exhibitions 🚇 Porte de Versailles

Public Transport

Buses are good for sightseeing, and routes are clearly marked on bus stops and in the buses. People with limited mobility may also find buses useful, although they can get unbearably crowded at rush hour. However, the transport of choice is the Métropolitan or RER, two separate but linked systems. The RER is a suburban rail network that passes through the city centre, while the "Métro" (underground) has

14 lines and more than 300 stations. Both are cheap and efficient. Both systems function in the same way and the tickets are interchangeable. For transport information in English, call 08 92 68 77 14 or visit the website: www.ratp.fr

How to Use the Métro

■ **There is a Métro map inside the back cover of this book.**
■ **Métro lines** are identified by their end-station, a colour and a number.
■ The Métro operates from 5:30am to around 1am (2:15am Fri and Sat). If possible, **avoid rush-hours** 8–9:30am and 4:30–7pm.
■ The city is divided into **five fare zones**, but for everything covered in this book you will just need zone 1, apart from La Défense (zone 3), the excursions and the airports (zone 4: Orly, zone 5: Roissy).
■ Buy a *carnet* **of ten tickets** for zone 1. This costs roughly the same as seven tickets bought individually.
■ You can also get an unlimited *Mobilis* pass for one day, or a *Paris Visite* travel pass for one, two, three or five days. Tickets are available from all stations.
■ **Validate your ticket** when you enter the station. To do this, place it in the slot on the side of the barrier and remove it from the second slot at the top before passing through the turnstile. Keep hold of it until you exit, as ticket inspectors make spot checks and fine ticketless travellers.
■ Watch out for **pickpockets**.

Batobus

Travelling by batobus (www.batobus.com) – a river shuttle boat – is a fun way to see the key river sights. It operates all year except January every 25 to 30 minutes 10–10, in summer (7pm in spring and autumn); 10:30–4, in winter, stopping at the Eiffel Tower, Musée d'Orsay, St-Germain-des-Prés, Notre-Dame, Hôtel de Ville, Louvre, Jardin des Plantes and the Champs-Élysées.

Taxis

Taxis can be hailed in the street if the white roof sign is illuminated, or are at most main sights in taxi ranks. Radio taxi companies include Taxis Bleus (tel: 08 91 70 10 10) and G7 (tel: 01 47 39 47 39).

Car

Parking is difficult and expensive (especially if you get clamped), filling stations are hard to find, and the one-way systems can make driving a nightmare. You will need your driving licence, car registration and car insurance documents. The speed limit in the city is 50kph (30mph), seatbelts must be worn in front seats (and in rear seats where fitted) – and remember to drive on the right.

Car Rental

All the main car-rental companies have desks at Roissy CDG airport, and in the city centre. Contact Avis (tel: 08 20 05 05 05), Hertz (tel: 08 25 86 18 61) or Europcar (tel: 08 25 35 83 58) for details.

Discount Passes

A *Paris Museum Pass* offers unlimited access to over 60 sights in Paris and the Île de France (not temporary exhibitions) over a two-, four- or six-consecutive day period. It is available at tourist offices, railway stations and museums.

Admission Prices

The cost of admission is indicated by the following:

Inexpensive up to €5   **Moderate** €5–8   **Expensive** over €8

Accommodation

From luxurious palaces to more humble family-run establishments, Paris offers visitors a range of accommodation possibilities – only be sure to reserve well in advance, particularly in the spring and autumn.

Reservations

A useful website for finding accommodation is www.webtourist.net Another excellent reservation service for both hotels and restaurants is provided by the website of the Paris Tourst Office (www.parisinfo.com) which offers discounts, as well as suggestions for special occasions.

Multinational Chains

Anonymous multinational chains are encroaching here as elsewhere, and though their hotels offer relatively good standards of accommodation, they are rather soulless, without real national identity. Often, because of their size, they offer standards of service that are more automated than personal. However, they are a useful standby when the city gets booked up during trade fairs in spring and autumn. **Holiday Inn** (www. ichotelsgroup.com central reservations within France, tel: 0800 90 59 99; from the UK tel: 0800 405060) is a chain with 25 hotels in the city and its outlying districts. There are three types available in Paris. The Holiday Inn is currently at the top of the scale. There are also more informal Holiday Inn Garden Courts, and Holiday Inn Express, primarily geared towards business use but without leisure facilities. Two of the Holiday Inns in Paris have an indoor swimming-pool. **Ibis** (central reservations within France, tel: 08 92 68 66 86) have 51 hotels scattered throughout Paris offering up-to-date, simple, clean and compact accommodation ideally suited to the budget traveller.

Apartments

Whether it's for one night or a longer stay, renting an apartment makes practical and financial sense: it is like having your own private address, and the facilities are excellent. All are serviced on a daily basis. Rooms are comfortable and spacious, with lots of storage spaces. Bathrooms are up to date and well maintained. Galley kitchens provide the necessary crockery, cutlery, plates, pots and pans for self-catering. **Paris Appartements Services** (20 rue Bachaumont, 75002, tel: 01 40 28 01 28; www.paris-apts.com) offers a good selection.

Hostels

The city also offers budget accommodation in the form of hostels where rooms are generally shared with several others and may not have their own bathrooms. The majority are geared towards the young, or at least the under-35s. The best contact point is the main tourist office: **Office de Tourisme de Paris**, 25 rue des Pyramides, 75001, tel: 08 92 68 30 00, Jun–Oct daily 9–7; rest of year Mon–Sat 10–7, Sun and public hoildays 11–7. Métro: Pyramides, Tuileries. You need to arrive as early in the day as possible because lengthy queues soon build up. Youth hostels in the city include **Auberge Internationale des Jeunes**, in Bastille (10 rue Trousseau, 75011, tel: 01 47 00 62 00; www.aijparis.com Métro: Bastille, Ledru Rollin), with rooms for two, three or four people, and **Auberge de Jeunesse de Paris Jules Ferry** (8 boulevard Jules Ferry, 75011, tel: 01 43 57 55 60, Métro: Goncourt), with rooms for two, four or six.

Bed-and-Breakfasts

For bed-and-breakfast and sometimes an evening meal in private homes, contact: **France Lodge**, 2 rue Meissonier, 75017, tel: 01 56 33 85 85, Métro: Wagram.

The selection on ▶ 38–40 represents a small cross-section of some of Paris's best and most characterful hotels.

Expect to pay per double room:
€ under €120   €€ €120–250   €€€ €250–350   €€€€ over €350

Hôtel Agora €

In a good central location close to Les Halles and the Centre Pompidou, this establishment has an early 20th-century façade and a delightful interior that blends ancient and modern. There are five floors, served by lift; the bedrooms on the top floor are the most characterful, with sloping ceilings. Most rooms have shower/WC only, but some have baths, for which there is an extra charge.

➕ 200 C1 ✉ 7 rue de la Cossonnerie, 75001 ☎ 01 42 33 46 02; fax: 01 42 33 80 99 🚇 Les Halles

Hôtel Beaumarchais €€

One of the bargains among reasonably priced Parisian hotels, this was tastefully redesigned in the late 1990s. All rooms have bathrooms, with walls and fabrics in fun, primary colours or soothing ochres. Italian glass lamps are another feature. The lobby also bears some of these hallmarks. The 24-hour room service includes breakfast, though you'd be missing out on the treat of the flower-filled courtyard where coffee and croissants are served. Strategically located between the Bastille, the Marais and hip Oberkampf night-spots, this hotel is gay-friendly but not exclusively gay.

➕ 201 F2 ✉ 3 rue Oberkampf, 75011 ☎ 01 53 36 86 86; fax: 01 43 38 32 86; www.hotelbeaumarchais.com; email: reservations@hotel.beaumarchais.com 🚇 Oberkampf

Hôtel Caron de Beaumarchais €€

This historic hotel is named after the author of *The Marriage of Figaro* which inspired Mozart to write his famous opera. Take a romantic yet comfortable journey back to the 18th century in this delightful place; the hotel's 19 rooms are soundproofed and equipped with all modern conveniences: private bathroom/WC, air-conditioning, satellite TV, high-speed wifi Internet connection, breakfast is served until noon.

➕ 201 E1 ✉ 12 rue Vielle du Temple, 75004 ☎ 01 42 72 34 12; fax: 01 42 72 34 63; www.carondebeaumarchais.com 🚇 Hôtel de Ville

George V €€€€

Owned by the Four Seasons Group, this exclusive hotel maintains the impeccable standards you'd expect. Though named after an English king, it is very much a Parisian hotel with an international air. Grand high-ceilinged public rooms contain antique furniture, 17th-century tapestries, *objets d'art* and paintings, and lovely flower arrangements. High standards of service are provided in both the sumptuous suites and the bedrooms.

➕ 197 F3 ✉ 31 avenue George-V, 75008 ☎ 01 49 52 70 00; fax: 01 49 52 70 10; www.fourseasons.com/paris 🚇 George V

L'Hôtel €€€€

Formerly the Hôtel d'Alsace, this is where, on 30 November, 1900, Oscar Wilde died. Restored and re-opened in 1968 by the present owners, it retains many original features including a reconstruction of Wilde's modest room. By contrast, bedrooms are now spacious, air-conditioned and equipped with all the usual modern facilities. There's room service till 2am and even a *hamman* and indoor pool.

➕ 194 C5 ✉ 13 rue des Beaux-Arts, 75006 ☎ 01 44 41 99 00; fax: 01 43 25 64 81; www.l-hotel.com 🚇 St-Germain-des-Prés

Hôtel du Jeu de Paume €€–€€€

At the heart of Île St-Louis, this unique hotel was once a 17th-century royal indoor tennis court. Public areas are at different levels, with a comfortable mezzanine lounge and cellars with sauna, Jacuzzi and fitness equipment. The 28 bedrooms are quaint, cosy and comfortable; the staff very polite and friendly.

🚇 195 F4 | ✉ 54 rue St-Louis-en-l'Île, 75004 ☎ 01 43 26 14 18; fax: 01 40 46 02 76; www.jeudepaumehotel.com
🚇 Pont Marie

Hôtel du Levant €–€€

This family run hotel in the heart of the Latin Quarter, a 5-minute walk from Nôtre-Dame, is full of Parisian charm. The 46 rooms have shower or bath and WC, air-conditioning, satellite TV and Internet access. The breakfast is buffet style and there is a cosy lounge. Direct RER trains to the airports and Gare du Nord.

🚇 195 D4 | ✉ 18 rue de la Harpe, 75005 ☎ 01 46 34 11 00; fax: 01 46 34 25 87; www.hoteldulevant.com
🚇 Saint-Michel

Hotel du Louvre €€€€

This historic hotel, facing the Opéra Garnier and the Louvre Museum, was built in 1855 at the behest of Napoleon III and, at the time, was considered France's foremost luxury hotel. Past guests include artist Pisarro, who painted the opera house from the room now named the Pisarro Suite. The French Empire style has been preserved in all 177 recently renovated rooms and the hotel is currently offering a special "Da Vinci Code" package (following the success of Dan Brown's bestselling thriller), which includes a junior suite, Louvre Museum passes and a special "Da Vinci Code" map.

🚇 199 F2 | ✉ place André Malraux, 75001 ☎ 01 44 58 38 38; fax: 01 44 58 38 01; www.hoteldulouvre.com
🚇 Palais Royal-Musée du Louvre

Hôtel Meurice €€€€

Overlooking the Jardin des Tuileries, the building dates from 1907, the golden age of the palace hotel. It quickly became a favourite of the Imperial Court. Ambitious refurbishment has brought a spa and even more splendour to the hotel. Antique furniture, fresh flowers and original paintings add individuality to the luxurious bedrooms.

🚇 199 E2 | ✉ 228 rue de Rivoli, 75001 ☎ 01 44 58 10 10; fax: 01 44 58 10 15; www.meuricehotel.com ▸ Tuileries

Hôtel Montalembert €€€€

Now restored to its original 1926 splendour, the hotel incorporates many luxury materials in its construction and design. On the ground floor are an elegant bar, relaxing lounge and delightful patio garden. A fine marble staircase leads up to the 56 bedrooms, some modern, others in Louis-Philippe style. A few smaller rooms are less expensive. Bathrooms are opulent, with marble and chrome.

🚇 194 A5 | ✉ 3 rue de Montalembert, 75007 ☎ 01 45 49 68 68; fax: 01 45 49 69 49; www.montalembert.com
🚇 Rue du Bac

Hôtel de la Place du Louvre €€

From rooms with a view at this laid-back, welcoming hotel, you can admire the gargoyles of St-Germain l'Auxerrois and the elegant façade of the Louvre. Each of the comfortably spacious, individual bedrooms comes complete with a sparkling bathroom, and is named after a modern artist such as Monet or Modigliani. Although simple French breakfasts are served in the atmospheric Musketeers' Cellar, sample the city's best croissants at Cador, a venerable *salon de thé* at the end of the street.

🚇 200 B1 | ✉ 21 rue des Prêtres St-Germain-l'Auxerrois, 75001 ☎ 01 42 33 78 68; fax: 01 42 33 09 95; www.esprit-de-france.com
🚇 Louvre-Rivoli/Pont Neuf

Hôtel Prima Lepic €€

A discreet entrance on a busy, winding street leads into a brightly lit foyer, which in turn opens onto a spacious breakfast room furnished with attractive white wrought-iron furniture. The walls are decorated with murals depicting local scenes. The 38 bedrooms are bright, and tastefully furnished. The quietest rooms overlook the inner courtyard; those facing the street let you commune with the bustle of

Parisian life. Sacré-Coeur and the Moulin Rouge are a short walk away.

🕂 202 B3 ✉ 29 rue Lepic, 75018
☎ 01 46 06 44 64; fax: 01 46 06 66 11;
www.hotelprimalepic.com
Ⓜ Blanche/Abbesses

Relais St-Germain €€€

Set in a charming 17th-century townhouse, this idyllic hotel almost feels as though it is in the countryside. This is due not only to soundproof double-glazing and an abundance of flowers, but also to carved stonework, parquet flooring and wooden beams in most rooms. Ranging from intimate standards to large suites, most of the 22 rooms have a separate bathroom, and are named after French writers. The hotel's literary theme is reinforced by an enticing reading room off the tasteful lobby, where you can pick classics by Balzac and Flaubert off the shelves.

🕂 194 C4 ✉ 9 carrefour de l'Odéon, 75006 ☎ 01 43 29 12 05;
www.hotelrsg.com Ⓜ Odéon

Sofitel Arc de Triomphe €€–€€€€

This stylish, classical hotel is superbly located just off the Champs-Elysées and a stone's throw from the Arc de Triomphe and the city's main fashion district. Built during the Baron Haussmann era (➤ 30), it combines the best of traditional Haussmannian Paris with the conveniences of a modern hotel, with 134 rooms decorated in warm colours with period furniture and prints,

sumptuous beds and luxurious bathrooms. Each room contains the latest communications technology.

🕂 197 F4 ✉ 14 rue Beaujon, 75008
☎ 01 53 89 50 50; fax: 01 53 89 50 51
www.sofitel.com
Ⓜ Charles de Gaulle-Etoile

Terrass Hôtel €€€

At the foot of the Butte Montmartre and close to Sacré-Coeur, the Terrass has been run by the same family for four generations. The 100 comfortable bedrooms include 13 suites, and the 7th-floor restaurant (May–Sep only) has a superb view of the city, shared by front-facing rooms on the 4th to 6th floors. The restaurant on the ground floor is open year-round.

🕂 202 B3 ✉ 12 rue Joseph-de-Maistre 75018 ☎ 01 44 92 34 14; fax: 01 42 52 29 11; www.terrass-hotel.com
Ⓜ Blanche/Place-de-Clichy

La Villa Saint Germain €€€

For designer chic and cutting-edge décor, you can't go wrong with this gem, popular with celebrities. No period furnishings here – it's leather, stainless steel and polished granite all the way, but comfort is not sacrificed. Bedrooms and bathrooms are stylish and modern. There's a smart place-to-be-seen bar on the ground floor, plus well-stocked minibars in every room.

🕂 194 B5 ✉ 29 rue Jacob, 75006
☎ 01 43 26 60 00; fax: 01 46 34 63 63;
www.villa-saintgermain.com
Ⓜ St-Germain-des-Prés

Food and Drink

Paris enjoys an international reputation as the world capital of gastronomy. No trip to the city of lights would be complete without a serious look at some of its innumerable restaurants, brasseries, bistros and cafés.

For Parisians, gastronomy, or the art and science of good eating and drinking, is more than a pastime – it is a way of life in a city where the inhabitants spend a greater proportion of their income on food than they do on almost anything else.

Most restaurants open for lunch at noon and close at 2pm or 2:30pm, then open again at around 7pm for dinner until 10pm or 10:30pm. Note that many of the better restaurants close at the weekends, too, and nearly all for the whole of July or August.

A selection of restaurants is included at the end of each chapter.

Types of Cuisine

In his 32-volume *La France gastronomique*, Curnonsky, the famous French gastronome and author who died in 1956 aged 83, identified four distinct types of French cookery: "*La Haute cuisine, la cuisine Bourgeoise, la cuisine Régionale* and *la cuisine Improvisée*". Half a century later, his categories still stand.

- **Haute cuisine**, based on a solid classical foundation and built on long, hard-working and rigorous apprenticeships and great techniques, is professional cooking by chefs of the highest achievement. In current terms it describes accurately the cooking of multi-starred Michelin chefs such as Alain Ducasse (► 112) and Guy Savoy (► 21, 65).
- **Nouvelle cuisine** is (or was) a modern interpretation of *haute cuisine* in which top chefs reconstructed classic French dishes in response to demand in the 1980s for lighter, more decorative and fanciful food which relied heavily on much-reduced sauces to carry the flavours. In its original form, the style was short lived. However, *nouvelle cuisine* has left a distinctive mark on French *haute cuisine*, where classic dishes are now prepared in a much lighter vein than 25 years ago.
- By contrast, **cuisine improvisée** is peasant or rustic in origin and execution; in other words, old-fashioned farmhouse dishes using simple ingredients.
- But it is the two remaining categories that have most shaped the culinary map of Paris. **Cuisine bourgeoise**, or French provincial cooking, is based on the simple day-to-day dishes of ordinary middle-class French cookery. **Cuisine régionale**, meanwhile, features the great regional specialities of France, reflecting the produce of the various regions, with classic dishes such as *bouillabaisse* and *estouffade de boeuf* (beef stew) from Provence, pike with *beurre blanc* from the Loire, *coq au vin* from Burgundy and *cassoulet* from Toulouse.

Bistros, Brasseries and Restaurants

Visitors to Paris are often confused by the distinctions between bistros, brasseries and restaurants.

Bistros

- A bistro is basically a small, modest, often family-run establishment with a short menu of **traditional, home-style cooking**, together with a good selection of local cheeses.
- **Wine** is offered by the carafe or *pichet* (jug), with only a small selection available by the bottle.

Brasseries

- *Brasserie* is the French word for brewery, but the word nowadays describes a lively, smart, yet **informal** restaurant that serves food at any time of the day and often late into the night.
- **Beer** remains a feature, with some brasseries offering quite an extensive selection.
- **Typical dishes** are *choucroute*, a hearty blend of sauerkraut and assorted sausages, *blanquette de veau* (veal in a cream sauce) and steak *frites* (chips or fries) – frequently described as the national dish of France. Shellfish plays a major part, as witnessed by the mountainous displays outside many brasseries on Paris's more fashionable boulevards.

Restaurants

- Fully fledged restaurants offer elegant, classic *haute cuisine* in a more refined setting. Prices are higher, but frequently these restaurants offer **fixed-price menus** of surprisingly good value, especially at lunch-time.

- Some **specialise** in creative modern cooking, others in seafood or classic regional dishes.
- Whereas in a bistro or brasserie it is usual to order the house wine, restaurants often have long-standing **wine cellars** and *sommeliers* (wine waiters) who will happily give advice on what to order with the food.
- At top restaurants it is absolutely essential to **reserve your table** well in advance, often months.
- For dinner especially, both sexes should **dress smartly**, men with jacket and tie, though in trendier establishments ties are not *de rigueur*.

The Best Restaurant for...
...**Romance** – A. Beauvilliers, 75018 (➤ 158)
...**Ambience** – L'Ambroisie, 75004 (➤ 138)
...**Cuisine** – Pierre Gagnaire, 75008 (➤ 114)
...**Value for money** – À Deux Pas du Dos, 75003 (➤ 140)
...**Stylish indulgence** – Alain Ducasse, 75016 (➤ 112)

Cafés and Bars
- There are around **10,000 cafés and bars** in Paris. As French as the baguette, outdoor cafés with serried rows of outward-facing seats are ideal for people-watching. To adopt the café lifestyle just learn to nurse a beer or coffee for hours; waiters never seem to mind.
- **Coffee and beer** are the main drinks; tea is usually dreadful (except in *salons de thé*). Drink coffee black and order draught beer – *une pression* – it's cheaper. **Hot chocolate** (often made with real chocolate) is superb.
- Note that a **service charge** is automatically applied to all café bills, which you settle when you're ready to leave, and remember that *service compris* means "service is included".
- Staff should be addressed politely as "***monsieur***" or "***mademoiselle***": never call "*garçon!*" or snap your fingers.
- The hub of Paris café society is **St-Germain-des-Prés**: here you will find the world-famous **Café de Flore** and **Les Deux Magots**, once the haunts of bohemian existentialists but now highly sought-after tourist attractions, with prices to match.

Recommended Breakfast Venues
Café Beaubourg (➤ 138)
Le Cochon à l'Oreille 15 rue Montmartre, 75001 (➤ 15) – legendary workers' café near Les Halles, famous for its early snacks. ✚ 200 B2

Recommended Tea Salons
Angélina 226 rue de Rivoli, 75001 – great hot chocolate. ✚ 199 E2
L'Ébouillanté 6 rue des Barres, 75004 (www.restaurant-ebouillante.com) – tiny tea shop with delicious pastries. ✚ 195 F5
Ladurée 16 rue Royale, 75008 (www.laduree.fr) – old-fashioned tea room known for its macaroons. ✚ 199 D3
Mariage Frères (➤ 66)

Recommended Aperitif Venues
Café de la Musique 213 avenue Jean-Jaurés, 75019 – stunningly modern cocktail bar in the new Cité de la Musique complex. ✚ Off map
La Gueuze (➤ 87–88) – a temple to beer, with 130-plus different brands from around the world. ✚ 195 D3
Le Baron Aligre 1 rue Théophile Roussel, 75012 – part bar, part wine shop. ✚ Off map
Le Rouge Gorge 8 rue St-Paul, 75004 – country-style wine bar. ✚ 196 A4

Shopping

Paris excels in two notable areas: *haute couture* and *haute cuisine*. This is one of the style capitals of the world. Of the many pleasures of visiting this vibrant but often expensive capital, one that will not affect your pocket is window-shopping, admiring the exhilarating and fantastical displays on offer.

- Best for **exclusive shopping** is the Right Bank, in an area contained within boulevard de Sébastopol to the east, boulevard Haussmann to the north, and rue Washington and avenue George V to the west.
- The major **department stores** are also here (with the exception of Bon Marché in the 7th *arrondissement*, ➤ 67). These were the first in the world, designed as showplaces for affordable fashion and jewellery.
- Some of the more exclusive shops require you to be **dressed in a suitable manner**: scruffy attire is frowned upon.
- Shopping on the **Left Bank** is a more hit-and-miss affair, but the numerous narrow, crowded streets off boulevard St-Germain are worth exploring.
- To the east is the **5th** *arrondissement*, the student quarter, with its numerous bookshops.
- The **6th and 7th** *arrondissements* are home to a sumptuous array of antiques shops and individual boutiques, though the 7th, consisting largely of wealthy residential areas and government properties, lacks a good network of Métro connections: if you're prepared to do the legwork, however, there are some superb food shops to be discovered.

Cosmetics and Fragrances
- French cosmetics and fragrances can be either hugely less expensive or much the same price in France, so have your home stores' prices to hand to enable you to **make comparisons**.
- The major perfume houses often launch their new fragrances in the large department stores such as Galeries Lafayette: it's well worth paying them a visit to check out the **introductory offers**.

Gourmet Foods
- An increasing number of people flock to Paris in search of the finest and most delectable gourmet foods. It is a city of wonderful **pastry and chocolate shops**. Christian Constant (➤ 67) is a must for chocolate fans.
- For **cheeses** try Alléosse (➤ 116) in the 17th *arrondissement*, Androuët, Barthélémy and Marie-Anne Cantin all in the 7th (➤ 67), La Ferme St-Aubin (➤ 89) in the 4th and La Ferme St-Hubert (➤ 116) in the 7th.

Opening Hours
As a rule most shops are open until at least 7pm, but some close for lunch (noon–2) and on Mondays. The major chains are open continuously Monday to Saturday 9:30–7, usually with late nights till 10pm on Thursdays. Sunday opening is limited by law, but some supermarkets and small shops may open for at least some of the day, especially in more touristy areas.

Top Markets
Rue Mouffetard (Open: Tue–Sun 8–1, Métro: Monge) for foodstuffs.
Marché aux Fleurs (➤ 77) for all types of flowers.
Marché aux Puces de St-Ouen (➤ 157) seems to offer everything imaginable.
Marché aux Livres (Parc George Brassens, open: Sat and Sun 9:30–6, Métro: Porte de Vanves) for second-hand and antiquarian books.

Entertainment

The weekly *Pariscope* magazine is the essential guide for up-to-date listings of what's on in Paris. It contains *Time Out Paris* (www. timeout.com/paris/), a useful and informative six-page English-language insert at the back. There is also *l'Officiel des Spectacles*, available at news-stands.

Tickets

- For tickets to all events, including sport, classical music, jazz and rock, apply to **FNAC Spectacles** (136 rue de Rennes, 75006, tel: 08 92 68 36 22, Métro: St-Placide) or **Virgin Megastore** (52 avenue des Champs-Élysées, 75008, tel: 01 49 53 50 00, Métro: Franklin D Roosevelt). Book at least 14 days in advance.
- For discounted tickets on the day, be prepared to queue at **Kiosque Théâtre** (15 place de la Madeleine, 75008, Tue–Sat 12:30–8, Sun till 4. Closed Mon, Métro: Madeleine). Avoid the ticket agencies around the city.

Opera and Theatre

- Paris has **two opera houses** and four of France's **five national theatres**. In the latter you'll find French-language productions of the classics, including Molière, Goethe and Shakespeare.
- French theatre is very much geared towards **intellectual stimulation** rather than comedy and spectacle, the emphasis being on style and content of the spoken word rather than on action or characterisation.

Cinema

- Paris is the capital of the small **art house cinema**, with more than 300 films a week being screened in over 400 cinemas.
- The city's biggest screen is at the **Gaumont Grand Écran Italie** (30 place d'Italie, 75013, tel: 08 92 69 66 96, www.cinemasgaumontpathe.com Métro: Place d'Italie).
- **La Géode** at **Cité des Sciences et de l'Industrie** (► 156, 26 avenue Corentin Cariou, 75019, tel: 01 40 05 79 99) requires advance booking, but is worth it for its cinema-in-the-round special effects.
- For **arty, independent films** try cinemas in the MK2 chain (www.mk2.com).

Cabaret and Clubs

- Paris's cabarets and live shows feature **regularly renewed reviews** and are a plethora of glitter, dance-hall and transvestite vignettes nowadays geared towards an international audience. The most famous is the Moulin Rouge (► 152).
- The city's club scene begins around 1:30am, is expensive, and is geared towards the beautiful and **ultra-chic** – so definitely no trainers.

Sport

- There's plenty to entertain sports fans in Paris, from **Grand Slam tennis** at the Roland Garros tennis complex (2 avenue Gordon Bennet, 75016, tel: 01 47 43 48 00, www.rolandgarros.com) to **international football and rugby** at the Stade de France (St-Denis-la-Plaine, tel: 08 92 70 09 00, www.stadefrance.com). Major **horseracing** events take place at Longchamp racecourse in the Bois de Boulogne, and the celebrated **Tour de France** concludes in late July with hundreds of cyclists hurtling down the crowd-lined avenue des Champs-Elysées.

Eiffel Tower to St-Germain-des-Prés

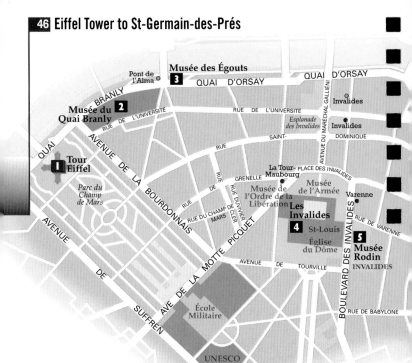

Getting Your Bearings

The Left Bank, or Rive Gauche, cradled by the Seine at the very heart of the city, oozes Parisian character and charm, with its bustling street markets, its long-aproned waiters in crowded cafés, its colourful street markets and sophisticated shopping, and its tiny candle-lit bistros with their cheery red-and-white checked tablecloths that take you back half a century or so. It is hardly surprising that it is an eternal favourite for visitors and one of the most sought-after residential districts in Paris.

In this chapter, the Left Bank includes the area south of the Seine from the Eiffel Tower in the west to the Jardin du Luxembourg in the east, but not the Latin Quarter. It contains many of the city's best known and most loved attractions, including the extraordinary Musée d'Orsay – an Industrial Age railway station audaciously converted into the capital's main Impressionist gallery; the atmospheric St-Germain-des-Prés *quartier* – the traditional intellectual and literary heart of Paris and a veritable paradise for gourmands, shoppers and coffee drinkers; and, of course, Eiffel's famous tower, which sits astride the urban landscape like a gigantic piece of Meccano.

Previous page: The Left Bank has long been home to many of Paris's most famous cafés

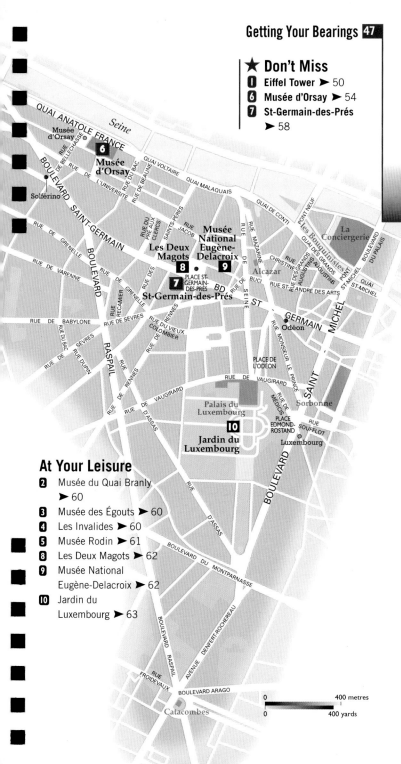

QUAI ANATOLE FRANCE
Seine
Musée d'Orsay

6

Musée d'Orsay

Solférino

BOULEVARD SAINT-GERMAIN

RUE DE BELLECHASSE
RUE DE L'UNIVERSITÉ
RUE DU BAC
QUAI VOLTAIRE
QUAI MALAQUAIS
QUAI DE CONTI
PONT NEUF
Les Bouquinistes
La Conciergerie
BOULEVARD DU PALAIS

RUE DE GRENELLE
RUE DE VARENNE
RUE DE BABYLONE
RUE DE SÈVRES
RUE DU BAC
SÈVRES
RUE DUPIN
RASPAIL
RUE DE RENNES
RUE RÉCAMIER
RUE DE GRENELLE
RUE DES SAINTS-PÈRES
RUE DU PRÉ AUX CLERCS
RUE JACOB
RUE DES SAINTS-PÈRES

Musée National Eugène-Delacroix

Les Deux Magots

8

9

RUE MAZARINE
RUE DE SEINE
RUE DE BUCI
CHRISTINE
RUE DAUPHINE
QUAI DES GRANDS AUGUSTINS
RUE DES GRANDS AUGUSTINS
RUE ST-ANDRÉ DES ARTS
PONT ST-MICHEL
QUAI ST-MICHEL
BOULEVARD ST-MICHEL

Alcazar

7

PLACE ST-GERMAIN-DES-PRÉS

St-Germain-des-Prés

BD
ST
GERMAIN
SAINT
MICHEL

Odéon

RUE DE VAUGIRARD
RUE DU VIEUX COLOMBIER
RUE DE RENNES
RUE DE VAUGIRARD
RUE D'ASSAS
RUE DE MÉDICIS
RUE MONSIEUR LE PRINCE
PLACE DE L'ODÉON
RUE SOUFFLOT
RUE

Palais du Luxembourg

10

Jardin du Luxembourg

PLACE EDMOND-ROSTAND
Sorbonne
Luxembourg

At Your Leisure

BOULEVARD DU MONTPARNASSE
BOULEVARD RASPAIL
AVENUE DENFERT-ROCHEREAU
RUE FROIDEVAUX
BOULEVARD ARAGO
RUE D'ASSAS

Catacombes

0 ___ 400 metres
0 ___ 400 yards

Enjoy a leisurely day of strolling on the Rive Gauche, taking in some of the finest pleasures the capital has to offer.

Eiffel Tower to St-Germain in a Day

9am

Arrive early (9am mid-June to August; 9:30 am rest of year) at the **⋯ Eiffel Tower** (▶ 50–53, right), beat the crowds and be among the first to reach the top for truly breathtaking views of the capital and the countryside beyond. On a clear day they say you can see as far as Chartres, over 70km (45 miles) away.

10am

Stroll down the Champ-de-Mars past *boules*-playing locals, children on ponies, lovers entwined on benches and camera-clicking tourists (the views from here of Eiffel's old iron lady are particularly photogenic). Continue on to **⋯ Les Invalides** (▶ 60) – it's the last resting place of Napoléon Bonaparte (left) and it's also one of the world's most comprehensive museums of military history.

12 noon

Arrive at the famous **⋯ Musée d'Orsay** art gallery (▶ 54–57, right) in plenty of time for lunch at the museum's excellent Café des Hauteurs. Then, for dessert, feast on Manets, Monets and other Impressionist treasures.

3:30pm

Make your way westwards along the Seine to browse in the tattered, green wooden booths of second-hand books and prints that line the river, known as *les bouquinistes* (➤ 24, left).

4pm

Explore the maze of streets south of *les bouquinistes* and you'll soon discover why **7 St-Germain-des-Prés** (➤ 58–59), centred on its famous church (right), is considered a shoppers' paradise, with its myriad tiny galleries, antiques dealers, chic interior design shops and fashion boutiques.

6pm

If by now you've run out of energy on your shopping spree, recharge your batteries with a coffee (or a refreshing *citron pressé* on a hot day) at the famous but touristy café, **8 Les Deux Magots** (➤ 62, left) on boulevard St-Germain. If possible, find a table outside overlooking the church of St-Germain-des-Prés. The bars and cafés of St-Germain have long been associated with Parisian intellectual life and, although the heydays of Hemingway and Sartre are gone, Les Deux Magots still draws a fascinating crowd of would-be writers, actors and philosophers.

8pm

St-Germain really comes alive by night. Head south of boulevard St-Germain and you'll be spoilt for choice of restaurants for dinner.

❶Eiffel Tower

Strange to think that Gustave Eiffel's famous tower, the universally beloved symbol of France, was considered a hideous eyesore when it was constructed more than 100 years ago. Yet since its inauguration in 1889, over 200 million people have climbed the tower, and today the "iron lady" attracts around 6 million visitors annually, making it one of the world's premier tourist attractions.

The lacy wrought-ironwork of this masterpiece of engineering is amazing and most visitors find soaring skywards in a double-decker glass lift both exciting and alarming. Writer Irwin Shaw saw it as a giant phallic symbol, while Hitler, passing through the city in 1940, was unimpressed: "Is that all it is? It's ugly!" Whatever your reaction, no visit to Paris is complete without seeing this awesome 7,000-tonne structure of gleaming brown metal, and the views from the top on a clear day are unforgettable.

Above: Gustave Eiffel also designed the frame of the Statue of Liberty in New York

In 1885, Paris held a competition to design a 300m (985-foot) tower as the centre-piece for the Centennial Exhibition of 1889. Gustave Eiffel, nicknamed the "magician of iron", won the contest with his seemingly functionless tower, beating 107 other

Left: The Eiffel Tower – high-point of the 1889 Exhibition

✚ 197 E1 ✉ Champ de Mars, 75007
☎ 01 44 11 23 23; www.tour-eiffel.fr
🕐 2 Sep to mid-Jun daily
9:30am–11:45pm; rest of year
9am–12:45am. Last access 45 mins
before closing 🍴 Café (Level 1) €;

Jules Verne restaurant (Level 2; ➤ 65)
€€€€ 🚇 Bir-Hakeim 🚆 RER Champ-
de-Mars 🛗 By elevator: 1st floor
inexpensive; 2nd floor moderate; 3rd
floor expensive. On foot (1st & 2nd
floors only) inexpensive

proposals, including one for a giant sprinkler and another for a monster commemorative guillotine.

It took less than two years to build the tower. Initially it grew at a rate of 10m (33 feet) a month, speeding up to nearly 30m (98 feet) a month as it neared the summit. Yet on the day it opened, none of the lifts worked. Eiffel and his 60-strong party of officials had to climb the 1,710 steps to place the French flag at the top. (There are now 1,665 steps to the top, but the staircase leading to the third level is closed to the public.)

For years the finished product remained a world-record breaker, twice the height of any other building (until New York's Chrysler building went up in 1930). For the first six months it drew a staggering 12,000 visitors a day. However, it was not without its critics, who slated it as "scrap metal" even as it was being built.

Local residents objected to this "overpowering metal construction" that straddled their district, fearing it would sway and collapse, crushing their homes beneath it. Author Guy de Maupassant was a regular at the second-floor restaurant, swearing that it was the only spot in Paris from which you could not see the tower! Together with 300 other prominent members of the intelligentsia of the time (including Charles Garnier, Charles Gounoud and Alexandre Dumas), he launched a petition against its

VITAL STATISTICS

WEIGHT: 7,300 tonnes
TOTAL HEIGHT: 324m (1,063 feet) (15cm/ 6 inches higher on hot days due to metal expansion)
NUMBER OF METAL SECTIONS: 18,000
NUMBER OF RIVETS: 2.5 million
NUMBER OF RIVET HOLES: 7 million
NUMBER OF STEPS: 1,710

❏ **Visibility from the top:** 75km (47 miles)
❏ **Maximum sway at the top:** 12cm (5 inches)

erection, describing it as a "monstrous construction", a "skeleton", a "hollow candlestick" and a "bald umbrella", and condemning it as a "crime against history and against Paris". On a more positive note, the playwright Jean Cocteau described it as the "Queen of Paris".

The tower was originally designed to stand for 20 years.

EIFFEL TOWER: INSIDE INFO

Top tips Visit early in the morning or late at night to avoid the worst of the crowds. **For the best views**, arrive one hour before sunset.
• The tower itself looks at its **best after dark** when every girder is illuminated.
• Get your postcards stamped with the famous **Eiffel Tower postmark** at the post office on level one (daily 10–7:30).
• The tower celebrated the **Millennium** with a **sparkling show**. This lighting effect has now become a permanent feature; the **glittering lights** come on for the first 10 minutes of every hour, from nightfall until 2am in summer, 1am in winter.

Fast track Climb the stairs to the first level (57m/187 feet; it takes about 5 minutes). Catch your breath in the *cineiffel* (a short film recounts the tower's history), then walk or take the lift to level two (115m/377 feet). (Tickets for both stages from the ticket office at the bottom of the southern pillar – Pilier Sud.)

Fortunately, its height was to be its salvation – the tall iron tower proved to be a marvellous antenna. The first news bulletin was broadcast from the Eiffel Tower in 1921, and the first television broadcast in 1935. It was also used to measure atmospheric pressure and, after being reclaimed from its German occupiers in 1944, to decipher German World War II radio codes. In 1937, it was the venue for a beauty contest, at which the minimum height required of contestants was 1.75m (5 feet 7 inches), as a token of respect for the tall iron lady!

Over the years, countless eccentrics have jumped off the tower with various home-built flying machines, hang-gliders and parachuting kit. In 1977, a crazy but skilful American

Previous page and below: On a clear day you can see for 75km (47 miles) from the top of the tower

pilot flew between the legs of the tower and promptly lost his flying licence.

TAKING A BREAK
Try the impressive regional cooking at **Altitude 95** (1st floor Eiffel Tower, tel: 01 45 55 20 04, open daily noon–2:30, 7–11).

5 Musée d'Orsay

If you visit only one art gallery during your stay, make it the Musée d'Orsay, a feast of 19th-century art and design, including a hugely popular collection of Impressionist paintings. The originality of this amazing museum lies in its presentation of a wide range of different art forms – painting, sculpture, decorative and graphic art – all under the lofty glass roof of a former Industrial Age railway station.

The museum occupies the former Gare d'Orsay, built by Victor Laloux on the site of the Palais d'Orsay, which was destroyed during the Paris Commune in 1871 (➤ 9). The station was inaugurated in 1900 but ceased operating in 1939 with the dawn of electric trains, and remained empty for several decades. It was subsequently used as an auction room by Drouot-Richelieu, then as a theatre, and was saved from demolition by the skin of its teeth in 1973, thanks to the public outcry over the destruction of the historic pavilions at Les Halles food market (➤ 133). It was finally converted into a museum in 1986.

The Gare d'Orsay had always been an admirable piece of architecture. Even at its inauguration the monumental iron-and-glass edifice of cathedral-like proportions was considered so striking that painter Édouard Detaille suggested it should be converted into a museum or art gallery. Thankfully, much of the original architecture, including its crowning glory – the beautiful vaulted glass roof, enhanced today by a marvellous statue-lined promenade running the full length of the building – has been retained.

The station's two massive clocks have also been restored. One provides the backdrop for the Café des Hauteurs on the top floor. Watching its giant minute hand clunk round the hour ensures a swift lunch here! In its heyday, the Gare d'Orsay took

Above: Everything about the Musée d'Orsay is striking – even the building is a work of art

---

🔢 199 E1
✉ 1 rue de la Légion d'Honneur, 75007
☎ 01 40 49 48 14; www.musee-orsay.fr
🕐 Tue–Sun 9:30–6 (Thu until 9:45pm). Ticket sales stop 30 minutes before closing time.

Closed 1 Jan, 1 May, 25 Dec
🍴 Self-service cafeteria €; café €; restaurant €€
Ⓜ Solférino
🚉 RER Musée d'Orsay
💶 Moderate. Free on the first Sunday of the month.

Left: A bird's-eye view inside the Musée d'Orsay

Fine furnishings on display in the Musée d'Orsay

great pride in its hotel. Its expansive *belle époque* dining-room has been preserved on the first floor, complete with gilded mirrors and candelabras, offering sensational views across the Seine to the Rive Droite.

Seeing the Museum

The precious art collections span the years from 1848 to 1914, conveniently starting where the Louvre (► 96–101) leaves off and ending where the Centre Pompidou (► 124–127) begins. They are **organised chronologically on three levels**, with additional displays throughout clarifying the various contexts in which the art was created.

The skylit upper level houses the biggest crowd-puller – a dazzling collection of Impressionist and post-Impressionist treasures. It would be impossible to list all the star attractions, but favourites include Monet's *Coquelicots* (*Poppies*) and *La Rue Montorgueil – Fête du 30 juin 1878*, Renoir's *Danse à la ville* (*Town Dance*) and *Danse à la campagne* (*Country Dance*), Van Gogh's *La Chambre à Arles* (*Room at Arles*) and Matisse's pointillist *Luxe, calme et volupté*. Montmartre

The Ugolin statue by Carpeaux

Sculpture

Throughout the museum you will find priceless sculptures at every turn, especially along the central aisle. The 26 caricature busts of members of parliament here by satirist Honoré Daumier are especially entertaining. The middle floor includes treasures by Rodin, including the plaster version of *La Porte de l'Enfer* (*Gateway to Hell*), a vast bronze that occupied the last 37 years of his life but remained unfinished at his death. Many of the Degas bronzes on the top floor were cast from wax sculptures found in his studio after his death, but the beautiful and unique *Danseuse habillée* (*Clothed Dancer*) was exhibited during his lifetime.

fans will especially enjoy Renoir's *Bal du Moulin de la Galette*, Degas' *L'Absinthe* and Toulouse-Lautrec's *Danse au Moulin Rouge*, all inspired by local scenes.

The close juxtaposition of paintings and sculptures on the ground floor illustrates the huge stylistic variations in art from 1848 to 1870 (the key date when Impressionism first made its name). Look out in particular for Courbet's *L'Origine du monde* (*Origin of the World*) and early Impressionist-style works such as Boudin's *La Plage de Trouville* (*The Beach at Trouville*) and Monet's *La Pie* (*The Magpie*). Here, too, are the "opera rooms" – devoted to architect Charles Garnier and his *pièce de résistance*, the Opéra de Palais Garnier (➤ 107) – and a fantastic bookshop.

The Church at Auvers clearly demonstrates the bold, distinctive style of Vincent Van Gogh

The middle level features *objets d'art* of the art nouveau movement, displaying the sinuous lines – epitomised here in furniture by Charles Rennie Mackintosh and jewellery and glassware by Lalique – that led the French to nickname the movement *style nouille* (noodle style).

MUSÉE D'ORSAY: INSIDE INFO

Top tips Be sure to **pick up a plan of the museum** as the layout is not clearly signed and can be rather confusing.

• Buy a copy of the excellent ***Pocket Guide***. It provides a succinct outline of the most important works of the collection. For a more comprehensive look at the collection, the beautifully illustrated ***Guide to the Musée d'Orsay*** is a must for all self-respecting art-buffs.

• If you are pressed for time, **ignore the lower floors** and head straight to the upper level to see the famous Impressionists on the river side of the gallery.

Tickets and tours Tickets for the permanent exhibits are valid all day, so **you can leave and re-enter** the museum as you please.

• There are **separate fees** for temporary exhibitions. Prices vary depending on the exhibition. There are plans for ticket machines, which should cut down the often lengthy queues.

• **English-language tours** (charge: moderate) begin daily (except Sun and Mon) at 11:30am. Ask for a ticket at the information desk.

• **Audioguides** – cassette tours (charge: moderate, available in six languages from just beyond the ticket booths on the right) – steer you round the major works, many of which had a revolutionary impact on 19th-century art. Both these and the English-language tours are excellent.

❻ St-Germain-des-Prés

Chic, lively and centrally located, St-Germain-des-Prés represents everyone's idea of the "Left Bank". It bursts with cafés, restaurants, antiques shops, art galleries and fashion boutiques, and is peopled by students, arty types, the "*caviar gauche*" – the wealthy socialist intelligentsia – and the simply rich, who come here to sample the bohemian life.

St-Germain's eventful history dates back to the 6th century with the founding of the Benedictine Abbey of St-Germain-des-Prés, a powerful ecclesiastical complex throughout the Middle Ages. After the Revolution of 1789 only the **church of St-Germain-des-Prés** survived, a fine example of the Romanesque style and the oldest church in Paris. Its graceful bell tower is a useful landmark for visitors.

The area around the church was first developed in the late 1600s, but today it is celebrated for its 19th-century charm. It gained its reputation as the intellectual and literary heart of Paris between the two world wars, when just about every notable Parisian artist, writer, philosopher and politician frequented three now-legendary cafés on boulevard St-Germain – the **Café de Flore** (No 172, ► 16), **Brasserie Lipp** (No 151) and most famous of all, **Les Deux Magots** (No 170, ► 15, 62). Later, in the 1950s, the area became the hot spot for the jazz generation.

You'll find plenty to tempt the taste-buds at the colourful rue de Buci market

The main artery of boulevard St-Germain stretches east–west from the Latin Quarter to the staid government buildings and mansions of the Faubourg St-Germain. It also divides St-Germain-des-Prés neatly into two halves. To the north, you will find traditional cafés, hundreds of art galleries and antiques shops and the **École des Beaux-Arts**; to the south lie trendy bars, eateries and shopping streets containing such gems as **Bon Marché** (► 67), the city's first department store.

Today, St-Germain is uncertain whether to cling to its pre-war intellectual days or to move with the times as part of the new, forward-looking capital. It is still the literary and artistic heart of Paris, with the École des Beaux-Arts and most publishing houses established here, and with countless antiques dealers still thriving on selling the past. But the spotlight has been turned on to fashion, and the area is now considered a luxury shopping district with such designers as Giorgio Armani, Kenzo, Christian Lacroix, Yves Saint Laurent and Sonia Rykiel moving in from the Rive Droite. Yet despite its *nouveau-glamour*, St-Germain still retains its arty atmosphere, a slower pace of life than the Rive Droite, and its popularity. (See also walk on pages 178–179.)

Opposite: The ancient church of St-Germain-des-Prés – a gem of Romanesque architecture

➕ 194 B/C5 ✉ 75006 🚇 St-Germain-des-Prés

ST-GERMAIN-DES-PRÉS: INSIDE INFO

Absolute musts Treat yourself to **a picnic** from the rue de Buci market (mornings only) or the covered Marché St-Germain.

• Soak up the atmosphere of tiny, tranquil **place Furstenberg**.

• **Window-shop** in the streets of the Carré Rive Gauche, the grid of streets around rue de Beaune, famous for high-quality antiques.

• **People-watch** in one of the great literary cafés (► 15).

• Browse through *les bouquinistes*, the ramshackle old green booths of second-hand literary treasures that line the banks of the Seine (► 24).

At Your Leisure

2 Musée du Quai Branly

Designed by Jean Nouvel and surrounded by landscaped public gardens, the stunning new ethnological museum devoted to the arts and civilisations of Africa, Asia, Oceania and the Americas offers visitors a new approach to non-Western cultures. The exhibits came from the Musée de l'Homme in the Palais de Chaillot (➤ 110) and from the former Musée des Arts d'Afrique et d'Océanie on the edge of the Bois de Vicennes. Temporary exhibitions (often displaying works lent by museums from all over the world), shows, concerts, workshops and activities for all ages bring life to this decidedly 21st-century museum.

🚯 197 F1/2 ✉ 27, 37 and 51 quai Branly; 206, and 218 rue de l'Université, 75007 ☎ 01 56 61 70 01; www.quaibranly.fr ⏰ Tue–Sun 10–6:30 (Thu until 9:30). Last access 45 mins before closing. Closed public hols 🍴 Café €, restaurant €€ 🚇 Alma-Marceau 🚉 RER Pont de l'Alma

3 Musée des Égouts

Immortalised in *Les Misérables* as an escape route for Jean Valjean, and the location of the phantom's lair beneath the Opéra Garnier in the hit show *Phantom of the Opera*, the sewers of Paris form a sophisticated 2,100km (1,300-mile) maze of subterranean tunnels, masterfully constructed by Baron Haussmann in the late-19th century. You, too, can discover the mysteries of underground Paris in what is undoubtedly the smelliest museum in Paris.

🚯 198 A2 ✉ Pont de l'Alma, rive gauche (entrance in front of 93 quai d'Orsay), 75007 ☎ 01 53 68 27 81 ⏰ Sat–Wed 11–5, May–Sep; 11–4, rest of year. Closed two weeks in Jan for maintenance 🚇 Alma-Marceau 🚉 RER Pont de l'Alma 🎟 Inexpensive

4 Les Invalides

The imposing architectural ensemble of Les Invalides, constructed around a grand church and housing several museums, is a must, especially for anyone interested in French military history. It is best approached from Pont Alexandre III, up the long grassy esplanade, with its fountains carefully

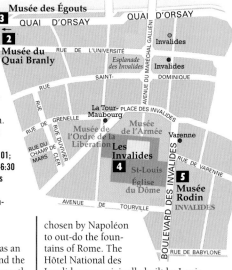

chosen by Napoléon to out-do the fountains of Rome. The Hôtel National des Invalides was originally built by Louis XIV as a convalescent home for wounded soldiers. Its austere 195m (640-foot) long slate and stone façade is a splendid example of 17th-century classical architecture. In its heyday, the complex resembled a small town.

Though still home to war veterans, Les Invalides stands today as a memorial to the endless battles and campaigns that have marked French history, all vividly portrayed in the **Musée de l'Armée** – one of the most comprehensive museums of its kind in the world. Of particular interest is the **Museum of Relief Maps** with its models of fortified towns, illustrating the art of siege from Louis XIV to Napoléon III, and the

Above: The Sun King's Église du Dome
contains Napoléon's tomb
Below: *Le Penseur* (The Thinker) by Rodin

exhibition spanning the two world
wars. Admission to the museum also
covers the **Musée de l'Ordre de la
Libération** and the **Église du Dôme**.
This masterpiece of 17th-century
church architecture rises high above
the Hôtel des Invalides. Inside, the
centrepiece is Napoléon's mausoleum:
a circular crypt containing coffins
within a red porphyry sarcophagus.
Adjoining the Dôme, and originally
part of it, the **Soldiers Church** is far
more tasteful, decorated only by a row
of poignantly faded *tricolore* pennants.

🔲 193 E5 ✉ esplanade des Invalides,
75007 ☎ 01 44 42 38 77;
www.invalides.org ⏰ Apr–Sep saily
10–6; rest of year 10–5; mid-Jun to mid-
Sep Dôme open until 7. Closed 1st Mon
of month 🍴 Café € 🚇 La Tour-
Maubourg/Varenne/Invalides 🚉 RER
Invalides 🎫 Moderate

Napoléon Bonaparte

Napoléon is associated with this
district of Paris more than any other
French ruler. Here he celebrated his
military successes, staging grandiose
parades on the Champ-de-Mars. He
used the esplanade outside Les
Invalides to show off his war spoils –
guns captured in Vienna in 1803 and
a lion statue plundered from St Mark's
Square in Venice – and he honoured
his victorious armies in Les Invalides
and the nearby École Militaire, where
he himself had trained as a young
officer. His passing-out report noted:
"If the circumstances are right, he
could go far".

5 Musée Rodin

Nowhere is more pleasurable on a
sunny day than the sculpture-studded
gardens of the Musée Rodin, an open-
air museum dedicated to the best-
known sculptor of the modern age.
Rodin lived and worked in the adjoining elegant mansion – Hôtel Biron –
alongside Cocteau and Matisse. Built
in 1730, the house was a dance hall,

convent and school before
becoming artists' studios. On
Rodin's death, it became
the Musée Rodin.

Inside are 500
Rodin sculptures,
including such
masterpieces as *The
Kiss*, and *The Age
of Bronze*, whose
realism so
startled the crit-
ics that they
accused him of
having impris-
oned a live boy
in the plaster.

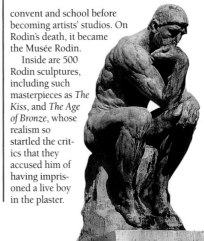

LE PENSEVR

You can see Rodin's most celebrated work, *The Thinker* (➤ 61), in deep contemplation in the garden he loved so much. Today it provides an intimate setting for such major works as the *Burghers of Calais* and *Balzac*, as well as sculptures by Camille Claudel, his one-time pupil, model and lover.

🔶 193 E5 ✉ 77 rue de Varenne, 75007 ☎ 01 44 18 61 10; www.musee-rodin.fr 🕐 Apr–Sep Tue–Sun 9:30–5:45 (last entrance 5:15, park closes at 6:45); rest of year Tue–Sun 9:30–4:45 (last entrance 4:15, park closes at 5). Closed Mon, 1 Jan, 25 Dec 🍴 Café (9:30–5:30, Apr–Sep; 9:30–4:30, rest of year) € 🚇 Varenne 🎟 Moderate (garden only inexpensive)

🗓 Les Deux Magots

Described by journalist Albert Thibaudet as "an intersection of roads, an intersection of professions, an intersection of ideas", Les Deux Magots was founded in 1881 and named after the wooden statues of two Chinese dignitaries (*magots*) who sit atop boxes of money on a pedestal inside the café. It was a particular favourite of Picasso and Hemingway, who would read his works aloud here. Jean-Paul Sartre and Simone de Beauvoir, however, preferred

Visit the intimate Musée Delacroix and wind the clocks back to 19th-century Paris

Café de Flore near by (No 172, ➤ 16), while **Brasserie Lipp** (No 151, ➤ 65) was a favourite of St-Exupéry, Camus and President Mitterrand. Nowadays, the cafés are popular tourist haunts, but legends die hard and they still attract a surprising number of celebrities and members of the literary élite.

🔶 194 B5 ✉ 170 boulevard St-Germain, 75006 ☎ 01 45 48 55 25 🚇 St-Germain-des-Prés

🗓 Musée National Eugène-Delacroix

Hidden off the road in a charming cobbled courtyard, this tiny museum was the last home and studio of the great French Romantic painter, from 1857 until his death, at the age of 60, in 1863. Among the modest belongings on display are Delacroix's paintboxes and palettes, some of his sketches, self-portraits and animal paintings and lots of letters. In many ways, his airy, generously windowed studio is an attraction in itself. As Delacroix himself wrote, "My lodgings are indeed charming. The sight of my small garden and the cheerfulness of my studio always give me pleasure."

🔶 194 C5 ✉ 6 rue de Furstenberg, 75006 ☎ 01 44 41 86 50; www.musee-delacroix.fr 🕐 Wed–Mon 9:30–5 🚇 St-Germain-des-Prés 🎟 Inexpensive; free 1st Sun of month

⑩ Jardin du Luxembourg

Numerous artists, poets, writers and philosophers have paid tribute to the beautiful Jardin du Luxembourg, one of the oldest parks in Paris, designed in the formal French style with precisely planted rows of trees, trim hedges, immaculate lawns, fountains, ponds and bench-lined gravel paths. It remains a favourite rendezvous for students and residents of the Latin Quarter.

The Medici Fountain is always a favourite corner in the Luxembourg Gardens

brief interlude during World War II, when the German occupying forces made it their headquarters.

🏠 194 C3 ✉ boulevard St-Michel, 75006 ☎ 01 42 34 23 89
🕐 Daily 7:30/8:15–dusk
Ⓜ Odéon
🚇 RER Luxembourg
🆓 Free

The grand Palais du Luxembourg overlooking the gardens was built for Marie de' Médicis, widow of Henri IV. It was completed in 1627, but she lived there for only five years before being expelled from France by Cardinal Richelieu. It remained a royal residence until the Revolution, when it was used as a prison. Since 1879, it has been the seat of the French Senate, with a

For Kids

• The dizzying heights of the **Eiffel Tower** (➤ 50–53).
• **Puppet shows** in the Champ-de-Mars (daily at 3:15pm and 4:15pm during school holidays).
• **Musée des Égouts** (➤ 60) – Paris's underground sewer system.
• **Jardin du Luxembourg** (➤ above) – for adventure playground, pony rides, carrousel, model yachts, street entertainers, puppet shows and other treats.
• **The Catacombs** (➤ 9) – Paris's most ghoulish chamber of horrors (not recommended for young children).

Where to...
Eat and Drink

Prices
Expect to pay per person for a meal, excluding drinks:

€ up to €25 €€ €25–50 €€€ €50–100 €€€€ over €100

L'Affriolé €€

This intimate bistro's name comes from the Old French word for "to tempt", and the inventive brasserie-based cuisine conjured up by Alain Atibard does just that. Varied dishes bursting with flavour and based on seasonal produce, like stuffed rabbit with green pea purée and baked apple with pine nuts, are served stylishly on beautiful ceramic-tiled tables. As an original touch, home-candied orange peel and crack-your-own walnuts round off every meal. Lesser-known regions are favoured on the extensive wine list.

🕇 198 A1 ⊠ 17 rue Malar, 75007 ☎ 01 44 18 31 33 ⓖ Tue–Sat noon–2:30, 7:30–10:30. Closed Aug Ⓜ Invalides

Alcazar €€€

Terence Conran has hit Paris and scored a roaring success at this hip restaurant whose mezzanine resounds to funky sounds and clinking cocktail glasses every Saturday evening. Soothing jazz or blues often accompany lunch and dinner, while the popular Sunday brunch has a Japanese-style massage included. The food will be familiar to Conran fans, as will the vibrant, postmodern décor of white ceilings and pillar-box red columns, with flower displays dangling above the tables. Starter salads are massive, almost a meal in themselves, while the main courses include fish and chips and confit of duck as symbols of gastronomic *entente cordiale*. Vegetarians are properly catered for. Book ahead at weekends.

🕇 194 C5 ⊠ 62 rue Mazarine, 75006 ☎ 01 53 10 19 99; www.alcazar.fr ⓖ Lunch Mon–Sat noon–3, brunch Sun noon–3:30, dinner Mon–Sun 7–1 Ⓜ Odéon

L'Arpège €€€€

Located in a quiet street mainly of government offices, the restaurant interior is sombrely yet stylishly, minimalist with its largely unadorned curved pearwood panelling. In this setting Alain Passard's traditional cooking positively glows with originality, his style honed from stints with Boyer in Reims and Senderens at Lucas Carton. It's all excellent value, expensive though it is, and of course very popular, so make sure you book in advance.

🕇 193 F5 ⊠ 84 rue de Varenne, 75007 ☎ 01 47 05 09 06; www.alain-passard.com ⓖ Noon–2, 6–10. Closed Sat, Sun Ⓜ Varenne

Barocco €€

In contrast to other Parisian restaurants of a South American colour where kitsch and fun are *de rigeur*, Barocco has cosy décor with comfortable, velvet armchairs, elegant tableware and an interesting library. The food is equally good, mixing Brazilian zest and French delicacy. The fish and seafood cooked in coconut milk, lamb and sweet potatoes. There is live music from Sunday to Thursday.

➕ 194 C5 ☒ 23 rue Mazarine, 75006 ☎ 01 43 26 40 24; www.restaurant-latino.com ⊚ Mon–Sat noon–3, 7–2am, Sun 7–2am ⊜ Odéon

Les Bistrot du 7ème €

What could be more pleasant on a cool evening than a candlelit dinner in this cheerful little bistro a stone's throw from Les Invalides? The cuisine is traditional with a slight regional influence: *foie gras* and *duck à l'orange*, fillet of scorpion fish Provençal style, kidneys in mustard sauce. There is a choice of meats at very reasonable prices and a large selection of wines. Expect a cosy convivial atmosphere and a warm welcome.

➕ 198 B1 ☒ 56 boulevard de la Tour-Maubourg, 75007 ☎ 01 45 51 93 08 ⊚ Daily noon–2:20, 7–10:30. Closed Sat and Sun lunch ⊜ La Tour-Maubourg

Les Bouquinistes €€

One of Guy Savoy's satellite restaurants, this trendy Left Bank bistro is named after the *bouquinistes* (booksellers) on the *quai*. Décor is a blend of creamy hues with small colourful highlights gouged out of the plastered walls. The minimalist setting complements a short, modish menu. A blackboard lists a selection of the day's specials. Dishes are innovative and prepared with attention to detail. Service is pleasant and friendly.

➕ 195 D5 ☒ 53 quai des Grands Augustins, 75006 ☎ 01 43 25 45 94; www.lesbouquinistes.com ⊚ Mon–Fri noon–2:30, 7–11, Sat 7–11. Closed Christmas ⊜ St-Michel

Le Cherche Midi €€

The ideal place to take refuge from chic shopping in the neighbourhood boutiques, this is a good old-fashioned cram-them-in and feed-them-well trattoria. The tasty menu holds no surprises – antipasti, pasta, grilled meats and veal escalopes – but servings are hearty, and the Montepulciano flows copiously. Meats are served with perfectly cooked vegetables plus *polenta*. The décor is that of a former boulevard bistro, but there's a small terrace for the warmer months. The puddings belong to the familiar repertoire of Italian specials (*pannacotta* and *tiramisu*) but you can also sample the famous Berthillon ice-cream.

➕ 194 A4 ☒ 22 rue du Cherche-Midi, 75006 ☎ 01 45 48 27 44 ⊚ Daily noon–3, 8–11:45 ⊜ Sevres-Babylone

Le Divellec €€€€

Jacques Le Divellec is one of the capital's prime exponents of contemporary fish cooking, the juxtaposition of raw fish and *joie gras* being his creation. His lobster press is based on the Tour d'Argent's famous duck press. The dining room overlooks the Esplanade des Invalides and the décor has a nautical theme, complementing the simple yet innovative cuisine.

Elaborate sauces and unnecessary garnishes are shunned in favour of the quality and flavour of the fish.

➕ 202 B1 ☒ 107 rue de l'Université 75007 ☎ 01 45 51 91 96; www.le-divellec.com ⊚ Mon–Fri noon–2, 7:30–9:30. Closed 1 week at Christmas ⊜ Invalides

Jules Verne €€€€

You need to book two months in advance to secure a table for dinner (one week for lunch) in this stunning location on the second level of the Eiffel Tower, reached via a dedicated elevator. At 115m (375 feet) above the city, the superb views complement the highly imaginative and sophisticated cuisine by Alain Ducasse. The black décor and artwork provide minimum distraction from the Parisian panorama, day or night.

➕ 197 E1 ☒ Second floor, Tour Eiffel, 75007 ☎ 01 45 55 61 44 ⊚ Daily 12:15–3.30, 7:15–9:30 ⊜ Bir Hakeim/Champ de Mars

Mariage Frères €

A chic and expensive tea shop which offers more than 460 teas from 20 countries. The colonial Indian atmosphere of the elegant upstairs dining-room of the 17th-century building is the setting for an imaginative menu focused almost entirely on tea. As well as delicious afternoon teas, it's ideal for lunch. The original shop is at 30 rue du Bourg-Tibourg in the Marais.

✚ **195 D5** ◻ **13 rue des Grands-Augustins, 75006** ☎ **01 40 51 82 50; www.mariagefreres.com** Ⓖ **Daily noon–7** Ⓜ **Odéon**

Le Petit St-Benoît €

To rub shoulders with the locals – signed photos testify to past visits from great writers and intellectuals – this is the place to come, but don't confuse it with similarly named restaurants near by. Old-fashioned dishes like *petit salé aux lentilles* or rabbit with mustard are mainstays at this fussily scruffy place. Soups and terrines are made to centuries-old recipes, while main courses usually come with a heap of mashed potatoes or pasta. Good bread and fruity house wines are bonuses, as is the terrace for summer lunch-times – watching passers-by here is part of the fun. No credit cards.

✚ **194 B5** ◻ **4 rue St-Benoît, 75006** ☎ **01 42 60 27 92** Ⓖ **Mon–Sat noon– 2:30, 7–10:30. Closed Aug** Ⓜ **St-Germain-des-Prés**

Le Récamier €€

A favourite of politicians and publishers, this is a snug, comfortable restaurant specialising in hearty Burgundian dishes such as *jambon persillé* (ham with parsley in aspic), *oeufs en meurette* (eggs in red wine with garlic, onions and bacon bits), and a wonderful *boeuf bourguignon* with fresh noodles. The wine list features vintages of claret, burgundy and Rhône wines from the 1950s.

✚ **194 A4** ◻ **4 rue Récamier, 75007** ☎ **01 45 48 86 58** Ⓖ **12:30–2:30, 7:30–10:30. Closed Sun** Ⓜ **Sèvres-Babylone**

La Rôtisserie d'En Face €€

Tucked away down a narrow street and across the road from his main nearby eponymous restaurant at 14 rue des Grands-Augustins (tel: 01 43 26 49 39), this is one of Jacques Cagna's cheaper dining options (the other one is L'Espadon Bleu). The setting is lively and informal with a good choice of dishes bearing the Cagna hallmark of care and quality. The suckling pig and spit-roast chicken from the *rôtisserie* are delicious. Look for game in season, and for dessert opt for the delicious fruit tart of the day.

✚ **194 C5** ◻ **2 rue Christine, 75006** ☎ **01 43 26 40 98; www.jacques-cagna.com** Ⓖ **Mon–Fri noon–2:30, 7–11 (Fri 11:30), Sat 7–11:30** Ⓜ **Odéon/St-Michel**

Vagenende €–€€

This fine Listed building, designed as a brewery at the turn of the 20th century, is now an elegant brasserie boasting a stunning art nouveau décor. The French cuisine is prepared with fresh market produce in true regional tradition: seafood pie with lobster sauce, *foie gras* with Gewurztraminer wine, traditional Alsace-style *choucroute*.

✚ **194 C4** ◻ **142 boulevard St-Germain, 75006** ☎ **01 43 26 68 18; www.vagenende.fr** Ⓖ **Daily noon–1am** Ⓜ **Odéon**

Le Violon d'Ingres €€€

Christian Constant, former head chef at Les Ambassadeurs in the Hotel de Crillon, now combines *haute cuisine* with a more down-to-earth rusticity at his comfortable and extremely fashionable Left Bank bistro. Prices, though not exorbitant, reflect the painstaking care put into the highly skilled preparation of the food and the exemplary standards of service. (See also Christian Constant, ▶ 67.)

✚ **197 F1** ◻ **135 rue St-Dominique, 75007** ☎ **01 45 55 15 05; www.leviolondingres.com** Ⓖ **Tue–Sat noon–2:30, 7 –10:30. Closed 3 weeks Aug** Ⓜ **École Militaire**

Where to...
Shop

The 6th is one of the most quintessentially Parisian of the *arrondissements*, famous for its shopping and attracting designers, including Armani, Hermès, Lacroix and Kenzo, in the wake of Sonia Rykiel. Rue de Buci and its environs are a food shopper's paradise, with a daily market groaning under piles of cheese, fruit, meat and vegetables.

Rue du Bac stretches from the Seine to the *arrondissement* to the smart, largely residential 7th, where rue du Pré-aux-Clercs and rue Cler are worth investigating, but the main shopping streets are rue de Grenelle and rue St-Dominique.

Department Store

Le Bon Marché (24 rue de Sèvres, 75007, tel: 01 44 39 80 00, Metro: Sèvres-Babylone) on the Left Bank and houses the Grande Epicerie food hall.

Food

Androuët (83 rue St-Dominique, 75007, tel: 01 45 50 45 75, Metro: Invalides) is one of the foremost Parisian cheese shops, while nearby **Barthélemy** (51 rue de Grenelle, 75007, tel: 01 45 48 56 75, Metro: Rue du Bac) sells cheeses ripened to perfection. **Marie-Anne Cantin's** celebrated cheese shop (12 rue du Champ-de-Mars, 75007, tel: 01 45 50 43 94, Metro: Ecole Militaire) is round the corner from the market on rue Cler. For chocolate, try **Christian Constant** (37 rue d'Assas, 75006, tel: 01 53 63 15 15, Metro: Notre-Dame-des-Champs/St-Placide) and **Debauve et Gallais** (30 rue des Sts-Pères, 75007, tel: 01 45 48 54 67, Metro: St-Germain-des-Prés). **Oliviers & Co** (28 rue de Buci,

75006, tel: 01 44 07 15 43, www. oliviers-co.com Metro: St-Germain-des-Prés and Mabillon; branches in the seven other *arrondissements*) sells olives plus all manner of olive products. On Sundays, a wonderful but expensive **organic market** (*marché biologique*) livens up the boulevard Raspail near Rennes Metro station.

Fashion Accessories

Emporio Armani (149 boulevard St-Germain, 75006, tel: 01 53 63 33 50, www.armani.com Metro: St-Germain-des-Prés) has a store with a good coffee shop, not far from **Sonia Rykiel's** ready-to-wear fashion house, with its excellent accessories and cosmetics (175 boulevard St-Germain, 75006, tel: 01 49 54 60 60, www.soniarykiel.com Metro: St-Germain-des-Prés). **Yves Saint Laurent** for women is at 6 place St-Sulpice, 75006, tel: 01 43 29 43 00, www.ysl.com. The men's shop is at 12 place St-Sulpice, 75006, tel: 01 43 26 84 40, Metro: Mabillon. **Shu Uemura** (176 boulevard St-Germain, 75006,

tel: 01 45 48 02 55, www.shu-uemura.co.jp/shopinfo Metro: St-Germain-des-Prés) is the high-tech retail outlet of one of the world's leading make-up artists.

Gifts

Christian Tortu (6 carrefour de l'Odéon, 75006, tel: 01 43 26 02 56, www.christian-tortu.com Metro: Odéon) is the best florist in Paris. **Emilio Robba** (63 rue du Bac, 75007, tel: 01 45 44 44 03, www. emiliorobba.fr Metro: Rue du Bac) specialises in artificial flowers so exquisitely realistic they're displayed in water. **Souleiado** (78 rue de Seine, 75006, tel: 01 43 54 62 25, www. souleiado.com Metro: Mabillon/ Odéon) is a must for table and bed linen. Go to **Geneviève Lethu** (95 rue de Rennes, 75006, tel: 01 45 44 40 35, www.genevievelethu.fr Metro: St-Sulpice/Rennes) and **Le Cèdre Rouge** (116 rue du Bac, 75007, tel: 01 42 84 84 00, Metro: Rue du Bac/Sèvres-Babylone) for very French home furnishings.

Where to...
Be Entertained

This part of the city's Left Bank is virtually the world centre for alternative cinema, with a fantastic choice of films on offer. These art-house cinemas, mostly located in the 5th and 6th *arrondissements* (▶ 90) are all conveniently close to each other, and, though a few may have seen better days, it is still well worth checking the *Cinema* section of *Pariscope* for the most diverse choice of programmes on offer anywhere in the world. Theatre and night-clubs are far thinner on the ground in these parts, but there are one or two notable exceptions.

(▶ 90)

CINEMA

At any one time you'll find classics such as *Metropolis* and *Easy Rider* alongside masterpieces such as the late Stanley Kubrick's *A Clockwork Orange*. Following the outcry when it was released, Kubrick forbade its screening, and Paris was one of the few cities where the film could be seen in its entirety. More recent cult films are also frequently shown.

La Pagode (57 bis rue de Babylone, 75007, tel: 01 45 55 48 48, Métro: St-François Xavier) is probably the city's most charming cinema: shipped over in sections from Japan, it is wonderfully exotic, with velvet seats, painted screens and a Japanese garden. Cult classics and recent arty releases are shown in the original language on two screens. The following cinemas are also worth investigating:

Cinéma Christine (4 rue Christine, 75006, tel: 08 92 68 05 98, Métro: Odéon),

L'Arlequin (76 rue de Rennes, 75006, tel: 08 92 68 48 24, Métro: St-Sulpice),

Le St-Germain-des-Prés (22 rue Guillaume-Apollinaire, 75006, tel: 01 42 22 87 23, Métro: St-Germain-des-Prés),

Les Trois Luxembourg (67 rue Monsieur-le-Prince, 75006, tel: 08 92 68 93 25, Métro: Cluny La Sorbonne, RER: Luxembourg).

THEATRE AND CONCERTS

The **Théâtre du Vieux Colombier** (21 rue du Vieux Colombier, 75006, tel: 01 44 39 87 00, Métro: St-Sulpice) offers both classical and contemporary theatre by the world-famous Comédie-Française troupe (www.comedie-francaise.fr). **Odéon, Théâtre de l'Europe** (1 place Paul Claudel, 75006, tel: 01 44 85 40 00, www.theatre-odeon.fr, Métro: Odéon), stages classical and contemporary theatre from all over Europe, often in languages other than French. The **American Church in Paris** (65 quai d'Orsay, 75007, tel: 01 40 62 05 00, Métro: Invalides) holds free classical concerts. Concerts are not free at the **church of St-Germain-des-Prés** (3 place St-Germain-des-Prés, 75006, tel: 01 55 42 81 33, Métro: St-Germain-des-Prés), but the acoustics and setting are marvellous.

NIGHT-LIFE

Le Don Camilo (10 rue des Saints-Pères, 75007, tel: 01 42 60 82 84, Métro: St-Germain-des-Prés) dinner show begins at 8pm. **Le Trap** (10 rue Jacob, 75006, open Tue–Sun 11pm–4am, in summer. Métro: St-Germain-des-Prés) is one of the few gay clubs on the Left Bank, and has a reputation for being one of the most daring.

The Latin Quarter
and the Islands

Getting Your Bearings

The Latin Quarter has been the centre of learning in Paris for more than 700 years, home to prestigious schools and universities all clustered around their doyenne, the Sorbonne. Its name derives from the academic tradition of studying and speaking in Latin, but nowadays in this multi-ethnic district, this is just about the only tongue you're guaranteed *not* to hear.

Notre-Dame Cathedral (previous page) and Sainte-Chapelle (below) – two of the city's most dazzling landmarks

Today, despite the ever-increasing number of Greek restaurants, cheap shops and fast-food joints, the area is still a lively student district. It's a warren of cobbled medieval streets, overflowing with innumerable cafés, bookstores, cheap restaurants, quirky boutiques, cinemas, jazz clubs and smoky bars that stay open until late, preserving the quarter's legendary "bohemian" feel.

Of the two river islands beside the Latin Quarter, the Île de la Cité is the more historic – home to the earliest inhabitants of Paris, the Gallic tribe of the Parisii (hence the city's name) – and it also boasts such awe-inspiring sights as the jewel-like Sainte-Chapelle and Notre-Dame. By contrast, the more intimate Île St-Louis provides a tranquil retreat from the hustle and bustle of the city.

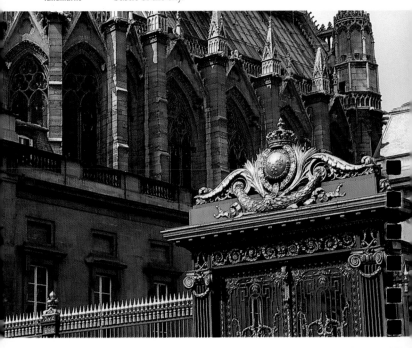

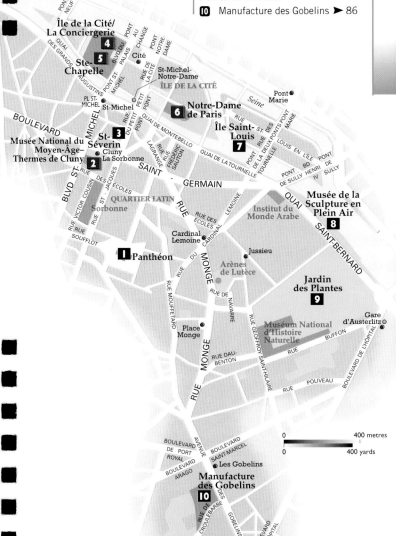

From churches and museums to a market and the guillotine (not to mention the best ice-cream in Paris), this varied day out offers something special for everyone. What's more, it should even keep the children entertained.

The Latin Quarter and Islands in a Day

9:15am

Start your day gently at the most serene museum in Paris, the **2 Musée National du Moyen-Âge** (➤ 74–75, left), whose medieval treasures are among the greatest collections from this era. You will find them displayed in a beautiful Gothic mansion, built on the ruins of an ancient Roman bathhouse.

11am

Stroll northwards towards the river, stopping off for morning coffee in one of many student bars nestling in the lively tangle of streets behind the church of **3 St-Séverin** (➤ 84).

12 noon

Cross the Petit Pont on to the **4 Île de la Cité** (➤ 76–77) to visit the mighty cathedral of **6 Notre-Dame** (➤ 80–83, right). Quasimodo had a fantastic view from the towers: it's a long, long climb to the top, but if the weather's fine it's well worth every step.

1 pm

Have lunch at the Jardin Notre-Dame (2 rue de Petit-Pont), within sight of **6 Notre-Dame** (➤ 80–83), or cross over to **7 Île St-Louis** (➤ 84, left) for lunch at le Fin Gourmet (➤ 87). For dessert join the locals waiting outside Berthillon for a taste of the most heavenly ice-cream in Paris.

3 pm

Return to the Île de la Cité, past the quaint **flower market** (➤ 77, right) in place Louis-Lépine and on to the **4 Conciergerie** (➤ 76), a fascinating museum full of gory tales from the days of the guillotine, and **5 Sainte-Chapelle** (➤ 78–79).

5:30 pm

Relax awhile in the peaceful, green **square du Vert-Galant** (➤ 28) at the westernmost end of the island, and watch the barges and tourist boats plying the river past the Louvre. Then why not hop aboard a *bateau-mouche* for a sightseeing cruise (➤ 172–174, left) as the sun sets over the city?

8 pm

The abundance of fresh air is bound to have given you a hearty appetite. So head back south of the river to the Latin Quarter for dinner at Les Bouquinistes (➤ 65), followed by a quick nightcap.

❷ Musée National du Moyen-Âge– Thermes de Cluny

Even if you're not a fan of medieval art and history, the National Museum of the Middle Ages, with exhibits spanning 15 centuries of Parisian history, is a must, if only for the remarkable building, which in itself is the architectural embodiment of this period.

Discover the real history of Paris in this beautiful museum

The collections are housed in two adjoining buildings – the remains of Gallo-Roman baths and the late 15th-century Hôtel de Cluny, the mansion of the abbots of Cluny and a masterpiece of Flamboyant Gothic style. Around AD 200, the wealthy guild of Paris boatmen built a complex of Roman baths here, only to have them destroyed by barbarians less than a century later. The unearthed remains

of the well-preserved "frigidarium" form a kind of basement gallery in the museum, exhibiting various Roman bits and bobs, including fragments of mosaics and frescoes that once decorated the bathhouse.

Centuries later, the monks of the abbey of Cluny in Burgundy built a mansion – the Hôtel de Cluny – on this spot as a residence for visiting abbots. As a contemporary

---

➕ 195 D4 ✉ 6 place Paul Painlevé, 75005 ☎ 01 53 73 78 00; www.musee-moyenage.fr 🕐 Wed–Mon 9:15–5:45   🚇 Cluny–La Sorbonne 🚈 RER B or C St-Michel–Cluny-Sorbonne   💰 Moderate; free 1st Sun of month

saying justly claimed: "Wherever the wind blows, the abbey of Cluny holds riches." Today, with its ornate turrets, gargoyles and cloistered courtyard (to which admission is free), it represents the finest remaining example of medieval civil architecture in Paris.

The many treasures in the museum reflect the richness and diversity of life in the Middle Ages, including furnishings, stained glass, jewellery, statuary, carvings, illuminated manuscripts, paintings and, most famous of all, the *Dame à la Licorne* (*Lady and the Unicorn*) tapestries. This exquisite series of six panels portraying a lady flanked by a lion and a unicorn, set against a pink flower-strewn background, provides a delightful reflection of the chivalrous world of courtly love. Each panel symbolises one of the five senses: (from left to right) taste, hearing, sight, smell and

touch. In the sixth and largest panel, entitled *À mon seul désir*, the lady returns the necklace depicted in the other five tapestries to its jewel casket, refusing to capitulate to the passions aroused by the senses.

Medieval tapestries count among the many priceless treasures here

TAKING A BREAK

Have lunch at **La Gueuze**, close to the Jardin du Luxembourg (➤ 87–88).

THE MUSEUM: INSIDE INFO

Orientation Pick up a leaflet at the ticket desk which **details the key sights** and provides a plan of the floors of the museum. Once inside, it's easy to find your way round as each room is clearly marked.

Must-sees Early stained glass from the Ste-Chapelle and Rouen Cathedral (ground floor, room 6).
• **Statues of the Kings of Judaea** from the façade of Notre-Dame (ground floor, room 8).
• The **Roman baths** (basement, room 9).
• The world-renowned *Lady and the Unicorn* tapestries (first floor, room 13).
• The Flamboyant Gothic **chapel of the monks of Cluny** (first floor, room 20).

Top tips Even if you don't have time to visit the museum, step inside the courtyard to admire its **ornate turrets, gargoyles and friezes**.
• You don't have to pay the price of a museum ticket to see the Roman remains: just **peer through the iron fence** from the boulevard St-Michel.

Hidden gems Gallic jewellery; 15th-century illuminated **Book of Hours**; 16th-century **Averbode altarpiece**, depicting three carved scenes including the Last Supper; 14th-century **winklepickers**; **medieval gardens**, inspired by the museum's collections.

4 Île de la Cité and the Conciergerie

The history of this small, boat-shaped island in the Seine is the history of Paris. Here, in around 300 BC, the earliest inhabitants of Paris (the Parisii tribe) settled, and it was here two centuries later that the Romans built the town of Lutetia, meaning "settlement surrounded by water". This was to become the seat of the ancient kings of France and the centre of political power, and in medieval times it also became the home of the church and the law.

For such a small island, the Île de la Cité boasts a remarkably high number of key sights including the Cathedral of **Notre-Dame** (➤ 80–83), **Ste-Chapelle** (➤ 78–79), and the **Conciergerie**.

The imposing cluster of buildings which stretch the entire width of the island at its western end were once the seat of royal power, and today house the Palais de Justice, the city's law courts. The Conciergerie occupies part of the lower floor of the complex and a couple of towers on the north bank of the island. Originally the residence of the governor of the king's palace – hence the name – it became a prison in 1391 (when the concierge became the chief gaoler) and remained so until 1914.

Lovers of lurid history will be in their element here. Starting in the impressive church-like Salle des Gens d'Armes (Hall of the Men-at-Arms), you continue along the "rue de Paris" (sinisterly named after the great executioner, Monsieur de Paris), to the Salle de la Toilette or

The execution of Marie-Antoinette

Île de la Cité
✚ 195 D/E5 🚇 Cité
The Conciergerie
✚ 195 D5 ✉ Palais de la Cité, 2 boulevard du Palais, 75001 ☎ 01 53 40 60 93;
www.monum.fr 🕐 Daily 9:30–6 (5 Nov–Feb) . Closed 1 Jan, 1 May, 25 Dec
🚇 Cité 🚌 Châtelet 💶 Moderate (a combined Conciergerie/Ste-Chapelle
ticket is available)
Marché aux Fleurs and Marché aux Oiseaux
✚ 195 E5 ✉ place Louis-Lépine, 75004 🕐 Mon–Sat 8–7; Sun 9–7
🚇 Cité 🚌 St-Michel

"preparation room". Here prisoners handed over their last possessions and were prepared for the guillotine – their hands tied behind their backs, their heads shaved to the nape of the neck and their shirt collars ripped apart. They were then escorted to the May courtyard, where they waited for the dreaded tumbrels (carts) to deliver them to the guillotine in place de la Révolution (today's place de la Concorde).

Among notorious pre-Revolution prisoners who awaited death here were Ravaillac, the assassin of Henri IV; Marquise de Brinvilliers, a mass poisoner who killed off the majority of her family; and Cartouche, the French equivalent of Robin Hood, who terrorised the streets of Paris.

During the Revolution, 2,780 people were guillotined – peasants, politicians, artists, nobles – among the most illustrious being Marie-Antoinette, who spent 76 days in a cell here before losing her head in 1793.

Painting the prison

TAKING A BREAK

Cross the Pont de l'Archevêché at the eastern end of the island to enjoy a traditional French meal at **La Rôtisserie du Beaujolais** (➤ 88).

Place du Parvis Notre-Dame

Not only is the Île de la Cité the heart of Paris, but it is also the heart of France. Set into the ground on the square outside the main portal of Notre-Dame, a bronze star marks the *point zéro des routes de France*, the point from which all distances are measured to and from Paris throughout France.

ÎLE DE LA CITÉ: INSIDE INFO

Top tip It's quite easy to **spend a whole day on the Île de la Cité** in order to enjoy all its treasures and diversions: Notre-Dame (➤ 80–83), Ste-Chapelle (➤ 78–79), the Conciergerie, attractive parks such as square Jean XXIII (➤ 82), the colourful flower market – Marché aux Fleurs – which on Sundays becomes a bird market (Marché aux Oiseaux), and the busy staging post for the *bateaux-mouches* that ply the Seine.

5 Sainte-Chapelle

Gaze up to heaven to the soaring navy-blue, star-painted ceiling

Sainte-Chapelle has to be seen to be believed. It is surely Paris's most beautiful church – a veritable Sistine Chapel of shimmering stained glass – and a remarkable fusion of art and religion, although it is not always rated as one of the top city sights.

It was built next door to the royal palace in 1248 by Louis IX – a king so devout that he came to be known as St Louis – to house a fragment of the Holy Cross and the entire Crown of Thorns. Louis had paid the outrageous sum of 1.3 million francs (the chapel itself only cost 400,000 francs) for these relics. He wanted the edifice to have the light, lacy aspect of a reliquary, and the result, which took a mere five years to build, was this bejewelled masterpiece of Gothic architecture.

The chapel is split into two levels. The **lower chapel**, dedicated to the Virgin Mary, was for the palace staff, while the upper chapel was originally linked to the palace by an outside walkway, so that the king and his entourage could enter it directly. The most striking feature of the upper chapel is its transparency. It seems as though there are no walls – only glowing stained-glass windows and clusters of slender columns

---

🖪 195 D5
✉ 6 boulevard du Palais, 75001
☎ 01 53 40 60 80; www.monum.fr
🕐 Daily 9:30–6 (5 Nov–Feb). Last entry 30 mins before closing. Closed 1 Jan, 1 May, 25 Dec

🚇 Cité/St-Michel
🚉 Châtelet-Les-Halles/
St-Michel–Notre Dame
✋ Moderate (combined Ste-Chapelle/
Conciergerie ticket is available)

SAINTE-CHAPELLE: INSIDE INFO

Top tips Try to visit when the **sun is shining**, flooding the interior with rich red, green, blue and gold rays of light.
• For a truly magical experience, attend one of the regular **candlelit chamber music concerts**. Ask for details at either the ticket office or at the tourist information office.

One to miss Don't bother with the lower chapel. **It pales into insignificance** beside the upper chapel.

rising to the vaulted ceiling. The verticality of the design is accentuated externally by the tall spire. The angel on the roof once revolved so that its cross could be seen everywhere in Paris.

It is something of a miracle that Sainte-Chapelle is still here for us to enjoy. During the Revolution, its chapel was neglected and its relics removed to Notre-Dame. Thereafter, it was used to store flour, then as a depot for the court archives, until it became so dilapidated that, in 1837, it was advertised for sale. Purchased, thankfully, by the State, it was restored and given a new spire. In 1871, the Communards (➤ 9) poured petrol over the entire chapel, failing to set it on fire only for lack of time.

Sainte-Chapelle's *pièce de résistance* is undoubtedly its stained-glass windows – a pictorial Bible illustrating 1,134 scenes from both the Old and New Testaments. The most famous, and best seen at sunset, is the gigantic rose window, which depicts the Apocalypse in 86 multi-coloured glass panels.

TAKING A BREAK

Make your way over to Île St-Louis for lunch at **Le Fin Gourmet** (➤ 87), working up your appetite by admiring the mouthwatering displays in many of the shops near by.

The beautiful stained-glass windows play both a decorative and an architectural role

⑥ Notre-Dame de Paris

Despite the inevitable crowds of tourists, the grandeur of this landmark cathedral, with its impressive sculpture-encrusted façade, its distinctive flying buttresses and its soaring nave, never fails to inspire.

In the early-12th century, as the population of Paris continued to expand, the Bishop of Paris decided to build one immense church here at the very heart of Paris to replace two old ones – the former Notre-Dame and the neighbouring St-Etienne, both of which were in a state of disrepair. The resulting cathedral was erected as an expression of profound religious faith on a site considered holy for many centuries, where the Romans had earlier built a temple to Jupiter. It took more than 150 years to complete (1163–1345) and has since suffered many alterations. During the Revolution, the statues of the Kings of Judaea on the façade were removed and decapitated by the mob, in the mistaken belief that they represented French monarchs. The originals, now on view in the Musée National du Moyen-Âge–Thermes de Cluny (► 74–75), have been replaced with replicas.

Notre-Dame Cathedral – at the geographical and historical heart of Paris

Inset: One of the famous gargoyles

Over the centuries, the cathedral has fulfilled many roles, serving as a place of worship, and as a community hall. It was even the setting for lavish banquets and amateur theatrical productions. At one point it was abandoned altogether but, thanks largely to Victor Hugo's *Hunchback of Notre-Dame*, it was finally saved from total ruin by Viollet-le-Duc who, under Napoléon III, carried out extensive renovations, all in keeping with the original style.

As a result, today we are able to enjoy one of the world's most beautiful examples of early Gothic architecture. **The façade** is particularly remarkable. It seems perfectly proportioned, with its two towers narrower at the top than at the base, giving them the illusion of great height. Look closer, however, and you will notice the north (left) tower is wider than the south tower and that each of the three main

✚ 195 E4
✉ 6 Parvis Notre-Dame, 75004
☎ 01 42 34 56 10;
www.cathedraledeparis.com
🕐 Daily 7:45–6:45; sacristy:
Mon–Sat 9:30–6, Sun 1:30–5:30.
Closed some religious feast days
Ⓜ Cité
Ⓡ RER St-Michel–Notre Dame
⚑ Free; sacristy inexpensive;
tower moderate

Did You Know?
The interior is 130m (430 feet) long, 48m (160 feet) wide and 35m (115 feet) high.
402 spiral steps lead to the top of the 70m (230-foot) high south tower.
12 million people visit each year, of whom 6,000 attend services.
The main bell, the "Emmanuel", rang in 1944 to celebrate the liberation of France.

Square du Jean XXIII

Every year pairs of kestrels nest in the towers of Notre-Dame, and some years, around late June, local ornithologists set up a public hide in this delightful park behind the cathedral, with telescopes and even a video camera transmitting detailed shots of the adult birds feeding their offspring. The park also offers striking views of the cathedral's massive flying buttresses.

---

entrances is slightly different in shape. The bird's-eye view of central Paris and close encounter with the grotesque gargoyles atop the cathedral repay the climb to the **tops of the towers**.

Try to visit Notre-Dame on a sunny day, when **the soaring nave** is bathed in shimmering, multi-coloured lights, filtered through the astonishing stained-glass windows: **the rose windows** are particularly celebrated. In the transept, the window on the north side (to your left as you face the altar) depicts scenes from the Old Testament, while the one on the south (right) side shows Christ in the centre, surrounded by virgins, saints and the 12 apostles. The stunning red and blue west window (in the main façade) portrays the Virgin and Child and boasts a diameter of no less than 10m (33 feet).

Perfect proportions – the flying buttresses of Notre-Dame

Traces of Rome

Paris derives its name from the Parisii, the Celtic tribe living on the Île de la Cité in 52 BC, the year the Romans invaded, to stay for over five centuries. Traces of Roman settlement are still scattered around the area, including the baths at the Hôtel de Cluny and the ruins of an amphitheatre (les Arènes de Lutèce) where crowds of 10,000 once attended gladiator fights. Numerous remains discovered while building an underground car-park beneath Notre-Dame are atmospherically displayed in the Crypte Archéologique de Notre-Dame de Paris (1 place du Parvis Notre-Dame, 75004, tel: 01 55 42 50 10, open: Tue–Sun 10–6, inexpensive).

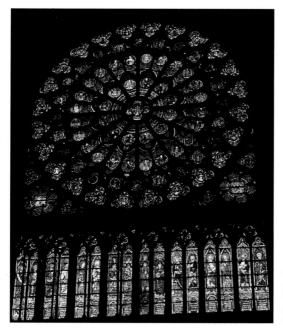

The shimmering
rose windows
in the transept
are particularly
delicate

NOTRE-DAME DE PARIS: INSIDE INFO

Once inside In the side chapels, note the **series of religious canvases** by
Charles Le Brun known as the *May* paintings; during the 17th and 18th centuries
the Paris guilds presented a painting to the cathedral on May Day each year.
• Against a pillar near the modern high altar stands a beautiful 14th-century
statue of the Virgin and Child, known as Notre-Dame de Paris (Our Lady of Paris).
• Beside the high altar is a **kneeling statue of Louis XIII**, who, after many years of
childless marriage, pledged to erect a high altar if an heir was born to him – but
although the future Louis XIV was born soon after, the altar was not built for
another 60 years.

One to miss Don't bother with the sacristy if you're short of time, unless you're a
particular fan of vestments, sacred vessels and other liturgical objects.

Top tips Visit early in the morning, when the cathedral is at its brightest and
least crowded.
• If you plan to climb the towers, remember to **wear sensible shoes** and **be
prepared to queue** (Jul–Aug daily 9–7:30 [until 11 Sat and Sun]; Apr–Jun,
Sep 9:30–7:30; rest of year 10–5:30. Last admission 45 mins before closing.
Closed 1 Jan, 1 May, 25 Dec). The entrance to the north tower is on rue du
Cloître Notre-Dame (turn right out of the main doorway and round the corner
of the façade).
• There are **free guided tours in English** on Wed and Thu at 2 and on Sat at 2:30.
• Try to attend one of the **free organ concerts** on Sundays in summer at 4:30pm.

At Your Leisure

1 Panthéon

Surprisingly, there's not as much to see as you'd expect in this massive domed landmark. Originally commissioned around 1750 as a church by Louis XV in thanks following his remarkable recovery from a grave illness, it remained unfinished until 1789 owing to lack of finance. Two years later, all Christian references were removed and it was converted into a secular mausoleum for the "*grands hommes de l'époque de la liberté française*" (great men of the age of French liberty). Since then Voltaire, Rousseau, Hugo, Zola, the Resistance leader Jean Moulin, Braille (inventor of the reading system for the visually impaired) and other great figures have been buried here. Nobel Prize-winner Marie Curie, the first woman to be interred in the Panthéon for her own achievements, was reburied here in 1995.

The Panthéon, where the illustrious rest

➕ 195 E3 ✉ place du Panthéon, 75005
☎ 01 44 32 18 00; www.monum.fr
🕐 Apr–Sep daily 10–6:30; rest of year 10–6, Last entrance 45 minutes before closing. Closed public holidays 🚇 Place Monge/Cardinal Lemoine 🚉 RER Luxembourg 🚶 Moderate

3 St-Séverin

Not only is St-Séverin one of the most beautiful churches in the capital, with one of the finest organs (popular for concerts), but it is also one of its best-kept secrets. It has a delightful blend of Flamboyant Gothic architecture and contemporary stained glass (depicting the Seven Sacraments) with one of the oldest bells in Paris, and an intimate garden enclosed by a cloister, all constructed on the site of the Left Bank's former parish church and graveyard. St Séverin, a 6th-century hermit, was closely associated with St Martin, patron saint of travellers, so parishioners would hang horseshoes here as a token of thanks on their safe return from a journey.

The old, cobbled streets surrounding St-Séverin are popular with students and tourists alike, full of cafés, shops and cheap eateries.

➕ 195 D4 ✉ 1 rue des Prêtres-St-Séverin, 75005 ☎ 01 42 34 93 50; www.saint-severin.com 🕐 Mon–Sat 11–7:30; Sun 9–8:30 🚇 St-Michel

7 Île St-Louis

When you tire of urban life, head for the Île St-Louis – an oasis of tranquillity at the heart of the city. The smaller of Paris's two islands, it has a village-like atmosphere, with tree-lined quays, matchless views of Notre-Dame and peaceful streets of elegant grey stone mansions, built in the 17th century as an annex to the fashionable Marais district. Little has changed since the writer Louis-Sébastien Mercier observed two centuries ago, "the island seems to have escaped the great corruption of the city, which has not reached here yet".

One of the attractions of the island is its main street, rue St-Louis-en-l'Île, with its luxury shops, including the legendary Maison Berthillon. There's always a queue outside, and for good reason; an ice-cream bought here is sure to a highlight of your day.

3 St-Séverin

Île Saint-Louis **7**

Musée de la Sculpture en Plein Air **8**

1 Panthéon

QUARTIER LATIN — Sorbonne

Institut du Monde Arabe

Jussieu

Arènes de Lutèce

🞧 195 F4 ⊠ Berthillon, 31 rue St-Louis-en-l'Île, 75004 ☎ 01 43 54 31 61 🕓 Wed–Sun 10–8. Closed Mon, Tue, school holidays (except Christmas) 🚇 Pont Marie

🎱 Musée de la Sculpture en Plein Air

This modern, imaginatively landscaped riverside promenade, running along quai St-Bernard from the Gare d'Austerlitz to the Institut du Monde Arabe, is dotted with over 40 avant-garde sculptures by Brancusi, César and Zadkine among others. With colourful barges often moored along the waterside, and beautiful views of Île St-Louis opposite, this is one of the most enjoyable stretches of the river for a daytime stroll, but an area probably best avoided after dark.

🞧 196 A/B3 ⊠ quai St-Bernard, 75005 🚇 Austerlitz

The stylish town houses of the Île St-Louis stand sentinel along the banks of the Seine

For Kids

• Notre-Dame de Paris (➤ 80–83) – **climb the tower** to see the monster gargoyles (you may even catch a glimpse of the hunchback). Tinies will enjoy feeding the pigeons in the cathedral square.

• Conciergerie (➤ 76; not recommended for young children) – the turreted prison **famous for torturing its prisoners** before they were beheaded.

• Île de la Cité (➤ 76–77) – **starting point for a river cruise** on a *bateau-mouche*.

• Île St-Louis (➤ 84–85) – for an **ice-cream at Berthillon**.

Architectural Wonder

The architecture of the Institut du Monde Arabe (Arab World Institute) must be seen to be believed. The main (south) façade of this striking 1988 glass-and-steel edifice by French designer Jean Nouvel consists of 240 mechanised metal panels that act like the aperture of a camera, opening and closing to let in just the correct amount of natural light, while at the same time creating a beautiful pattern reminiscent of *moucharabieh* (traditional Arab latticework). The restaurant on the 9th floor has one of the finest views in Paris.

🚏 195 F3　✉ 1 rue des Fossés-St-Bernard, 75005　☎ 01 40 51 38 38; www.imarabe.org　🕐 Tue–Sun 10–6　🚇 Cardinal Lemoine/Jussieu　💰 Moderate

One of the garden's founders – admiring his surroundings

9 Jardin des Plantes

Louis XIII's "Garden of Medicinal Herbs", established by two physicians in 1626, was first opened to the public in 1640. Today it is the city's official botanical garden. As well as magnificent walkways flanked by flowers, ancient trees and statues, it also has a stunning alpine garden with more than 2,000 species of plants from all over the world, a small zoo (set up during the Revolution to house survivors from the royal menagerie at Versailles), and the Muséum National d'Histoire Naturelle. The natural history and anthropology collections here are among the largest in the world. Of particular interest is the palaeontology gallery with its reconstructed skeletons of prehistoric mammals. The late 19th-century Grande Gallerie de l'Évolution, with its huge glass roof, and the palaeobotany and mineralogy gallery, telling the story of plants since their first appearance on Earth, are also worth a visit.

🚏 196 A2　✉ Park and Menagerie: 57 rue Cuvier, 75005; Muséum: 2 rue Buffon, 75005　☎ Menagerie: 01 40 79 37 94; Musée: 01 40 79 30 00 (recorded information); www.mnhn.fr　🕐 Park: daily 8–5:30 (8 pm in summer) (Jardin Alpin closed Sat, Sun); Menagerie: Apr–Sep daily 9–6; rest of year 9–5; Musée: Wed–Mon 10–5 (10–6, in summer). Grande Galerie: Wed–Mon 10–6　🚇 Jussieu/ Austerlitz　💰 Menagerie: moderate; Musée: moderate

Further Afield

10 Manufacture des Gobelins

The Manufacture des Gobelins began life as a humble dyeing workshop, set up by the Gobelin brothers in 1440 and converted into a small tapestry factory in the early-17th century. It owes its international reputation to Louis XIV who, when gathering together the greatest craftsmen of the day to furnish his new palace at Versailles in 1662, employed 250 Flemish weavers to work here. Tapestries are still made using traditional techniques.

🚏 195 F1　✉ 42 avenue des Gobelins, 75013　☎ 01 44 08 52 00　🕐 Open for guided tours only, Tue, Wed, Thu afternoons; phone for details　🚇 Les Gobelins　💰 Moderate

Where to...
Eat and Drink

Prices
Expect to pay per person for a meal, excluding drinks:
€ up to €25   €€ €25–50   €€€ €50–100   €€€€ over €100

L'Atelier de Maître Albert €€

Tucked away in a narrow street, this rotisserie, owned by Guy Savoy, has an elegant décor blending the traditional and new. Although light and modern, the cuisine is deeply rooted in French tradition, with a choice of spit-roasted meats and poultry: spit-roasted French beef sirloin with béarnaise sauce and potato gratin, skewered monkfish with braised carrots and onions savoured with hazelnut juice. Lively atmosphere, warm welcome.

🛨 195 E4 ☒ 1 rue Maître Albert, 75005 ☎ 01 56 81 30 01; www.ataeliermaitrealbert.com ⓖ Daily noon–2:30, 6:30–11:30 (1am Thu, Fri and Sat). Closed Sat and Sun lunch Ⓜ Maubert-Mutualité

Le Bar à Huîtres €€

One of a group of three oyster bars serving, among other dishes, wonderful shellfish and enormous seafood platters. The other branches are on boulevard Beaumarchais and boulevard Montparnasse.

🛨 195 D4 ☒ 33 rue St-Jacques, 75005 ☎ 01 44 07 27 37; www.lebarahuitres.com ⓖ Daily noon–1am Ⓜ Cluny-La Sorbonne

Brasserie Balzar €€

Located at the heart of the University district, this lively brasserie is the rendezvous of professors and students, of writers and publishers, of intellectuals and artists who flock here to have a meal in typically Parisian 1930s décor. The cuisine has been modernised but remains traditional, *steak au poivre*, calf's liver and *choucroute garnie* are among the favourite dishes.

🛨 195 D4 ☒ 49 rue des Écoles, 75005 ☎ 01 43 54 13 67; www.brasseriebalzar.com ⓖ Daily noon–2:30, 6:30–midnight Ⓜ Cluny-La Sorbonne

Chieng Maï €

This ranks among the city's best for Thai cooking, so it is always necessary to book in advance. The menu is true to its classic roots, though spicing is a little less fiery than is traditional, as a concession to the general French dislike of highly spiced foods. Pork satay, fish steamed in a banana leaf, and sautéed beef with basil are perennial favourites.

🛨 195 E4 ☒ 12 rue Frédéric Sauton, 75005 ☎ 01 43 25 45 45 ⓖ Daily noon–2:30, 7–11:30. Closed Aug Ⓜ Maubert-Mutualité

Le Fin Gourmet €€

At the quieter end of the magnificent thoroughfare that slices the Île Saint Louis lengthwise, this little bistro specialises in homestyle cooking like the speciality terrine of foie gras with onion and raspberry marmalade, followed by a flavoursome *boeuf Bourgignon*. The wines are reasonably priced. The lunch-time menus are unbeatable value for these parts.

🛨 196 A4 ☒ 42 rue St-Louis-en-l'île, 75004 ☎ 01 43 26 79 27 ⓖ Tue–Sun noon–2, 7–11 Ⓜ Pont Marie

La Gueuze €

Only a few steps from the Jardin du Luxembourg, the speciality here is the vast selection of some 150 beers from around the world, including 66 bottled Belgian beers with 13 more on draught. The menu features

Belgian staples served in generous portions, such as *moules marinières* (mussels in white wine) and *carbonnade flamande* (the Belgian national dish of beef in beer). A blackboard lists a few specials, grills and salads.

➕ 195 D3 ☒ 19 rue Soufflot, 75005 ☎ 01 43 54 63 00 Daily 11am–1am (Sun till 11pm) RER: Luxembourg

Mavrommatis €€

A far cry from the tourist-touting tavernas on the nearby rue Mouffetard, this classy Greek restaurant adds a sophisticated touch to traditional dishes like *tzatziki* and *stifado* (rabbit casserole). The subtly balanced menu includes preserved lamb and yoghurt with honey, vine leaves and moussaka. The desserts are clever adaptions of French dishes, incuding *nougat glacé* mousse with fresh figs, chestnut and vanilla with honey and *baklava*. Delicious Greek wines are the perfect accompaniment to the divine cooking.

➕ 195 F2 ☒ 42 rue Daubenton, 75005 ☎ 01 43 31 17 17; www.mavrommatis.fr Tue–Sat noon–2:15, 7–11 Censier-Daubenton

Marty €€

Right at the southernmost tip of the 5th *arrondissement* near the junction of avenue des Gobelins and boulevard de Port-Royal, the first-floor brasserie here, decorated in an elegant and evocative 1930s style, offers a fine selection of very fresh fish and shellfish, as well as a few good meat dishes. The ground-floor restaurant is a little more expensive.

➕ 195 E1 ☒ 20 avenue des Gobelins, 75005 ☎ 01 43 31 39 51; www.marty-restaurant.com Daily noon–3, 7–10 Les Gobelins

Chez Paul €€

Paul's jovial presence guarantees a welcome at this neighbourhood institution, with its delightful summer garden. This authentic restaurant, serving up favourites like *pot au feu*, *cochon au lait* (roast suckling pig) and *boudin aux pommes*, is worth the slight detour to La Butte aux Cailles. The menu justifiably boasts the best mashed potato (*purée*) in Paris. Terrines and soups loom large among the starters while classic desserts such as chocolate cake with *crème anglaise* are prepared to perfection.

➕ Just off map 195 ☒ 22 rue de la Butte-aux-Cailles, 75013 ☎ 01 45 89 22 11 Daily noon–2:30, 7:30–11 Place d'Italie/Corvisart

Le Pré Verre €–€€

The lunch menu at this small, modern, split-level *bistro à vins* near the Musée Cluny is especially good value and includes a glass of wine and coffee. Following five years training in Asia, Chef Philippe Delacourcelle is considered a master of spices, conjuring up such subtle flavour combinations as tuna with celery and sesame, and veal with ginger and polenta. To complete your meal, try some strawberries infused in parsley and *crème caramel poivre et sel* (pepper and salt).

➕ 195 E4 ☒ 8 rue Thenard, 75005 ☎ 01 43 54 59 47 Tue–Sat noon–2, 7:30–10:15 Cluny-La Sorbonne/Maubert Mutualité

La Rôtisserie du Beaujolais €€

Under the same ownership as La Tour d'Argent (▶ 89) across the road, this waterfront bistro enjoys a view of Notre-Dame from its covered terrace. Typical dishes featured on the menu include *escargots de Bourgogne* (snails), *saucisson de Sibilla* and pigs' trotters. The spit-roasted meats are wonderful, especially the duck.

➕ 195 F4 ☒ 19 quai de la Tournelle, 75005 ☎ 01 43 54 17 47 12:15–2:30, 7:30–10:15. Closed 24, 25 Dec Maubert-Mutualité

La Tour d'Argent €€€€

Established in 1582, La Tour d'Argent is the second-oldest restaurant in Paris, and one of the oldest in the world. Commanding spectacular views of the Seine, Notre-Dame and Île St-Louis, it is an absolute must for any once-in-a-lifetime visit to Paris – for those with deep pockets. The menu is traditional, with modern influences subtly incorporated. The speciality is duck, especially *duck à la presse*, which has been on the menu for more than 100 years and comes with a numbered certificate. (Do note that it is served on the rare side.) Other renowned dishes include lobster quenelles and *pêches flambées à l'eau de vie de framboise* (peaches in raspberry liqueur). The excellent wine cellar is almost without equal and includes a museum.

🚇 199 F4 🏠 6th floor 15–17 quai de la Tournelle, 75005 🕿 01 43 54 23 31; www.latourdargent.com 🕒 Wed–Sun 12:30–2:30, 7:30–9, Tue 7:30–9 🚇 Maubert-Mutualité/ Pont Marie

Where to... Shop

The 5th *arrondissement*, or Latin Quarter, remains the bohemian domain of students and is a paradise for book lovers. Other shops are a little down-market, with the exception of Les Comptoirs de la Tour d'Argent. Even if you can't dine at its famous restaurant (▶ left), you can buy from a splendid selection of gourmet produce and tableware. Shoppers can find all manner of goodies on Rue St-Louis-en-l'Île, the island's main thoroughfare, ranging from *foie gras* to designer ceramics.

Paris Jazz Corner (5 rue de Navarre, 75005, tel: 01 43 36 78 92, Métro: Place Monge) is the place to head for a great selection of second-hand jazz recordings.

Dalloyu (2 place Edmond Rostand, 75006, tel: 01 43 29 31 10, open daily 9–8:30, Métro: Cluny-la-Sorbonne), founded 200 years ago, sells delicacies (*foie gras*, truffles, chocolates, macaroons) There is also a tea room.

Diptyque (34 boulevard Saint Germain, 75005, tel: 01 43 26 77 44, www.diptyqueparis.com, open Mon–Sat 10–7, Métro: Maubert-Mutualité) sells an amazing variety of subtly scented candles, soaps and *eau de toilettes*, including unusual fragrances such as "firewood" and "new mown hay".

La Ferme St-Aubin (76 rue St-Louis-en-l'Île, 75004, tel: 01 43 54 74 54, closed Mon, Métro: Pont-Marie) has some 200 cheeses (French and European varieties) on offer, all in luscious, peak condition.

La Tuile à Loup (35 rue Daubenton, 75005, tel: 01 47 07 28 90, open Tue–Sat 10:30–7, Mon 1–7, Métro: Censier-Daubenton), specialises in traditional rustic, French provincial arts and crafts.

Librairie Ulysse (26 rue St-Louis-en-l'Île, 75004, tel: 01 43 25 17 35, open Tue–Sat 2–8pm, Métro: Sully Morland) stocks a wealth of travel information, including books (new and used), maps and magazines on almost every country.

Gibert Jeune (5 place St-Michel, 75005, tel: 01 56 81 22 22, www.gibertjeune.fr, open Mon–Sat 9:30–7:30, Métro: St-Michel) is one of the largest bookshops in Paris, selling many food-related books.

Librairie Gourmande (4 rue Dante, 75005, tel: 01 43 54 37 27, www.librairie-gourmande.fr, open Mon–Sat 10–7, Métro: St-Michel) has books on food history, cu¹ antiques, drawings and li¹

Shakespeare & Co Bûcherie, 75005, tel¹ 13, mobile; open dɐ midnight, Métro: s mine of new and c language books.

Where to...
Be Entertained

A stroll along the winding rue Mouffetard, running north–south almost parallel to rue Monge, through the very centre of the Latin Quarter, is almost an entertainment in itself. It is packed with a diversity of eye-catching little gift and food shops, while numerous restaurants also beckon with mouthwatering window displays, soft candlelight, and often live music within.

CONCERTS AND CABARET

The church of **St-Julien-le-Pauvre** (79 rue Galande, 75005, tel: 01 43 54 52 16, Métro: St-Michel), facing the Seine, stages occasional concert recitals: arrive about 30 minutes early in order to ensure good seats. At **Paradis Latin** (28 rue du Cardinal Lemoine, 75005, tel: 01 43 25 28 28; www.paradis-latin.com open 8pm–midnight, closed Tue, Métro: Cardinal Lemoine/Jussieu) the nightly live cabaret show can be preceded by dinner.

JAZZ

Established in 1946 in medieval cellars, the **Caveau de la Huchette** (5 rue de la Huchette, 75005, tel: 01 43 26 65 05, open Mon–Thu 9:30pm–2:30am, Fri till 3:30am, Sat till 4am, Métro: St-Michel) is busy at weekends, filled with those who come to listen and dance to a lively mix of swing, boogie and rock. **Le Petit Journal** (71 boulevard St-Michel, 75005, tel: 01 43 26 28 59, open Mon–Sat 8:30pm–1:30am; closed Aug, RER: Luxembourg) offers a programme of trad jazz from first-class performers.

Les Trois Maillets 56 rue Galande, 75005, tel: 01 43 54 42 94, open daily 5pm–dawn, Métro: St-Michel) is a terrific jazz café located in the narrow streets between the Seine and boulevard St-Germain.

Look out for **Le Franc-Pinot** (1 quai de Bourbon, 75004, tel: 01 46 33 60 64, Métro: Pont Marie) on the Île Saint-Louis, which offers a varied programme of jazz music at 7 and 9:30pm.

CINEMAS

Among the art-house cinemas, most within walking distance of each other, **Studio Galande** (42 rue Galande, 75005, tel: 08 92 68 06 24, Métro Cluny La Sorbonne) shows independent and cult films, such as *The Rocky Horror Picture Show*. **Le Cinéma du Panthéon** (13 rue Victor-Cousin, 75005, tel: 01 40 46 01 21, Métro: Cluny La Sorbonne/Odéon, RER: Luxembourg), opened in 1907, is the city's oldest remaining cinema.

Others include **Action Écoles** (23 rue des Écoles, 75005, tel: 08 92 68 05 98, Métro: Maubert-Mutualité), **Le Champollion** (51 rue des Écoles, 75005, tel: 01 43 54 51 60, Métro: St-Michel), **Grand Action** (5 rue des Écoles, 75005, tel: 08 92 68 05 98, Métro: Cardinal Lemoine/Jussieu) and **Studio des Ursulines** (10 rue des Ursulines, 75005, tel: 08 92 68 09 78, Métro/RER: Luxem-bourg). Check the weekly *Pariscope* for current screenings.

CLUB

Le Saint (7 rue St-Séverin, 75005, tel: 01 43 25 50 04, open Tue–Sun 11pm–6am, Métro: St-Michel), not far from place St-Michel, is a small, comfortable dance club playing a wide range of music including techno and R&B.

The Louvre to the Arc de Triomphe

Getting Your Bearings

From the Louvre to the Arc de Triomphe, this area of western Paris is not noted for its charm but rather for its grandeur. It is the plutocratic plethora of luxury hotels, elegant squares, formal gardens and fashion emporiums that lend this part of the city its special character.

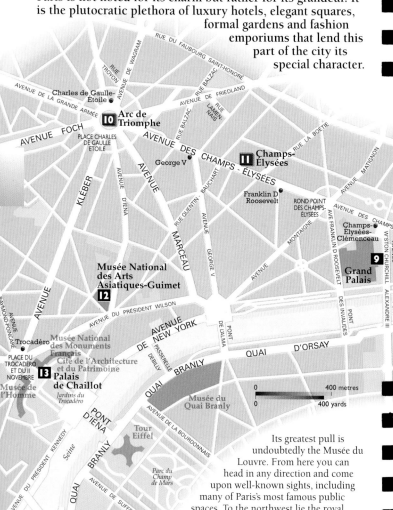

Its greatest pull is undoubtedly the Musée du Louvre. From here you can head in any direction and come upon well-known sights, including many of Paris's most famous public spaces. To the northwest lie the royal Jardin des Tuileries, place de la Concorde (venue for countless beheadings), the Champs-Élysées, the Arc de Triomphe and the Grande Arche de la Défense.

Previous page:
The Arc de Triomphe – vibrant hub of the Right Bank

Immediately north of the Louvre you'll discover two of the city's most magnificent shopping streets, the rue de Rivoli and rue St-Honoré, with their expensive boutiques, *grands magasins* (department stores) and old-fashioned shopping arcades – it's a veritable shoppers' paradise. In the evenings, there's fine dining, sophisticated night-clubs, the Paris Opéra or the world-renowned Comédie-Française, not to mention some of the city's most romantic night-time promenades and viewpoints.

★ Don't Miss

At Your Leisure

Further Afield

This is a day for art lovers, photographers and everyone who wishes to visit some of the greatest sights Paris has to offer.

The Louvre to the Arc de Triomphe in a Day

9am

Make sure you arrive at the 🚇 **Louvre** (above and right, ➤ 96–101) really early (preferably before the doors open at 9) to get a head start on the average 25,000 to 30,000 visitors who traipse through the galleries daily. Once inside, take your time and be selective.

12 noon

If you're feeling extravagant, have a light lunch at the stylish Café Marly (➤ 14–15) in the courtyard of the Louvre overlooking the glass Pyramid. Alternatively, try l'Incroyable 1793, a tiny, great-value bistro (26 rue de Richelieu, 75001, tel: 01 42 96 24 64, closed Sunday).

2pm

Where better to walk off your lunch (or take an afternoon siesta) than the delightful and typically French, statue-studded **6 Jardin des Tuileries** (left, ➤ 102–103). If you have not yet had your fill of art for the day, take your pick from the **Musée de l'Orangerie** (➤ 103) which houses Claude Monet's crowning glory, the waterlily series, or the **Jeu de Paume**, featuring temporary exhibitions inside a former real tennis court (➤ 103).

3pm

Cross the majestic **7 place de la Concorde** (➤ 108) and head up the **11 Champs-Élysées** (below, ➤ 104–105) – once an aristocratic pleasure park, but now thoroughly commercialised. Nevertheless, there is still a certain thrill associated with sauntering up one of the world's most famous streets. If you'd rather not walk, you can take the Métro from Tuileries or Concorde to Charles de Gaulle-Etoile.

5pm

High atop the **10 Arc de Triomphe** (left) is undoubtedly the best place to be during rush hour, 50m (165 feet) above the noise and traffic of the 12 major avenues that radiate from the largest triumphal arch in the world (➤ 104–105). The views are truly sensational.

7pm

Treat yourself to dinner at Le Fouquet's (➤ 113).

❶ Musée du Louvre

The centuries-old Musée du Louvre contains one of the largest, most important art collections in the world. Whether you find your visit here breathtaking, overwhelming, frustrating or simply exhausting, one thing's for sure – you would need a lifetime to see everything. Defeated in advance, many visitors to Paris skip it altogether. The key to a successful visit is to pace yourself, be selective and enjoy: there's nothing to stop you returning tomorrow for more.

The Louvre is a treasure house of great masterpieces

The museum took its name, according to one theory, from the Latin word *luperia* ("wolf lodge" or "hunting lodge"), when the 12th-century king Philippe Auguste built a lodge here and, fearing a Viking invasion while he was away fighting in the Crusades, ordered it to be surrounded by fortified walls. (The massive walls of the twin towers and drawbridge support of this fortress can be seen today, impressively floodlit, in the excavated basement of the Sully Wing.) After the Hundred Years' War, the fortress became a royal residence.

Throughout the following four centuries, a succession of kings and emperors all attempted to improve on or enlarge the palace complex. François I replaced the imposing keep with a Renaissance-style building and also started the Louvre's collections with 12 stolen Italian works of art, including the *Mona Lisa*. Henri IV ordered the construction of the Grande Galerie to link the palace with the Tuileries.

The Louvre's artistic heyday arrived in the

➕ 200 A1
✉ 34–6 quai du Louvre, 75001
☎ 01 40 20 50 50; 01 40 20 53 17 (information desk);
www.louvre.fr
🕐 Wed–Mon 9–6; Wed and Fri until 10pm. Closed 1 Jan, 1 May, 25 Dec
🍴 Cafés (€); restaurant (€€)
🚇 Palais Royal-Musée du Louvre/Louvre Rivoli
🎫 Expensive (reduced rate Wed and Fri after 6pm moderate). Free first Sun of every month

17th century under Louis XIV, a great patron of the arts, who considerably enhanced the collections, adding works by Leonardo da Vinci, Raphael and Titian. Napoléon, too, although notorious for having the most deplorable taste of any leader in the history of France, filled the palace with artworks looted during his victorious years. The Louvre's collections were first opened to the public after the Revolution, in 1793.

Henri IV
Much to the annoyance of his wife Marie de' Médicis, Henri accommodated his many mistresses and their children at the Louvre until his decadent life came to an abrupt end in 1610. Stabbed by an assassin in the streets, he was rushed back inside the Louvre, where he became the only king to die within its walls.

More recent architectural additions to the Louvre include the controversial pyramid entrance (1989) and the stunning renovation of the Richelieu wing, with its two modern glass-covered courtyards (1993). Not only are they impressive examples of the late President Mitterrand's predilection for grand civic architecture (► 31), but they have also, with exhibition space almost doubling to 60,000sq m (645,900 square feet), fulfilled Louis XIV's wish that the Louvre should be the largest museum in the world.

Tackling the Louvre
Rule number one – be patient: there are more than 35,000 works of art displayed in an enormous exhibition space which today covers 60,600sq m (652,300sq feet).

It's easy to spend hours exploring the cavernous galleries

Allow at least half a day. Even then, by the time you've queued for a ticket, queued at the information desk for a map, and left your coats, bags and umbrellas in the cloak-room, you'll probably only have a couple of hours left for the galleries themselves.

One saving grace is that the galleries are clearly marked (each room bears a number), and it is hard to get lost. However, if you don't want to tackle the museum on your own, ask at the information desk under the pyramid about the daily tours (in English and French) or rent an audio guide (moderate: available in six languages at the access to any of the wings).

In such a huge museum, it is impossible to see everything. If this is your first visit to the Louvre, you may like to buy the *Louvre Visitor's Guide*, which steers you round some of the main attractions (and see the Star Attractions box below).

You may prefer to concentrate on a particular period in greater depth: among the most dazzling collections are the **Greek, Etruscan and Roman Antiquities** (Denon, ground floor, rooms 5–30); **16th- to 17th-century Italian paintings** (Denon, first floor); **French sculpture from the early Middle Ages to the 19th century** (Richelieu, ground floor, Cour Puget and Cour Marly separated by the Passage Richelieu); **18th- to 19th-century French School of painting** (Sully, Richelieu second floor, rooms 36–73). The **Arts of Africa, Asia, Oceania** and the **Americas**, temporarily exhibited in the Louvre, are now permanently displayed in the new **Musée du Quai Branly** (► 60).

Putting his Foot In It

According to his mistress Françoise Gilot, Picasso once stepped on what he took to be an old canvas protecting the floor in a Louvre storage room – only to realise it was a priceless 10 by 6m (33 by 20 feet) Delacroix ceiling painting destined for one of the galleries.

Right: New perspective on the Louvre, through I M Pei's striking glass pyramid

---

Star Attractions
• Leonardo da Vinci's ***Portrait of Mona Lisa***, also called *La Gioconda* (1503–06, Denon, first floor, is back in room 6 after complete renovation).
• Théodore Géricault's moving shipwreck, ***The Raft of the Medusa*** (1819, Denon, first floor, room 77).
• ***The Lacemaker*** by Jan Vermeer (left, 1670–71, Richelieu, second floor, room 38), an exquisite portrayal of everyday domestic life in Holland.
• Michelangelo's ***Dying Slave*** (1513–20, Denon, ground floor), sculpted for the tomb of Pope Julius II in Rome.
• The unrivalled ***Venus de Milo*** (2nd century BC, Sully, ground floor, room 12), found in 1820 on the Greek island of Milo.
• The ***Winged Victory of Samothrace*** (190 BC, Denon, first floor), probably once a ship's figurehead and poised for flight at the head of a staircase.
• The wild ***Marly Horses*** by Guillaume Coustou (1740–45, Richelieu, Cour Marly).
• The **Gallery of Apollo** (Denon, first floor, room 66) recently renovated, the gallery that served as a model for the celebrated Hall of Mirrors at Versailles (► 167).

The airy glass pyramid adds to the beauty of the interior

For a comprehensive catalogue, try the weighty, well-illustrated *Louvre: The Collections* (available in the bookshop under the pyramid).

The Wings – Finding Your Way Around

The Collections are divided between three main wings – the **Sully** (named after Henri IV's Chancellor of the Exchequer); the **Richelieu** (eminent Cardinal and minister to Louis XIII); and the **Denon** (first director of the Central Arts Museum under

Napoléon I). Each wing has four levels, on which are arranged eight departments, each represented by a colour: yellow for Oriental Antiquities; dark green for Art of Islam; light green for Egyptian Antiquities; blue for Greek, Roman and Etruscan Antiquities; red for Paintings; pink for Prints and Drawings; purple for Decorative Arts; light brown for Sculpture; dark brown for the History of the Louvre/ Medieval Louvre.

TAKING A BREAK

The **Café Marly** makes a pleasant lunch stop (➤ 14–15).

The Pyramid

The Chinese-American architect Ieoh Ming Pei designed the extraordinarily modern glass pyramid in the Louvre's main courtyard, which now forms the main entrance to the museum. Made of glass in order to be "transparent and reflect the sky", this now much-loved landmark is 21.6m (71 feet) high and contains 793 panes of glass. It even boasts its own robot, designed especially for the weekly cleaning.

The *Mona Lisa*

If you are going to the Louvre solely to see the small portrait of a Florentine noblewoman known as the *Mona Lisa* or *La Giaconda* (as many visitors do), you may be disappointed to find her enigmatic smile encased behind bullet-proof glass and surrounded by masses of tourists – all eagerly taking snapshots as souvenirs. Every art thief must dream of stealing this Leonardo da Vinci masterpiece, and in 1911, a former museum worker named Vincenzo Perugia succeeded. Unsure how to sell it, he hid it under his bed in Florence, until it was discovered two years later and safely returned to the Louvre.

MUSÉE DU LOUVRE: INSIDE INFO

Getting in Four entrances – via the pyramid, via the Richelieu passage (off the rue de Rivoli), via the Porte des Lions, by the Seine, or via the Carrousel du Louvre shopping complex (closed Friday).

How to avoid the queues Visit **early in the morning**, 9 am, or Wednesday or Friday evening. Avoid Sunday, when the museum is at its most crowded.
• If you have a Museum Pass (▶ 36) or purchase your ticket in advance on the website or from one of the city's FNAC or Virgin stores (the nearest one is in the Carousel du Louvre), you can **enter the fast track** at the Richelieu entrance.
• If, like most people, you don't already have a ticket or a Museum Pass, go in by the **Carrousel entrance**: the queues are usually shorter here.

Once inside Your ticket will get you into any of the wings **as many times as you like** during one day.
• **Wear comfortable shoes** (you will have probably walked several kilometres by the end of your visit) and set yourself a few viewing priorities.

Top tips Pick up a **museum plan from the information desk** before you tackle any of the galleries. There's a special map available for visitors with disabilities, documentation in Braille, a dedicated tactile gallery and monthly guided visits in French (and sometimes British) sign language. Tel: 01 40 20 59 90.
• If you visit on Friday evening, ask at the information desk for the special booklet *Nocturnes du vendredi* which, even though it's in French, suggests an easily manageable route around 26 key treasures, including the *Mona Lisa*.
• **The museum shop is a great source** of books, souvenirs and museum gifts.
• Consider purchasing an **audio guide** (charge: moderate) with commentary on around 1,000 artworks, or take a guided **"Discovery Visit"** (inexpensive, plus entrance fee), at 11am, 2pm and 3:45pm in English daily (11:30 only on Sunday; not on the first Sunday of the month).

6 Jardin des Tuileries

When you've had your fill of museums and monuments, take a relaxing stroll through the Tuileries gardens, one of the oldest and most beautiful public gardens in Paris. Stretching along the right bank of the Seine, it offers unforgettable views embracing the Louvre, place de la Concorde, the Arc de Triomphe and, across the river, the Musée d'Orsay and the Eiffel Tower.

Hours of fun messing about with boats in the Jardin des Tuileries

The garden was first created in the 16th century by Catherine de' Médicis as an adornment in the Italian style to her pleasure palace, the Palais des Tuileries (once adjoining the Louvre but burned down during the Commune of 1871). The location of concerts and other entertainments, it also proved a useful spot for introducing to the French the Florentine fashion for horse-drawn carriages.

In the 17th century, the garden was transformed by Louis XIV's architect, André Le Nôtre (of Versailles fame, ► 165–167) into a *jardin à la française* – a formal and symmetrical garden, studded with ornamental statues, and embellished with carefully manicured lawns, orderly box-edged flower beds, topiarised trees and gravel walkways. Le Nôtre also laid out a long, straight path leading from the palace, through the middle of the gardens and way beyond to the west. This later became the

✚ 199 E2 ✉ Jardin des Tuileries, 75001 ☎ 01 40 20 90 43 🕔 Jul–Aug daily 7:30am–11pm; Apr–Jun and Sep 7:30am–9pm; rest of year 7:30am–7pm Ⓜ Tuileries/Concorde

Champs-Élysées and the first section of the city's famous Voie Triomphale, or Triumphal Way, which today stretches from the **Louvre** (➤ 96–101) to **La Défense** (➤ 111), 9km (6 miles) away.

Le Nôtre's gardens were the first in France to open to the public. Instantly popular as a place to see and be seen, they soon became the model for public gardens throughout Europe, and still remain a firm favourite with locals and tourists alike. Children especially love the pony rides and the large pond towards the eastern end of the garden, where they can sail old-fashioned toy boats (which can be rented from a nearby kiosk).

Once a real tennis court, the **Jeu de Paume** (on the rue de Rivoli side, www.jeudepaume.org) housed the city's Impressionist collection until it was moved to the **Musée d'Orsay** (➤ 54–57) in 1986. Today it stages temporary exhibitions of contemporary visual arts, photography and multimedia. The **Orangerie** (on the river side), reopened in 2006, provides an intimate setting

for a small collection of Impressionist paintings including Claude Monet's lovely and unmissable water-lily series.

A local artist captures the garden's riverside views on canvas

TAKING A BREAK

Try **Lescure** (7 rue de Mondovi, 75001, tel: 01 42 60 18 91, open Mon–Fri noon–2:15, 7–10:15. Closed Aug) for traditional home cooking in a rustic restaurant, family run since 1919.

JARDIN DES TUILERIES: INSIDE INFO

Top tips Enter the gardens either through the Arc de Triomphe du Carrousel at the Louvre end or **through the grand golden gates** on the edge of place de la Concorde.

• For information on **free guided tours** (45 minutes, summer only), see the notice board or phone 01 42 96 19 33.
• The **Jeu de Paume** (tel: 01 47 03 12 50, moderate) is open Tue noon–9, Wed–Fri noon–7, Sat and Sun 10–7.
• Following extensive renovation, the **Musée de l'Orangerie** (tel: 01 44 77 80 07, moderate, free first Sun of the month) is open Wed–Mon 12:30–7 (9 on Fri).

Hidden gem Look out for the **fine series of bronze figures** by 20th-century sculptor Aristide Maillol that decorate the pathways.

10 Arc de Triomphe
11 Avenue des Champs-Élysées

The Arc de Triomphe rises majestically at the head of the city's most famous avenue, the Champs-Élysées. Planned by Napoléon I as a monument to his military prowess, the colossal arch was not finished until 15 years after his death, in 1836. The Tomb of the Unknown Soldier beneath the archway makes it also a place of remembrance.

Two hundred and eighty-two steps up a narrow spiral staircase will lead you to the 50m (165-foot) high terrace. Here, the breathtaking view highlights the city's unmistakable design – the Voie Triomphale from the Louvre to La Défense, and the 12 avenues radiating out from the arch itself like the points of a star (hence the name place de l'Etoile, which stubbornly persists despite being changed officially to place Charles-de-Gaulle).

It is hard to believe that the broad and busy thoroughfare of the **Champs-Élysées** was just an empty field before Le Nôtre converted it into parkland as an extension of the Tuileries (▶ 102–103). For centuries it was a popular strolling ground, reaching its zenith in the mid-1800s, when a constant flow of horse-drawn carriages paraded up the street in order to allow ladies to show off

Street Celebrations

The Champs-Élysées has always been associated with grand parades and parties. In 1810 Napoléon I organised a lavish procession here (complete with life-size mock-up of the Arc de Triomphe, then under construction) to celebrate his marriage to his second wife Marie Louise. The avenue's patriotic status was confirmed by the World War I victory parade of 14 July, 1919. Twenty-five years later, Charles de Gaulle followed the same triumphal route at the end of World War II. It remains the venue for national celebrations – the last leg of the Tour de France cycle race every July ends here, and it is the scene of great pomp on Bastille Day (14 July) and Armistice Day (11 November).

Arc de Triomphe
✚ 197 E4 ✉ place Charles-de-Gaulle-Etoile, 75008
☎ 01 55 37 73 77; www.monum.fr
🕐 Apr–Sep daily 10am–11pm; rest of year 10am–10:30pm
Ⓜ Charles-de-Gaulle-Etoile
💲 Moderate

Champs-Élysées
✉ 198 C3 Ⓜ George V/Franklin D Roosevelt/Charles-de-Gaulle-Etoile

ARC DE TRIOMPHE: INSIDE INFO

Top tips The best time to visit the Arc de Triomphe is early in the day, when the **morning light emphasises the details** of the sculptures, or late afternoon as the sun sets over the roof-tops. In the evening, as shimmering lights map out the city.
• **Don't try to cross the road** to reach the arch. Access is via a subway at the top of the Champs-Élysées.
• Take plenty of film with you as **the views are stupendous**. An orientation table at the top of the arch makes spotting the key landmarks easy.

Did you know? Beneath the vault of the archway, the **flame of remembrance** has burned daily since 11 November, 1923.

One to miss The **small museum at the top of the arch** is not particularly inspired.

their finest fashions. Today, with its brash shops, cinemas and fast food joints, the avenue that was once the "most beautiful street in the world" has lost much of its magic, glamour and prestige, yet it still retains an aloof grandeur and unique appeal.

The Champs-Élysées – the most famous of Parisian boulevards

TAKING A BREAK

Have lunch or dinner at the bar or terrace of **Fouquet's** (► 113).

At Your Leisure

2 Palais Royal

Tired of sightseeing? Step through the gates of the Palais Royal into a haven of peace, and leave the noise and bustle of the city behind. The buildings of this 17th-century palace, commissioned by Cardinal Richelieu, Louis XIII's minister, today house the French Ministry of Culture and are closed to the public. However, the lovely arcaded gardens, where on 12 July, 1789, a revolutionary named Camille Desmoulins made the fiery speech that kick-started the city's revolt, are always open. At the southern end of these lovely gardens (and still a subject of great controversy) is an incongruous courtyard of ugly black-and-white striped columns (Colonnes de Buren) and fountains containing revolving silver spheres, erected in 1986.

🖂 200 A2 ⊠ place du Palais Royal
🚇 Palais Royal

Map labels:
BLVD MONTMARTRE
RUE DE RICHELIEU
RUE VIVIENNE
Grands Boulevards
Bourse
Les Galeries
4
RUE VIVIENNE
RUE DES PETITS CHAMPS
Sentier
RUE DE RICHELIEU
Jardin du Palais Royal
Place des Victoires 3
Palais Royal 2

3 Place des Victoires

Anyone who enjoys window-shopping should visit the graceful, circular place des Victoires. Designed by Versailles architect Jules Hardouin-Mansart, it is more famous today for its designer shops than for the victories of Louis XIV that it commemorates, but the Sun King does feature in an equestrian statue at the centre of the square. The harmony and symmetry of the surrounding architecture now create a showcase for such cutting-edge fashion designers as Kenzo.

🖂 200 B2 ⊠ place des Victoires
🚇 Sentier/Bourse

4 Les Galeries

Since Paris has always led the world in chic shopping, it comes as no surprise to discover that shopping arcades are a Parisian invention. The fashion began in 1785, when the Duke of Orléans, in need of money, decided to sell the arcades he had constructed in his garden at the Palais Royal (► left). A variety of merchants set up shop and the arcade instantly became a commercial success. You can still find several of these early 19th-century *galeries* dotted around the district, with their

Three Places to Picnic
• The courtyard of the Palais Royal
• Jardin des Tuileries (► 102–103)
• Square de la Tour St-Jacques (► 28)

Ancient and modern – colonnades and columns of the Palais Royal

Sophisticated Square

The Sun King was so thrilled with Mansart's masterpiece, the place des Victoires, that he ordered him to design a second square – the nearby place Vendôme. Elegant, snobbish and a perfect example of 17th-century urban architecture, it now has glittering window displays of stylish jewellers to dazzle visitors *en route* to stay, or more likely to gaze, at the deluxe Ritz hotel.

high glass roofs and ornate cast-iron structures forming covered passageways from one street to the next. In the 19th century they fell into disuse, but many were dramatically revived in the 1970s, once again becoming a popular rendezvous for journalists, designers and couturiers. Among the most charming are **Galerie Véro-Dodat** (antiques, bookshops and galleries), **Passage des Panoramas**, lit with fairy lights (cafés, boutiques), **Passage Verdeau** (drawings, engravings, old books and postcards), **Passage Jouffroy** (speciality shops – dolls' houses, cinema posters, toys and books) and, most sophisticated of all, **Galerie Vivienne** (fashion, interior design and an excellent *salon de thé*).

Galerie Véro-Dodat

🔲 200 B2 ✉ 19 rue Jean-Jacques Rousseau, 75001 🚇 Louvre-Rivoli, Palais Royal-Musée du Louvre

Passage des Panoramas

🔲 200 B4 ✉ 11 boulevard Montmartre/10 rue St-Marc, 75002 🚇 Richelieu-Drouot, Grands Boulevards

Passage Verdeau

🔲 200 B4 ✉ 31 bis rue du Faubourg Montmartre, 75009 🚇 Le Peletier

Passage Jouffroy

🔲 200 B4 ✉ 10 boulevard Montmartre, 75009 🚇 Richelieu-Drouot, Grands Boulevards

Galerie Vivienne

🔲 200 A3 ✉ 4 rue des Petits-Champs, 75002 🚇 Bourse

🛐 Opéra Garnier

From the outside, the Opéra Garnier looks more like a wedding cake than a world-renowned opera house.

Designed by Charles Garnier to show-case the splendour of Napoléon III's France, its exuberant design represents the climax of 19th-century classical and baroque architecture in Paris, and one of the crowning glories of the urban redevelopment plans of Baron Haussmann (▶ 30). The extravagance continues inside, with the lavish foyer and grand staircase illuminated by chandeliers, and the ceiling of the intimate red-and-gold auditorium painted by Marc Chagall with scenes from operas and ballets.

Galerie Vivienne – undoubtedly the city's most stylish arcade, with chic shops to match

Following an attempt on Napoléon III's life in 1858, Garnier added a pavilion equipped with a curved ramp so that the emperor could step from his carriage straight into the rooms adjoining the royal box. The Palais Garnier was inaugurated in 1875, five years after the fall of the Empire. A small museum which tells the story of opera through an extensive collection of musical memorabilia, including scores, manuscripts, sets and photographs. Tarot cards and ballet slippers of the legendary Russian dancer Nijinsky are also here. The museum ticket includes a visit to the opera house, unless there is a rehearsal or performance in progress.

➕ 199 F4 ✉ place de l'Opéra, 75009
☎ Opera house: information and box office: 08 92 89 90 90 (within France); 01 72 29 35 35; museum and library: 01 40 01 23 39; www.opera-de-paris.fr
🕐 Museum: daily 10–5; tours: phone 01 41 10 08 10 for details (expensive)
🚇 Opéra 🎫 Moderate

7 Place de la Concorde
This spacious cobbled square was laid out between 1755 and 1775, with a giant 3,300-year-old pink granite obelisk as its centre-piece (originally brought from the Temple of Rameses at Luxor, Egypt) and eight female statues representing France's largest

The Paris Opera – "a monument to art, to luxury, to pleasure" (Charles Garnier)

cities adorning its four corners. The north side is lined by the Hôtel de la Marine (headquarters of the French Navy) and Hôtel de Crillon (► 19), one of the city's most exclusive hotels.

In 1793, the square – renamed place de la Révolution – was the scene of the execution of Louis XVI (► 7), and during the following two years a further 1,343 "enemies of the Revolution" were guillotined here, including Marie-Antoinette and, six months later, revolutionary leaders Danton and Robespierre. At the end of this "Reign of Terror", the square was given its present name evoking peace – ironically now, as it's one of the city's busiest squares.

➕ 199 D2 🚇 Concorde

8 La Madeleine
This immense neo-classical church is one of Paris's great landmarks. Construction began in 1764, and the finished church was dedicated to Mary Magdalene in 1845. In between came numerous attempts to convert it into a bank, parliament buildings and a Temple of Glory to the armies of Napoléon (hence its resemblance to a Greek temple, surrounded by giant columns supporting a sculpted frieze).

As you enter the lavish marble and gilt interior, topped with three skylit cupolas, note the bas-reliefs depicting the Ten Commandments on the massive bronze doors. As you leave, admire the striking vista (from the south side), down rue Royale to place de la Concorde across to its architectural counterpart, the Palais-Bourbon (home of the Assemblée Nationale, the French parliament) on the far side of the Seine.

🔢 199 E3 ✉ place de la Madeleine, 75008 ☎ 01 44 51 69 00 🕐 Mon–Sat 8:30–7, Sun 7:30–7 🚇 Madeleine

🕐 Grand Palais: Wed–Mon 10–8 (until 10 Wed); Petit Palais: Tue–Sun 10–6
🚇 Champs-Elysées-Clemenceau

9 Grand Palais and Petit Palais

These two attractive art nouveau-style buildings were constructed as temporary galleries for the World Fair of 1900. A century later, they are still two of Paris's major exhibition spaces.

The most striking feature of the Grand Palais is its curved glass roof; at night it glows with the interior lighting. The eastern side of the palace hosts popular art exhibitions, while the western side has a science museum called the Palais de la Découverte.

The Petit Palais houses the Musée des Beaux-Arts de la Ville (Municipal Museum of Fine Arts).

🔢 Grand Palais: 198 B3; Petit Palais: 198 C3 ✉ avenue Winston-Churchill, 75008 ☎ Grand Palais: 01 44 13 17 30

Place de la Madeleine

Place de la Madeleine is always the first port of call for foodies in Paris, for the luxury caviar, champagne and handmade chocolates sold in the specialist shops surrounding the Madeleine church. Pride of place goes to Fauchon (▶ 116), which earns epithets such as "the Harrods Food Hall of Paris" and "millionaire's supermarket", with its mouth-watering showcase of French food. Just opposite Fauchon is a small and attractive flower market (daily except Sunday).

Majestic place de la Concorde – once scene of the bloody guillotine

Impressive fountains, studded with bronze and stone statues, adorn the Trocadéro gardens

12 Musée National des Arts Asiatiques-Guimet

The National Museum of Asian Art-Guimet was opened in 1889, the brainchild of Emile Guimet (1836–1918), a Lyons industrialist and fine arts fanatic. Now, following renovation work, it is considered to be among the world's foremost museums of Asiatic art. Its dazzling collection of 45,000 rare religious and secular items spans more than 3,000 years. The free 90-minute audioguide (in seven languages) steers you round a selection of masterpieces, including Cambodian Khmer Buddhist sculptures from Angkhor Wat, the Begram Treasures of Afghanistan and the Calmann and Grandidier collections of Chinese porcelain.

➕ 197 E2 ✉ 6 place d'Iéna, 75016
☎ 01 56 52 53 00; www.museeguimet.fr
🕒 Wed–Mon 10–6 (last entry 5:30)

Musée National des Arts Asiatiques-Guimet 12

AVENUE RAYMOND POINCARÉ
AVE KLÉBER
AVENUE DU PRÉSIDENT WILSON
Trocadéro
Musée National des Monuments Français
Cité de l'Architecture et du Patrimoine
AVENUE DE NEW YORK
PASSERELLE DEBILLY
PLACE DU TROCADÉRO ET DU II NOVEMBRE
13 Palais de Chaillot
Musée de l'Homme
Jardins du Trocadéro
PONT D'IÉNA
BRANLY
AVENUE DU PRÉS KENNEDY
Seine
QUAI
Tour Eiffel

🚇 Iéna, Trocadéro, Boissière
🎫 Moderate

13 Palais de Chaillot

Built high above the banks of the Seine for the Paris exhibition of 1937, the two curved, colonnaded wings of this honey-coloured art deco cultural centre house a theatre and two museums. The **Musée de l'Homme** (tel: 01 44 05 72 72, www.mnhn.fr open Wed, Fri and Mon 9:45–5:15, Sat and Sun 10–6:30, moderate) traces human evolution through displays of prehistoric artefacts from all over the world, underlining the common origins of Mankind. The **Musée de la Marine** (tel: 01 53 65 69 69, www.musee-marine.fr open Wed–Mon 10–6, moderate) portrays the thrilling history of the French navy through a series of model ships and other nautical paraphernalia.

The biggest crowd-puller here, however, is the view from the tumbling Trocadéro gardens below the palace, which affords a quintessentially Parisian panorama across the Seine and past the Eiffel Tower to the Champ-de-Mars. If possible, visit these lovely gardens by night, when the sculptures and fountains are floodlit.

➕ 197 D2 ✉ 17 place du Trocadéro, 75016 🚇 Trocadéro

For Kids
Arc de Triomphe (➤ 104–105).
Jardin des Tuileries (➤ 102–103) –
swings, slides, toy boats, and a
funfair in summer.
Palais de Chaillot (➤ 110) – for the
model ships in the naval museum.
Grévin (10 boulevard Montmartre,
75009, tel: 01 47 70 85 05;
www.grevin.com, open daily 10–6:30,
expensive) – Paris's answer to
Madame Tussaud's.

Further Afield
Musée Marmottan Monet
If you have visited the Musée d'Orsay
(➤ 54–57) and Musée de l'Orangerie
(➤ 103) and still thirst for more
Impressionist art, this museum is for
you. Set in an elegant 19th-century
mansion near the Bois de Boulogne, it
contains the world's largest collection
of Monets, including *Impression – Soleil
Levant* (the work that gave the
Impressionist movement its name) and
such celebrated series as *Cathédrale à
Rouen* and *Parlement à Londres*, as well
as paintings by contemporaries of
Monet such as Gauguin and Renoir.
➕ 197 off D2 ✉ 2 rue Louis-Boilly,
75016 ☎ 01 44 96 50 33;
www.marmottan.com ⏰ Tue–Sun 10–6
🚇 La Muette 💰 Moderate

La Défense
This modern skyscraper district on the
western outskirts of Paris bristles with
around 60 ultra-modern high-rise
buildings which create an atmosphere
so different from the rest of the city
that it's worth a brief visit. Most of the
buildings are occupied by the offices of
more than 1,200 companies, including
the headquarters of over half of
France's 20 largest corporations.

The *pièce de résistance*, designed by
Danish architect Otto von Spreckelsen,
is the Grande Arche de la Défense – a
hollow cube of white marble and glass
symbolising a window open to the
world and measuring 112m (368 feet)
on each side. Inaugurated in 1989, it
forms the westernmost point of the
city's Grand Axis or Voie Triomphale
(➤ 31) running through the Arc de
Triomphe and the Champs-Élysées to
the Louvre (look closely, though, and
you will notice that it is actually
slightly out of alignment).

La Grande Arche
➕ 197 off D5 ✉ Parvis de La Défense
☎ 01 49 07 27 27, www.grandearche.
com ⏰ Summer daily 10–8; winter
10–7; last entry 30 mins before closing
🚇 Grande Arche de La Défense
🚉 RER La Défense 💰 Moderate

Transparent lifts take visitors up to the top
of La Grande Arche

Where to...
Eat and Drink

Prices
Expect to pay per person for a meal, excluding drinks:
€ up to €25   €€ €25–50   €€€ €50–100   €€€€ over €100

Alain Ducasse €€€€

Having achieved the highest critical acclaim for his Louis XV restaurant in Monaco, Alain Ducasse has now done virtually the same at the Hôtel Plaza Athénée. He has reinterpreted some of the classics of French *haute cuisine*, instilling into them a lighter influence that has been gleaned from the provinces. His choice of ingredients is absolutely first class, and is perhaps best illustrated in the fabulous stuffed pigeon and chicken with *cepes* and two kinds of pasta. As a crowning touch the service is superb.

✚ 198 A3 ✉ 25 avenue Montaigne, 75008 ☎ 01 53 67 65 00; www.alain-ducasse.com ⏰ Thu–Fri 12:45–2:15, 7:45–10:15, Mon–Wed 7:45–10:15 Ⓜ Alma Marceau

L'Angle du Faubourg €€€

Located near the place Charles-de-Gaulle-Étoile, this one-Michelin-star restaurant is decidedly contemporary; the décor is simple yet elegant with works of art hanging on the walls. The constantly updated menu includes such dishes as chilled cream of chanterelle soup, jellied oysters, grilled langoustines seved

with artichokes à l'orange, roast lamb with braised fennel and crystallised tomatoes and, for dessert, roast figs with blackcurrant and vanilla and delicious soft macaroons with pineapple. Great wines enhance this French cuisine at its best.

✚ 198 A5 ✉ 195 rue du Faubourg-St-Honoré, 75008 ☎ 01 40 74 20 20 ⏰ Mon–Fri noon–2:30, 7–10:30, closed Aug Ⓜ Charles-de-Gaulle-Étoile, Ternes

Bistrot du Sommelier €€€

The owner has won awards for the best *sommelier* (wine waiter) both in France and in the world. It therefore comes as no surprise that the wine list here is phenomenal. There is also a fabulous variety available by the glass. Wine is also the theme of the décor, and though food almost takes second place, it is nevertheless good. The menu is short and modish, with game available in season.

✚ 199 D4 ✉ 97 boulevard Haussmann, 75008 ☎ 01 42 65 24 85; www.bistrotdusommelier.com

⏰ Mon–Fri noon–2:30, 7:30–10:30. Closed 3 weeks Aug, 1 week Christmas Ⓜ St-Augustin/Miromesnil

Café de la Paix €

Famous customers have included Oscar Wilde, Emile Zola, Maurice Chevalier, Josephine Baker and, due its Opéra-side location, Maria Callas and Placido Domingo. The interior was designed by the Opéra's architect, Charles Garnier, and the walls are decorated with fine Second Empire frescoes. Forget the fairly uninteresting restaurant and grab a terrace table (shielded by glass in the colder months) and indulge in the impeccable *pâtisseries* and ice-cream sundaes. Enormous baguette sandwiches filled with pâté, ham or salami should fuel your shopping sprees, while the coffee is also top quality; but expect to pay for the view of the opera house and to observe the continuous flow of Parisian passers-by.

✚ 199 F4 ✉ 12 boulevard des Capucines, 75009 ☎ 01 40 07 36 36

**Daily restaurant 7am–12:30am
(lunch from noon); terrace
10am–12:30am** 🚇 **Opéra**

Café Ruc €€€

Opposite the Comédie Française, this Costes brothers extravaganza (they also run the Café Marly, ▲ 14–15 and the Café Beaubourg, ▲ 138–139) has a décor of scarlet fabric, neo-baroque gilt mirrors, flounced lampshades and tiled floors. Black-clad waiters serve reliable *steaks tartares*, Wiener schnitzels, herby sea bream and *pastilla* of pigeon. The wine cellar is an Aladdin's cave, featuring clarets and burgundies. As for dessert, try the giant éclair. Outside, the crimson-chaired terrace is an unbeatable vantage point.

🕀 **199 F2** 🖂 **159 rue St-Honoré,
75001** 🕿 **01 42 60 97 54** 🚇 **Daily
8am–2am** 🚇 **Palais Royal Musée du
Louvre**

Carré des Feuillants €€€€

Pearwood-panelled walls and Murano crystal chandeliers help to create an elegant setting just off the rue Rivoli for Alain Dutournier, the city's foremost exponent of the cooking of the region. Utilising the wonderful produce of the region, including *foie gras*, Chalosse beef and chicken, he has taken traditional recipes and reworked them yet retains much of their original character.

🕀 **199 E3** 🖂 **14 rue de Castiglione,
75001** 🕿 **01 42 86 82 82**
🚇 **Mon–Fri 12:15–2, 7:30–9.45.
Closed Aug** 🚇 **Tuileries**

Chez André €€

A typically old-fashioned Parisian brasserie in a prime location, five minutes' walk from the Champs-Élysées serving generous helpings of simple traditional French cooking; this is the secret of its success...mixed green salad with grilled goat's milk cheese, fish soup with croutons, roast chicken with tarragon sauce, roast salmon with sautéed mushrooms, duck breast with green pepper and potato gratin and, to finish, chocolate dumplings with crystallised orange peel or rhum baba generously sprinkled with Saint-James Rhum.

🕀 **198 A3** 🖂 **12 rue Marbeuf, 75008**
🕿 **01 47 20 59 57** 🚇 **Daily
noon–2:30, 7–midnight** 🚇 **Franklin-Roosevelt**

Chez Jean €€–€€€

This formal but friendly restaurant, run by two alumni of Taillevent (one of the city's top restaurants, ▲ 114), specialises in classic dishes with a refreshingly modern twist. Try the *foie gras* with rhubarb and caviar, followed by slow-cooked farmhouse pork with a chutney of apricots, preserved lemons and sage. The cuisine is refined, the presentation exquisite, and the service second to none.

🕀 **200 A5** 🖂 **8 rue Saint-Lazare,
75009** 🕿 **01 48 78 62 73**
🚇 **Mon–Fri noon–2:30, 8–10:30**
🚇 **Notre Dame de Lorette/Trinité**

Fouquet's €€€

A real Paris institution that's listed as a historic building. Well placed on the Champs-Élysées, nowadays it is very much a place in which to see and be seen. For the famous, the veranda is the place to head for. The menu is that of a *brasserie de luxe*, offering a selection of generally well-prepared classics such as *foie gras terrine* and *hachis Parmentier* (Gallic shepherd's pie). A snack menu is available all day in the bar or on the terrace 11am–11pm.

🕀 **197 F4** 🖂 **99 avenue des
Champs-Élysées, 75008** 🕿 **01 47 23
50 00** 🚇 **Daily noon–3, 7–midnight**
🚇 **George V**

Harry's New York Bar €

A legendary bar just off the avenue de l'Opéra, Harry's is said to be where the Bloody Mary was first concocted in the 1920s. With its English-speaking bartenders, it can make for a welcome refuge if your French is limited. Cocktails are the reason to come here

is taken up by Le Cercle, which offers a simpler menu than that of the grander establishment upstairs.

✚ **198 C3** 🏠 **avenue Dutuit, 75008** ☎ **01 53 05 10 01** 🕐 **Tue–Fri 12:30–1:45, 8–9:45, Mon 8–9:45. Closed Aug** Ⓜ **Champs-Élysées-Clemenceau**

Pierre Gagnaire €€€€

Hailed by many in the know as one of the most creative chefs in France, and indeed in Europe, Pierre Gagnaire's extraordinarily inventive cooking combines unparalleled skills at the stove with consummate artistry on the plate. His imagination appears to be limitless, but there is nothing in any of his dishes that is not perfectly harmonious. Be prepared for a magical assault on your tastebuds. Such is the demand for a table here that you need to book a very long time in advance.

✚ **197 F4** 🏠 **6 rue de Balzac, 75008** ☎ **01 58 36 12 50** 🕐 **Mon–Fri noon–3:30, 7:30–9:30, Sun 7:30–9:30. Closed Sat, Aug** Ⓜ **George V**

and some argue that the dry martinis are the best in the city. Snack lunches (sandwiches, salads or *croques mon-sieur*) are served during the daytime, but at night you won't be allowed in unless you're smartly dressed (live music on some evenings). It may not be a typical French bistro but it's such an institution it's worth at least one visit during your stay.

✚ **199 F3** 🏠 **5 rue Daunou, 75002** ☎ **01 42 61 71 14; www.harrys-bar.fr** 🕐 **Daily 10:30am–2am (Fri and Sat 3am. Closed 25 Dec** Ⓜ **Opéra**

Ledoyen €€€€

This is one of the city's most historic restaurants that in the past has been patronised by Robespierre, painted by Tissot, and written about by Maupassant. It opened in 1792 in a pavilion near the Petit Palais in the Jardin des Champs-Elysees, and the elegant first-floor dining-room looks out over the gardens. Modern dishes, described without undue elabora-tion, are prepared with painstaking attention to detail. The ground floor

sauerkraut garlanded with sausages and pork) to Mediterranean *bouill-abaisse*, a fish stew flavoured with saffron. True to the brasserie tradition, the draught beer, shellfish and wine list are superb. A sumptuous 1920s décor and white-aproned, stern waiters rein-force your first (or last) taste of Paris.

✚ **202 E1** 🏠 **23 rue de Dunkerque, 75010** ☎ **01 42 85 05 15** 🕐 **Daily breakfast 8am, lunch from 11am, closes 1am** Ⓜ **Gare du Nord**

Willi's Wine Bar €€

Englishman Mark Williamson's splendid bistro/wine bar is not far from place des Victoires. On offer is a wonderful selection of Côtes du Rhône and Bordeaux wines in par-ticular, with a choice of eating in the chic bar, which offers an excellent wines by the glass, or in the dining room, where a short, daily-changing menu favours seasonal dishes.

✚ **200 A3** 🏠 **13 rue des Petits-Champs 75001** ☎ **01 42 61 05 09** 🕐 **Mon–Sat noon–2:30, 7:30–11 (bar open noon–midnight)** Ⓜ **Bourse**

Taillevent €€€€

The city's most enduring "grand" restaurant, whose panelled walls and discreet service help to create a civilised and refined ambience favoured by the great and the good of the city's establishment. There is a wonderfully old-fashioned and classic basis to the cooking, with only a few modern trends. Specialities include *foie gras*, lobster and truffles. The white truffle sorbet with chocolate *croquant* will round off your meal in style.

✚ **198 A4** 🏠 **15 rue Lamennais, 75008** ☎ **01 44 95 15 01; www.taillevent.com** 🕐 **Mon–Fri 12:15–2, 7:15–9.30. Closed Aug, public holidays** Ⓜ **George V**

Terminus Nord €€

Eurostarrers rightly see this venerable institution as a real godsend – it's con-veniently opposite the Gare du Nord, open all hours and it's also a bastion of delicious French cooking. The whole country is represented, from Alsace's *choucroute garnie* (a mountain of subtle

Where to...
Shop

This is the area to head for if you are in search of gifts or perfumes, or perhaps a little designer number such as a Hermès scarf or tie, from the city that is the epicentre of the world of high fashion. The *crème de la crème* of *haute couture* and one of the most exclusive shopping streets anywhere, is rue St-Honoré in the 1st *arrondissement* (which becomes rue du Faubourg St-Honoré in the 8th). A stroll westwards from Palais-Royal reveals a roll-call of famous designer names.

Colette is the place to go for leading designs in both fashion and home furnishings – from Alexander McQueen to Tom Dixon and the latest from Sony. The "Water Bar", which has more than 100 brands of bottled water, in the basement is a good place for a light snack. **Façonnable** offers a good selection of men's co-ordinated separates, while **Lanvin** features immaculate classic design for men and women.

Carita is one of the city's best ladies' hair stylists. **Annick Goutal** on rue de Castiglione is a tiny and exquisite perfume salon, and round in place Vendôme is **Cartier** with its top-quality jewellery. Rue Cambon, crossing rue St-Honoré, is where **Chanel** is based – not the place for clothing bargains, though the accessories are a little more affordable. If you continue westwards along rue du Faubourg St-Honoré, turn down avenue Matignon with its fine antiques shops and cross the rond point des Champs-Élysées, you will arrive at avenue Montaigne, a street of immense chic lined by the likes

of **Christian Dior, Dolce e Gabbana, Celine, Nina Ricci, Ungaro, Valentino** and **Louis Vuitton. Givenchy** is fairly close by on avenue George V. **Guerlain**, one of the most famous French perfumers, has a beauty salon on the avenue des Champs-Élysées, while it's easy to spot **Louis Vuitton**'s store on the Champs-Élysées by the lengthy queues outside.

Another small enclave of superior designer boutiques is located around place des Victoires, which joins rue des Petits Champs and rue Étienne Marcel. A branch of Jean-Paul Gaultier's main store (**Galerie Gaultier** is located here in Galerie Vivienne. Gaultier is one of the most innovative of French designers, offering the under 40s bespoke high fashion and dazzling ready-to-wear. His flagship store is at 44 rue George V.

At the **Salons du Palais Royal Shiseido**, make-up artist Serge Lutens offers a range of exclusive perfumes and make-up in a beautiful setting.

The **Musée des Arts Décoratifs** in the northwest wing of the Louvre has a bookshop and gift shop offering selections of unusual fine gifts.

On the same street, **Nature et Découvertes** is a fun New Age store, part of a chain selling camping gear as well as decorative games and pastimes and an assortment of fascinating instruments for stargazing.

No serious shopping trip would be complete without a visit to at least one of the department stores. **Galeries Lafayette** and **Au Printemps** are glamorous neighbours offering perfumes, jewellery and ready-to-wear fashion.

In rue Coquillière, just north of the domed Bourse du Commerce, the remarkable **E Dehillerin** has supplied cookware of all shapes and sizes to the great chefs since 1820. It helps if you are able to speak a little French.

Alléosse, off avenue des Ternes, is one of the finest cheese shops in the city, where Camembert, *époisses*, reblochon and goat's cheese are brought to the peak of maturity. It can be rather crowded on Saturdays. **Les Caves Augé**, on boulevard Haussmann, is the oldest wine shop in Paris. **La Ferme St-Hubert**, near Trocadero, is the realm of Henry Voy, a cheese connoisseur *par excellence*. Place de la Madeleine is home to two of the greatest luxury gourmet emporiums, **Fauchon** and **Hédiard**. These are a must for all *épicures*.

Alléosse
13 rue Poncelet, 75017
01 46 22 50 45
Closed Sun afternoon, all Mon
Ternes

Annick Goutal
14 rue de Castiglione, 75001
01 42 60 52 82
Tuileries/Concorde

Carita
11 rue du Faubourg St-Honoré, 75008
01 44 94 11 00;
www.carita.fr Concorde

Cartier
23 place Vendôme, 75001
01 44 55 32 20; www.cartier.com
Closed Sun Opéra/Tuileries

Les Caves Augé
116 boulevard Haussmann, 75008
01 45 22 16 97 St-Augustin

Le Cèdre Rouge (►67)
25 rue Duphot, 75008
01 42 61 81 81
Madeleine

Celine
36 avenue Montaigne, 75008
01 56 89 07 92; www.celine.fr
Franklin D Roosevelt

Chanel
31 rue Cambon, 75001
01 42 86 28 00; www.chanel.com
Concorde/Madeleine

Christian Dior
30 avenue Montaigne, 75008
01 40 73 54 44; www.dior.com
Alma-Marceau

Christian Lacroix
73 rue de Faubourg St-Honoré, 75008 01 42 68 79 04; www.christian-lacroix.com Miromesnil

Colette
213 rue St-Honoré, 75001
01 55 35 33 90; www.colette.fr
Palais-Royal/Tuileries/Pyramides

Dolce e Gabbana
22 avenue Montaigne, 75008
01 42 25 68 78 Alma-Marceau

E Dehillerin
18 rue Coquillière, 75001
01 42 36 53 13 Closed Sun
Les Halles

Façonnable
9 rue du Faubourg St-Honoré, 75008 01 47 42 72 60;
www.faconnable.com Concorde

Fauchon
26–30 place de la Madeleine, 75008 01 70 39 38 00; www.fauchon.fr Closed Sun Madeleine

La Ferme St-Hubert
14 rue des Sablons, 75016 01 45 53 15 77 Closed Sun
Trocadero

Galeries Lafayette
40 boulevard Haussmann, 75009
01 42 82 34 56; www.galerieslafayette.com Chaussée d'Antin

Giorgio Armani
41 avenue George V, 75008 01 56 89 06 50; www.giorgioarmani.com George V

Givenchy
3 avenue George V, 75008 01 44 31 50 00; www.givenchy.com
Alma Marceau

Guerlain
68 avenue des Champs-Élysées, 75008 01 45 62 52 57; www.guerlain.fr Franklin D Roosevelt

Hédiard
21 place de la Madeleine, 75008 01 43 12 88 88; www.hediard.fr
Closed Sun Madeleine

Where to...
Be Entertained

The capital's greatest diversity of entertainment venues is located within this area on the Right Bank. One inexpensive form of entertainment is people-watching, and Parisians love doing just that, either sitting at an outdoor café or strolling casually down the Champs-Elysées on a balmy summer's evening.

Le Balzac and **Le Lincoln**, both on streets just off the Champs-Elysées, are two excellent art-house cinemas. Le Balzac is famous for its programme of American independents (shown in the original language) and for the debates which often follow the projections.

The Orchestre Nationale de France – known as the best

orchestra in Paris – is based at **Maison de Radio-France**, close to the Seine, which also offers numerous free classical concerts and operas throughout the year, as well as radio shows open to the public. The elegant **Théâtre des Champs-Elysées** hosts opera, ballet, classical and chamber music orchestras. The **Opéra National de Paris-Palais Garnier** is not only one of central Paris's most imposing buildings, but it also enjoys near-perfect acoustics for a repertoire of beautifully staged operas and ballets. A visit here is a splendidly grand occasion.

The **Salle Gaveau** at the very centre of the 8th *arrondissement* is a favoured venue for chamber music and recitals, while the **Salle Pleyel** is the home of the Orchestre de Paris.

Hermès
⊠ 24 rue du Faubourg St-Honoré, 75008 ☎ 01 40 17 47 17;
www.hermes.com
Ⓒ Closed Sun Ⓜ Concorde

Jean-Paul Gaultier
⊠ 6 rue Vivienne, 75002
☎ 01 42 86 05 05;
www.jeanpaulgaultier.com
Ⓜ Bourse/Palais Royal

Lanvin
⊠ 22 (Femme), 15 (Homme) rue du Faubourg St-Honoré, 75008 ☎ 01 44 71 31 73 (Femme), 01 44 71 31 25 (Homme); www.lanvin.fr Ⓜ Concorde

Louis Vuitton
⊠ 101 avenue des Champs-Élysées, 75008 ☎ 08 10 81 00 10;
www.louisvuitton.com Ⓒ Closed Sun
Ⓜ George V

Musée des Arts Décoratifs
⊠ 107 rue de Rivoli, 75001 ☎ 01 44 55 57 50; www.lesartsdecoratifs.fr
Ⓒ Closed Mon Ⓜ Palais Royal

Nature et Découvertes
⊠ Carrousel du Louvre, 99 rue de Rivoli, 75001 ☎ 01 47 03 47 43
Ⓒ Closed Aug Ⓜ Palais Royal

Nina Ricci
⊠ 39 avenue Montaigne, 75008
☎ 01 40 88 64 51; www.ninaricci.com
Ⓜ Alma Marceau

Printemps Haussmann
⊠ 64 boulevard Haussmann, 75009
☎ 01 42 82 50 00;
www.printemps.com
Ⓜ Havre-Caumartin

Les Salons du Palais Royal Shiseido
⊠ 142 Galerie de Valois, Jardin du Palais-Royal, 25 rue de Valois, 75001 ☎ 01 49 27 09 09; www.shiseido.com
Ⓜ Palais Royal

Valentino
⊠ 17–19 avenue Montaigne, 75008
☎ 01 47 23 64 61;
www.valentino.com
Ⓜ Alma Marceau

The **Comédie Française**, located at the junction of avenue de l'Opéra and rue de Richelieu, presents high-quality productions of the classics by masters of the genre such as Molière and Shakespeare.

By contrast, one of the most stylish nude revues takes place nightly at the **Crazy Horse Saloon**, while the **Lido de Paris** offers an optional dinner preceding a spectacular show that features the famous Bluebell Girls and an astonishing array of special effects.

Queen Club is a gay club which is the haunt of outrageous drag queens while remaining straight-friendly. Expect house and garage mixed by international DJs.

La Scala is a huge club on three levels offering funk, dance, deep house and R&B (women get in free), while the best DJs (including Laurent Garnier) come to the **Rex** to spin house and techno.

A cruise (▶ 172–174) up and down the city's stretch of the Seine is a must on most visitors' itineraries and the *bateaux-mouches* run every 30 minutes from 10am to 11pm during summer months with possible additional trips. From October to March boats run every 45 minutes between 11am and 9pm. Cruises last for 1 hour.

Le Balzac
1 rue Balzac, 75008 ☎ 01 45 61 10 60 ⓜ George V/Charles de Gaulle-Étoile

Bateaux-mouches
Embarcadère pont de l'Alma, Right Bank ☎ 01 42 25 96 10; www.bateaux-mouches.fr ⓜ Alma Marceau

Crazy Horse Saloon
12 avenue George-V, 75008 ☎ 01 47 23 32 32; www.lecrazyhorseparis.com Shows: Apr–Jun 8:30pm, 11pm Sun–Fri and Sat 8pm, 10:15pm, 12:15am; Jul–Aug nightly 8:30, 11pm; rest of year Sun–Fri 8:30, 11pm, Sat 7:30, 9:45, 11:50pm ⓜ Alma-Marceau

Comédie-Française
1 place Colette, 75001 ☎ 01 44 58 15 15; www.comedie-francaise.fr Closed Jul–Sep ⓜ Palais Royal

Le Lincoln
14 rue Lincoln, 75008 ☎ 01 42 25 45 80 ⓜ George V/Franklin D Roosevelt

Lido de Paris
116 bis avenue des Champs-Élysées, 75008 ☎ 01 40 76 56 10; www.lido.fr Shows 9:30, 11:30pm ⓜ George V

Maison de Radio-France
116 avenue du Président-Kennedy, 75016 ☎ 01 56 40 15 16 ⓜ Ranelagh

Opéra National de Paris- Palais Garnier
place de l'Opéra, 75009 ☎ 08 92 89 90 90; www.opera-de-paris.fr Closed Aug ⓜ Opéra

Orchestre de Paris
252 rue du Faubourg St-Honoré, 75008 ☎ 01 42 56 13 13; www.orchestredeparis.com ⓜ Ternes

Queen Club
102 avenue des Champs-Élysées, 75008 ☎ 08 92 70 73 30; www.queen.fr Daily midnight–dawn ⓜ George V

Rex Club
5 boulevard Poissonnière, 75002 ☎ 01 42 36 10 96; www.rexclub.com 11pm–6am. Closed Aug ⓜ Bonne Nouvelle

Salle Gaveau
45 rue La Boétie, 75008 ☎ 01 49 53 05 07; www.sallegaveau.com Closed Jul–Aug ⓜ Miromesnil

La Scala
188 bis rue de Rivoli, 75001 ☎ 01 42 61 64 00; www.lascala.fr Wed–Sun 11pm–dawn ⓜ Palais Royal/Tuileries

Théâtre des Champs-Élysées
15 avenue Montaigne, 75008 ☎ 01 49 52 50 50; www.theatredeschampselysees.com Closed Jul–Aug ⓜ Alma Marceau/Franklin D Roosevelt

Le Marais
and Bastille

Getting Your Bearings

The ancient, maze-like Marais ("swamp") quarter, once an uninhabitable stretch of marshy ground used for market gardening, is now one of Paris's most historic and sought-after residential districts – home to chic Parisians, to the city's oldest Jewish community and to a vibrant gay community.

The pace of life in the Marais is slow and laid-back compared with the rest of the city. This gives you time to appreciate its narrow cobbled streets, studded with small squares and gardens, and to enjoy the modish boutiques, art galleries, intimate restaurants, bars and cafés – not to mention such noteworthy museums as the Musée Picasso and Musée Carnavalet that are housed in some of the magnificent Renaissance mansions that are so characteristic of the neighbourhood.

To the west lies the bustling Beaubourg district, with its ultra-modern and highly controversial Les Halles shopping centre, and of course the Centre Pompidou, one of the world's most famous museums of modern art, more than a quarter of a century old now and still architecturally outrageous. To the east, the trendy Bastille district, once famed for the prison that was stormed so notoriously on 14 July, 1789, is today known for its plethora of ethnic restaurants, its funky bars and clubs and the prestigious new Bastille Opera.

Previous page: Futuristic Centre Georges Pompidou is an imposing landmark in Le Marais

St-Eustache **2** Les Halles

Forum des Halles **3**

Louvre-Rivoli RUE ST-HONORÉ RUE DE L'ARBRE SEC Châtelet-Les Halles

PL DU LOUVRE **1**

RUE DES HALLES

St-Germain l'Auxerrois Pont Neuf PONT NEUF QUAI DE LA MÉGISSERIE RUE

PONT AU CHANGE

Window on the square – place

★ Don't Miss

At Your Leisure

Further Afield

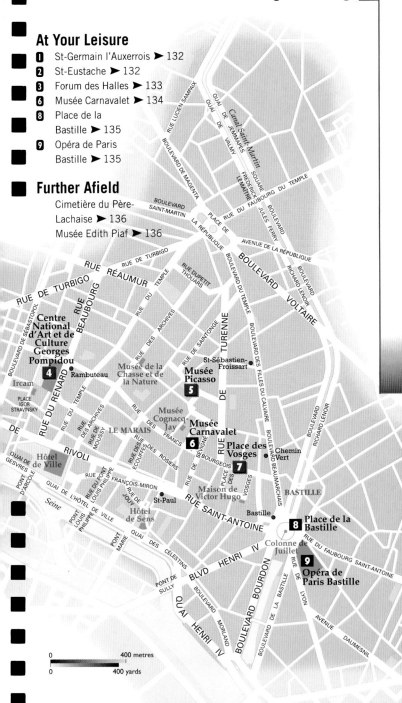

A fun-packed day of shopping and sightseeing, and an absolute must for art lovers.

Le Marais and Bastille in a Day

9am

Start the day with leisurely coffee and croissants at the legendary designer Café Beaubourg (► 138) overlooking the ④ **Centre Georges Pompidou** (► 124–127). Pause awhile in the spacious square to watch the buskers, mime artists, fire-eaters and jugglers, sit and write those postcards beside the brightly coloured mechanical pop-art fountains in **place Igor Stravinsky** (below, ► 127) – or, for a laugh and a fun souvenir, why not have your portrait sketched by a street caricaturist?

11am

Spend a few moments admiring the remarkable transparent architecture of the Centre Georges Pompidou, before stepping inside to enjoy one of the world's most exhilarating and controversial museums of modern art.

1pm

Head eastwards along rue Rambuteau into the heart of the intriguing **7 Marais quarter** (▶ 130–131). Either follow the walk on pages 175–177 or stroll at random past its many fine aristocratic residences. Window-shop in the trendy boutiques and galleries on rue des Francs Bourgeois and be sure to try some Jewish specialities in the kosher delis and bakeries along rue des Rosiers as an *hors d'oeuvre* before lunch in one of the countless cosy bistros in the surrounding streets.

3pm

Tucked away inside the Hôtel Salé, a beautiful 17th-century mansion in rue de Thorigny, the **5 Musée Picasso** (▶ 128–129) – the world's largest collection of works by Spanish artist Pablo Picasso – deserves at least a couple of hours of your time. The museum also contains part of Picasso's personal art collection, including treasured canvases by Braque, Cézanne, Matisse and Degas.

5:30pm

Wind your way through the Marais, down rue Elzevir and along rue des Francs Bourgeois to **7 place des Vosges** (right, ▶ 130–131), a gracious square of symmetrical brick houses with steeply pitched slate roofs and ground-floor arcades, mainly occupied by art galleries and antiques shops. At Ma Bourgogne café on the corner, the waiters sport traditional black jackets and long white aprons. Where better to enjoy an aperitif?

7:30pm

If you're lucky, you may be able to get last-minute tickets to attend an opera at the **9 Opéra de Paris Bastille** (▶ 135). If not, the gleaming glass edifice is still well worth admiring (especially after dark when floodlit) before ending your day with dinner at Bofinger (▶ 138).

4 Centre Georges Pompidou

Known to Parisians as "Beaubourg", the avant-garde Centre Georges Pompidou is one of the world's most extraordinary museums, one of the city's most distinctive landmarks and one of its most visited attractions. An X-ray-style extravaganza of steel and glass, striped by brightly coloured pipes and snake-like escalators, it looks as if someone has turned the whole building inside out. What's more, it contains one of the largest collections of modern art in the world.

It was in 1969 that French President Georges Pompidou declared "I passionately want Paris to have a cultural centre which would be at once a museum and a centre of creation." The building caused an outcry when it was opened in 1977, in the heart of the then run-down Beaubourg district, and it has been the subject of great controversy ever since, but it is generally acknowledged as one of the city's most distinctive landmarks – a lovable oddity, and far more popular as a gallery than anyone could ever have anticipated. As a result, the building had to be closed for two years of major renovation work, reopening, appropriately, on New Year's Eve 1999 with an exhibition spanning the art of the 20th century.

Before you go inside, pause to admire the centre's unique external structure, designed by Richard Rogers and Renzo Piano. Glass predominates, giving the entire edifice a transparency that abolishes barriers between street and centre. To avoid using conventional upright columns, a riot of steel beams cross-strutted and hinged over the length and width of the entire building form an intriguing external skeleton. Inside, walls can be taken down or put up at will, enabling the various

Above: An architectural feat of multi-coloured steel and glass

Opposite: Memorable cityscape from the top floor

Below: The museum's vast lobby

Finding Your Way Around

The centre consists of six main floors:

• The **1st, 2nd and 3rd floors** house an information library, an exhibition area and a cinema.

• The **4th and 5th floors** house the permanent collections of the Musée National d'Art Moderne (MNAM). Works from 1905 to 1960 – the Collection Historique – are on the 5th, with the 4th reserved for more recent art – the Collection Contemporaine (1960–present) – and a video room for viewing video-art. (To reach the 5th floor, enter the museum on the 4th floor.)

• The **1st and 6th floors** are used for temporary exhibitions.

• The **basement** is used for all types of shows, films, meetings and documentation.

• On **level 0** there is a bookshop, a children's gallery and a design boutique.

➕ 201 D1   ✉ place Georges-Pompidou, 75004   ☎ 01 44 78 12 33; www.centrepompidou.fr
🕐 Wed–Mon 11–10; MNAM and exhibitions close at 9; last ticket sold at 8
🚇 Rambuteau   💲 MNAM and exhibitions: expensive

Spacious, uncluttered exhibition halls provide the perfect backdrop to the modern art on display

espaces d'art to change shape in order to accommodate different displays.

On the outside, the building reveals all its workings by way of multi-coloured tubes, ducts and piping in the "high-tech" style that was briefly popular in the 1970s but was already out of vogue by the time the building was completed. But far from being merely decorative, they are carefully colour-coded: green for water, blue for air-conditioning and yellow for electricity. To complete the pattern, swarms of visitors zigzag up and down on red escalators. Once inside, you will find there is so much natural light that it's almost like walking around an open-air gallery.

Musée National d'Art Moderne

The Centre Pompidou's main attraction is the Musée National d'Art Modern – more than 50,000 works of contemporary art (of which about 2,000 are on display at any one time), starting from the early-20th century, roughly where the Musée d'Orsay leaves off. Among the main early schools represented are Fauvism, Cubism and Surrealism, with works by Matisse, Derain, Chagall, Braque and Picasso. The collection also covers the futurists, surrealists, minimalists – you name it, it's here, and you will be pleased to hear that there are thoughtfully placed clusters of chairs throughout for you to collapse in *en route*. The displays change annually, so if there's a particular piece you're eager to view, visit the website to check that it's on show.

Look out for 1960s American pop-art, some startling video-artworks (notably Nam June Paik's extraordinary sub-aquatic *Video Fish*) and the eccentric works of French New Realists Klein, César, Arman and Ben, many of which involve smashing, tearing, burning or distorting mundane objects of everyday life in a huge spoof on society and, in particular, the world of highbrow art.

Surrounding Sights

The area around the Centre Pompidou is a great place to while away an hour or two, mingling with the mime artists, musicians, magicians, fire-eaters and jugglers who perform on the spacious sloping plaza immediately outside the gallery, or wandering beside Paris's most remarkable contemporary fountain, the **Stravinsky Fountain** (to the south in place Igor Stravinsky). This consists of a wacky assortment of sculptures, including a dragon, a treble clef, a rotund woman and a pair of red pouting lips, each named after one of the great composer's works and all spinning and jetting streams of water in every direction, with the Gothic church of St-Merri as a backdrop.

Beside the fountain, the Institut de Recherche et Coordination de l'Acoustique et de la Musique **(IRCAM)** is one of the world's leading centres of experimental music. Down rue Brantôme to the north of the Centre Pompidou is the modern Quartier de l'Horloge. Here you will find the city's newest public clock,

The "Defender of Time" timepiece

an impressive, albeit sinister-looking brass-and-steel mechanical sculpture under an archway, called *Le Défenseur du Temps*. This is France's answer to the German glockenspiel. Currently awaiting repair, the "defender" usually battles hourly (from 9 am to 10 pm) with the elements of air, water and earth in the form of savage beasts. At noon, 6 pm and 10 pm there are particularly lively combats, when all three are successfully defeated.

TAKING A BREAK

There is a café on the 1st floor and the ultra-cool restaurant, **Georges** (tel: 01 44 78 47 99), with sweeping views over the roof-tops of Beaubourg on the 6th floor.

CENTRE GEORGES POMPIDOU: INSIDE INFO

Tickets If you are planning on spending several hours here, consider a **"One Day at the Centre" pass**, which you validate in a Métro-style machine at the entrance to each gallery. For details, ask at the information desk on the ground floor. The **Museum and Exhibitions ticket** gives admission to all current exhibitions.
• Pick up the **bimonthly programme of events** (in French).

Top tips If you are limited by time, stick to the MNAM exhibits on the **4th floor**, which tend to be the more frivolous, outrageous and highly entertaining works.

Hidden gem *Josephine Baker* by sculptor Alexander Calder (1898–1976) is an early, elegant example of the mobile – a form that he invented.

5 Musée Picasso

One of Paris's best-loved museums, the Musée National Picasso, in a back street in one of the finest 17th-century mansions in the Marais, contains an unparalleled collection of works by the most acclaimed artist of modern times. They span his entire career, from formative childhood sketches to major works of his later years.

Pablo Picasso

Picasso used to describe himself as "the world's leading collector of Picassos", and kept the majority of his works himself. When he died in 1973, his heirs paid heavy death duties by donating to the State a staggering 3,500-plus paintings, drawings, sketch books, engravings, collages, reliefs, illustrated books, ceramic works and an exceptional collection of sculptures. They formed the basis of this museum, unique in the world for their sheer number and range – the most complete overview of the master's work, spanning his entire life.

A second contribution, added after his wife died in 1986, enhanced the museum still further. Together with numerous key works by Picasso himself, treasures from his private collection were also added, including works by Cézanne, Matisse, Miró, Renoir, Degas and Braque. Picasso's works are arranged chronologically, providing a fascinating journey through a remarkable 80 years of artistic output, from early Impressionist works, through his distinctive Blue and Pink periods, Cubism and neo-classical phases, before culminating in his grotesque, distorted and predominantly black final canvases. Every room is clearly marked and also contains information about the major events in Picasso's life.

The intermingled paintings, sculptures and works in other media vividly illustrate Picasso's astonishing versatility. Perhaps the most interesting part of the collection is represented by the Cubist period. Together with Georges Braque, he developed the Cubist technique of representing many different views of a

---

✚ 201 E1 ✉ Hôtel Salé, 5 rue de Thorigny, 75003 ☎ 01 42 71 25 21; www.musee-picasso.fr 🕓 Wed–Mon 9:30–6 (Oct–Mar until 5:30). (Last entrance 45 minutes before closing.) Closed 1 Jan, 25 Dec 🚇 St-Paul/Chemin Vert/St-Sébastien-Froissart 💶 Expensive

Grand Hôtel Salé

Even if you aren't a Picasso fan, you should still visit the museum to see the interior grandeur of the Hôtel Salé, with its opulent cherub-encrusted ceilings and ornately carved staircase. The handsome chandeliers, chairs and tables throughout were designed specifically for the museum by Diego Giacometti.

The Hôtel Salé is the only mansion in the Marais not named after its 17th-century owner, in this case Pierre Aubert de Fontenay. Aubert – one of the King's partisans – made his fortune collecting salt taxes, hence the nickname *salé*, meaning both "salty" and, colloquially, "absurdly expensive".

subject in one picture: their pioneering works are well displayed here. You will also find numerous portraits of Jacqueline, Picasso's wife and muse for more than 20 years, and of various other female friends. (He had a reputation for seducing the wives of fellow artists.)

Picasso was also an innovative sculptor, and the garden shades many of his finest Cubist sculptures.

MUSÉE PICASSO: INSIDE INFO

Must-sees
Self-portrait (1901)
Portrait of Olga (1917)
The Bathers (1918)
Two Women Running on the Beach (1922)
Pan's Flute (1923)
The Crucifixion (1930)
Portrait of Jacqueline with Crossed Hands (right, 1954)
The Kiss (1969)

Top tip After a visit to the museum, the **summer café in the tiny garden** makes a pleasant spot for refreshments.

Hidden gems Don't miss the *Goat* and the bronze *Baboon*, its nose made out of a toy Renault car.

7 Le Marais and Place des Vosges

The history of the Marais dates back to the 14th century and Charles V, who moved the royal court here from the Île de la Cité. But it was not until the 17th century, when Henri IV laid out the place des Vosges, that the Marais became the place to live, and moneyed classes, keen to be associated with the monarchy, started to build the grand and sumptuous *hôtels particuliers* (mansions) that dot the neighbourhood today.

While away the day in the place des Vosges...

After the Revolution, the district sank into decay as the aristocracy moved towards the Tuileries and the Faubourg St-Germain. In the early 1960s, the area was a run-down, neglected corner of the capital, but following a major face-lift (sparked by the creation of the **Centre Pompidou** near by, ➤ 124–127), it has become one of the most lively, fashion-able and atmospheric *quartiers* of central Paris, a magnet for elegant shops, fine restaurants and bars. The district is especially busy on Sunday afternoons, when many of its trendy boutiques defy Sunday opening laws.

A number of its mansions have been restored and now house museums. As well as the **Musée Picasso** (➤ 128–129), **Musée Carnavalet** (➤ 134–135) and **Musée Cognacq-Jay** (➤ 176), these also include: the **Musée de la Chasse et de la Nature** (Hunting and Nature Museum, 60 rue des Archives, 75003) in the former residence of Louis XIV's Secretary of State; the **Maison Européenne de la Photographie** (5–7 rue de Fourcy, 75004), with exhibitions of contemporary photography.

The Marais' *pièce de résistance* is undoubtedly the place des Vosges, the oldest square in Paris and in many people's view the most gracious square. Its stately 17th-century town houses, laid out by Henri IV for his courtiers and built in alternate brick and stone with steeply pitched slate roofs, are arranged symmetrically around an immaculately kept park, once a popular venue for duels. Madame de Sévigné, famous for her letters, was born at No 1 in 1626. Victor Hugo lived at No 6 from 1832 to 1848, before going into exile. It is now a small museum dedicated to his memory. Otherwise, the graceful arcades nowadays house a variety of stylish galleries, antiques shops and elegant *salons de thé*.

To get a better overview of the area, see the walk on pages 175–177.

TAKING A BREAK

La Guirlande de Julie is ideal for a snack or a full meal (► 139). Weather permitting you can dine on the terrace.

...or enjoy some refreshment under the arches

LE MARAIS AND PLACE DES VOSGES: INSIDE INFO

Hidden gems The **Hôtel de Sens** is one of the city's few surviving medieval buildings, where Queen Margot, Henri IV's former wife, led a life of debauchery and scandal. Her poor complexion led her to start the fashion for wearing make-up in Paris, today a hugely successful industry (1 rue du Figuier, 75004).
• The **Hôtel de Sully** is a beautiful and meticulously restored 17th-century aristocratic mansion (62 rue St-Antoine, 75004, ► 176).

In more depth For seven centuries the Marais has had a vibrant Jewish community, focused around **rue des Rosiers** and **rue des Ecouffes,** which are lined with kosher shops and restaurants. Admire the synagogue (10 rue Pavée, 75004), renowned for its art nouveau architecture by Hector Guimard, designer of the famous Métro entrances, and visit the Jewish Art and History museum (Musée d'Art et d'Histoire du Judaïsme, 71 rue de Temple, 75004).

Did you know? Place des Vosges, originally called place Royale, received its present name in 1800 in honour of the Vosges *département*, the **first in France to pay taxes**.

At Your Leisure

❶ St-Germain l'Auxerrois

From the 14th century until the Revolution, when the adjacent Louvre was still a palace, St-Germain l'Auxerrois was the French royal family's parish church, and it still contains their pew. One of its most fascinating aspects today is its eclectic architectural styles: predominantly Gothic and Renaissance, it has been greatly altered over the centuries. At one point after the Revolution, it was used as a barn to store fodder.

The square tower rising beside the south transept contains the bell that was tolled to signal the start of the Saint Bartholomew's Day Massacre on 24 August, 1572, one of the bloodiest pages of French history. On the eve of the royal marriage of Henri of Navarre to Marguerite de Valois, thousands of Huguenots assembled in Paris for the wedding were slaughtered in a brutal massacre instigated by the ruthlessly ambitious Catherine de' Médicis and the Catholic Guise family.

🔢 200 B1 ✉ 2 place du Louvre, 75001
☎ 01 42 60 13 96 🕐 Daily 9–7; no visits during services 🚇 Louvre-Rivoli, Pont Neuf

❷ St-Eustache

This huge and imposing church, the second largest in Paris after Notre-Dame, was built for the congregation of Les Halles (see opposite) – once

One of St-Germain's original 16th-century stained-glass windows

the city's main market-place, today a modern shopping mall. Modelled on Notre-Dame, the church took 105 years to construct, and now stands as a gem of Renaissance architecture.

Many illustrious names have been associated with St-Eustache over the years: Cardinal Richelieu was baptised here; Louis XIV celebrated his first communion here; the composer Lully was married here; both the marriage and the funeral service for Mozart's mother Anna Maria were held here; and the playwright Molière was

For Kids
• **Centre Georges Pompidou** (➤ 124–127) contains a Galerie des Enfants (children's studio). Instruction is in French but the activities – arts and crafts workshops, mime- and puppet-shows – focus on actions rather than words. Telephone for times.
• The plaza surrounding the Centre Pompidou, with its street entertainers and the colourful **Stravinsky Fountain** (➤ 127).
• **Forum des Halles** (➤ opposite) and the surrounding streets abound with numerous children's boutiques and fast-food joints. There is also the Jardin des Enfants, an adventure playground aimed at 7–11 year olds.
• In winter months, there is an open-air ice-skating rink outside the **Hôtel de Ville** (➤ 177).

buried within its walls, later to be moved to the cemetery of Père-Lachaise (➤ 8 and 136).

Blessed with remarkable acoustics, St-Eustache boasts a long musical tradition. Here, Berlioz's *Te Deum* and Liszt's *Grand Mass* were first performed. In the mid-19th century the choir was directed by composer Charles Gounod, whose most outstanding chorister was an artistic child named Auguste Renoir. The gargantuan organ, installed in 1989, is the biggest double transmission organ in the world, making it especially suitable for the performance of 20th-century music. It is sometimes played weekdays from 5:30 to 6 pm, before evening Mass. There are organ recitals most Sundays from 5:30 to 6 pm. Concert schedules are posted on the church door.

🕂 200 B2 ✉ place du Jour, 75001
☎ 01 42 36 31 05; www.st-eustache.org
🕓 Mon–Sat 9:30–7 (Sat 10pm);
Sun 9–7:15 (8pm, in summer)
🚇 Les Halles
🚆 RER Châtelet-Les Halles

🔟 Forum des Halles

This was once the hub of Parisian daily life, and the city's main market-place – vividly described by Emile Zola as "the belly of Paris" – for nearly 800 years, until consumerism pushed aside centuries of local tradition in a trend the French today call *McDonaldisation*.

The market was removed to a modern, concrete complex in the suburb of Rungis near Orly Airport, and the elegant 19th-century iron-and-glass pavilions that had covered the stalls were bulldozed in 1969. They were replaced by the Forum des Halles – an ugly glass-and-chrome multi-level underground shopping centre, built around an open courtyard and crammed full of fast food

St-Eustache, parish church of Les Halles, is an unusual combination of Gothic structure and Renaissance decoration

Unusual sculpture at Les Halles

joints and French chain stores. It has proved surprisingly popular with Parisian shoppers. The area is best avoided after dark, when the atmosphere around the Les Halles complex can be decidedly menacing.

✚ 200 C2 ✉ Forum des Halles, 1–7 rue Pierre Lescot, 75001
🕐 Mon–Sat 10–7:30 🚇 Les Halles
🚉 RER Châtelet les Halles

6 Musée Carnavalet

It takes two vast Marais mansions to house the Musée de l'Histoire de Paris – 17th-century Hôtel le Peletier de St-Fargeau and the 16th-century Renaissance-style Hôtel Carnavalet (former home of Madame de Sévigné, whose prolific and witty letters to her daughter give a vivid insider's view of Louis XIV's court).

Together these two *hôtels particuliers* provide a magnificent setting for the extensive collections of historic paintings, sculptures, decorative art, documents, maps and costumes, which together provide a real taste of Parisian life over the centuries. Be warned, however – it's easy to get lost once inside. Essentially, the Hôtel Carnavalet covers the history of Paris from the Middle Ages to 1789, while the Hôtel le Peletier traces the history of the capital from the Revolution to the present day. The Orangery houses archaeological finds.

Highlights include keys to the Bastille, Napoléon I's death mask, an art nouveau jewellery shop moved intact from rue Royale, Proust's cork-lined bedroom from his apartment and the country's most important collection of memorabilia from the French Revolution. Allow at least two

The old Fouquet jewellery shop, re-created inside Musée Carnavalet

hours in this museum: with a grasp of the city's colourful history, you will find subsequent walks around Paris more rewarding.

🚹 196 B5
✉ 23 rue de Sévigné, 75003
☎ 01 44 59 58 58
🕐 Tue–Sun 10–6
🚇 St-Paul 🎫 Free

🟦 Place de la Bastille

The Bastille, built in the 14th century as a fortress to defend the eastern entrance to the city and transformed into a prison for political offenders, is the most famous monument in Paris that you cannot visit. It was demolished shortly after being stormed on 14 July, 1789 (▶ 6–7), which came to symbolise the start of the French Revolution. Its site is marked by the Colonne de Juillet (July Column), a 50m (164-foot) high bronze shaft surmounted by a statue of the Spirit of Liberty which commemorates those who died in two later uprisings, in 1830 and 1848. It stands on a hectic roundabout, with roads leading to other squares with equally evocative names – place de la Nation and place de la République.

The Bastille area was smartened up in celebration of the bicentennial of the Revolution, making it one of the trendiest *quartiers*, full of charming shops and galleries by day and lively bars, cafés and clubs by night.

🚹 196 C5 ✉ place de la Bastille, 75004 🚇 Bastille

🟦 Opéra de Paris Bastille

The austere glass and grey marble geometrical façade of the Bastille Opera towers over the place de la Bastille. It is one of Paris's newest buildings, controversial yet undeniably prestigious.

Built by President Mitterrand in what was then a rather run-down

district of Paris, it opened on 14 July, 1989 (the bicentenary of the French Revolution), as an affordable, accessible "opera of the people". However, tickets are still pricey and you have to book well in advance to guarantee a seat in the grey granite and oak 2,700-seat auditorium.

🚹 196 C4 ✉ place de la Bastille, 75012 (box office: 130 rue de Lyon) ☎ 01 40 01 19 70 (information); 08 92 89 90 90 (reservations, within France); www.opera-de-paris.fr 🕐 Box office: Mon–Sat noon–6:30. Guided visits some days, lasting 1 hr 15 mins. Phone for details

Colonne de Juillet – centre-piece of the place de la Bastille

Further Afield

Cimetière du Père-Lachaise

This must be the world's most fascinating cemetery – a silent village with countless occupants in higgledy-piggledy tombs, and the final resting place of the city's most prestigious names: painters Corot, Delacroix, Pissaro and Ernst; composers Bizet and Chopin; writers Apollinaire, Daudet, Balzac and Molière; singers Maria Callas, Edith Piaf and also former Doors lead vocalist, Jim Morrison, to name but a few. Pick up a map at the entrance or buy one at a local shop to see where they are buried.

In general, the more grandiose the tomb, the more obscure the occupant. Proust lies beneath a plain black marble slab in one of the cemetery's more modest quarters, and the notorious American dancer Isadora Duncan (who met an untimely death when her trailing scarf caught in the wheel of her Bugatti and broke her neck) is represented by a simple plaque among thousands of others lining the walls

of the crematorium. The exception to the rule is Oscar Wilde, whose grave is marked by a massive Epstein statue of a naked Egyptian flying skywards: the playwright would probably have considered the whole thing perfectly ludicrous, and therefore quite fitting.

Look out also for the artist Géricault (► 8), reclining on his tomb, palette in hand, admiring his masterpiece *The Raft of Medusa*; the recumbent statue of 19th-century journalist Victor Noir, as he was found after being shot by Napoléon III's cousin; and the tomb of François Raspail, a much-imprisoned partisan of the 1830 Revolution, shaped to resemble a prison cell.

The oldest residents are the celebrated 12th-century lovers Abelard and Héloïse, while the most moving monuments include that of the romantic poet George Rodenbach, depicted rising out of his tomb, often with a freshly picked rose placed in his outstretched hand, and, under a tiny willow tree, the grave of poet Alfred de Musset, bearing an inscription from one of his poems:

"My dear friends, when I die
Plant a willow at the cemetery
I love its weeping leaves
The pallor is sweet and precious
And its shadow will lighten
The earth where I shall sleep."

✚ 201 off F2 ✉ Boulevard de Ménilmontant, 75020 ☎ 01 55 25 82 10 ◷ Mid-Mar to 5 Nov Mon–Fri 8–6, Sat 8:30–6, Sun 9–6; rest of year Mon–Fri 8–5:30, Sat 8:30–5:30, Sun 9–5:30 Ⓜ Père-Lachaise, Philippe Auguste, Gambetta

Musée Edith Piaf

Born Edith Gassion in the working-class Bastille neighbourhood in 1915, this beloved *chanteuse* so famous for her powerfully emotional voice, took her stage name from her nickname, "the little sparrow". By the age of 15, she was singing in cafés, on the streets and in the cabarets of Pigalle, taking

Frédéric Chopin's grave – one of many poignant tombstones in Cimetière du Père-Lachaise

Edith Piaf, "the little sparrow"

her subject matter from the drugs, deaths and unhappy love affairs of her own life.

The atmospheric museum offers private tours around a two-room shrine to the great diva, crammed with kitsch memorabilia, from a life-size cardboard cut-out of the singer to her amazingly tiny suede shoes. The red walls are covered with original posters, photographs and portraits of *l'Ange Noir*, while immortal hits such as *La Vie en Rose* and *Je ne regrette rien* play on the gramophone.

🕇 201 off F2 ✉ 5 rue Crespin du Gast, 75011 ☎ 01 43 55 52 72 🕐 Mon–Thu 1–6. Closed Jun, Sep. Visits by prior appointment only Ⓜ Ménilmontant 💷 Donation

Canal St-Martin – a little-known highlight of residential eastern Paris

Off the Beaten Track

If you have time and the weather is fine, take a stroll along the **Canal St-Martin** (Métro: République, Goncourt, Château Landon, Jaurès), one of Paris's hidden delights. This picturesque 5km (3-mile) stretch of waterway – a long-time favourite of artists, novelists and film directors – links the Seine with a network of canals on the outskirts, providing a short-cut for river traffic between loops of the Seine. Walk along the tree-lined watersides fringing the canal, over locks and iron footbridges and past old factories and warehouses, or sit in a café watching the traditional barges chugging by. It's like winding the clocks back to the 19th century.

Where to...
Eat and Drink

Prices
Expect to pay per person for a meal, excluding drinks:
€ up to €25 €€ €25–50 €€€ €50–100 €€€€ over €100

L'Ambassade d'Auvergne €€

The rustic décor at this restaurant makes an appropriate setting for the authentic farmhouse cooking of the mountainous Auvergne region. Much of the produce used here comes from the region and is assembled to create warming and quite substantial dishes. Among the specialities are a wonderfully delicate cabbage soup ladled over a slice of Roquefort, cassoulet with Puy lentils and *boudin aux chataignes*, a rich, delicious black pudding with chestnuts accompanied by a chestnut sauce. The Menu Gourmand features specialities of the Auvergne and includes wines from the region too.

➕ 201 D2 ✉ 22 rue du Grenier St-Lazare, 75003 ☎ 01 42 72 31 22; www.ambassade-auvergne.com ⊙ Daily noon–2, 7:30–10 Ⓜ Rambuteau

L'Ambroisie €€€€

You have to book eight weeks in advance for a table in this elegant and exclusive town house restaurant in the beautiful 17th-century place des Vosges on the edge of the Marais. The main dining-room is lined with fabulous tapestries that, together with stone floors and much dark wood, add to the period atmosphere. The kitchen produces consistently superb food, dishes varying with the seasons.

➕ 196 B5 ✉ 9 place des Vosges, 75004 ☎ 01 42 78 51 45 ⊙ Tue–Sat noon–1:30, 8–9:30. Closed 2 weeks Feb, Aug Ⓜ Bastille/St-Paul/Chemin Vert

Aux Vins des Pyrénées €

This restaurant takes you back to the 1930s with gingham tablecloths and old family pictures on the walls. Fish and meat lovers are both catered for with dishes such as salmon *millefeuille* and grilled meat on the menu. For dessert, try crème brûlée or half-baked chocolate cake. The comprehensive wine list includes a selection from the Pyrenees.

➕ 196 B4 ✉ 25 rue Beautreillis, 75004 ☎ 01 42 72 64 94 ⊙ Sun–Fri noon–2:30, 8–11:30, Sat 8–11:30 Ⓜ St-Paul/Sully-Morland

Bofinger €€

A legendary brasserie, claiming to be Paris's oldest, close to place de la Bastille with an amazing turn-of-the-century *belle époque* interior. The classic dishes here are oysters and a wealth of other shellfish, *choucroute* (sauerkraut), duck *foie gras*, steak tartare and grills with delicious home-made desserts and ices to finish. The three-course fixed-price menu, including wine, is a popular choice and good value.

➕ 196 C5 ✉ 5–7 rue de la Bastille, 75004 ☎ 01 42 72 87 82; www.bofingerparis.com ⊙ Mon–Fri noon–3, 6:30–1am, Sat, Sun noon–1am Ⓜ Bastille

Café Beaubourg €€

All-in-black waiters bounding up the stairs with superhumanly laden trays, and 1980s-style split-level concrete, are hallmarks of this Costes brothers masterpiece, whose place-to-be-seen terrace affords a splendid view of the Pompidou centre. Don't be put off by the posiness of it all, because the food and drink are faultless – Italian-quality cappuccinos and espressos, bountiful brunches, perfectly mixed cocktails (to sip as you tap your feet to the groovy music), snacky delights such as tarama with blinis, and full-blown meals like the ever-popular seared steak tartare, not forgetting the fine array of *pâtisseries*.

🚇 201 D3 ⬛ **100 rue St-Martin, 75004** 🕿 **01 48 87 63 96** ⬛ **Daily 10am–1am** Ⓜ **Hôtel de Ville/ Rambuteau**

Chez Jenny €€

Named after the Alsatian Robert Jenny who established this venue in 1930, Chez Jenny pays tribute to the Alsace region of France with frescoes of its landscapes. Alongside the traditional *sauerkraut*, the menu features specialities such as saveloy sausage salad and iced *gugelhupf* with a vanilla-flavoured egg custard.

🚇 201 F2 ⬛ **39 boulevard du Temple, 75003** 🕿 **01 44 54 39 00** ⬛ **Daily noon–midnight** Ⓜ **République**

Chez Marianne €

If you can't make up your mind which of the many tempting Jewish delis in this neighbourhood to plump for, choose Marianne's. The second dining-room is calm and quaint, and in the summer there's a busy terrace. The service can be impatient but take your time to decide which of the delicious appetizers to have – you can concoct an assortment of four or more (be sure to have the hummus). The pastrami and smoked salmon are luscious, served on first-rate rye. To round it off, the deep cheesecake is wonderful but so are all the Central European-style pastries.

🚇 201 E1 ⬛ **2 rue des Hospitalières St-Gervais, 75004** 🕿 **01 42 72 18 86** ⬛ **Daily noon–midnight** Ⓜ **St-Paul**

Chez Nénesse €€

A splendid neighbourhood bistro with the laid-back and old-fashioned charm that is so typical of the Marais quarter. The cosy interior has an old stove and tiled floor

adding to its character. The excellent cooking is surprisingly modern, and the reasonable prices and a friendly atmosphere combine to ensure a popularity that means it is best to book well in advance.

🚇 201 E2 ⬛ **17 rue de Saintonge, 75003** 🕿 **01 42 78 46 49** ⬛ **Mon–Fri noon–2:15, 8–10:15. Closed public holidays, Aug, 1 week Christmas** Ⓜ **Filles-du-Calvaire/République/Oberkampf**

404 €€

This fashionable establishment, with its chic Berber décor reminiscent of the kasbah in Algiers, serves excellent North African food. It is forever busy and often crowded, but the food is capably prepared and authentic. *Tagines* and couscous feature as filling main courses, with the pigeon *pastilla* a must for anyone who hasn't tasted its delicious sweet and savoury flavours.

🚇 201 D2 ⬛ **69 rue des Gravilliers, 75003** 🕿 **01 42 74 57 81** ⬛ **Daily noon–2:30, 8–midnight. Closed Aug** Ⓜ **Arts et Métiers**

La Guirlande de Julie €–€€

In the same ownership as La Tour d'Argent (▶ 89) but at the opposite end of the price scale, Julie is open long hours and serves teas, snacks and meals. *Pot au feu* (boiled meat and vegetables), a classic winter warmer, is the speciality but the menu also includes mushroom ravioli, calves' liver with balsamic vinegar, and a superb *navarin* of lamb. Eat on the terrace in good weather.

🚇 196 B5 ⬛ **25 place des Vosges, 75003** 🕿 **01 48 87 94 07; www.latourdargent.com** ⬛ **Wed–Sun noon–3, 7.30–10:30** Ⓜ **Bastille/St-Paul/Chemin Vert**

Le Murano €€–€€€

The trendy restaurant of the Murano Urban Resort, one of Paris's avant-garde hotels located on the northern edge of the Marais, attracts a chic clientele. The bold contemporary décor, boasting deep red velvet seats in striking contrast with the simpe white tablecloths, is enhanced by background music and light effects. In preparing his innovative dishes, based on classic French cooking, the young chef often draws his inspiration from Eastern cuisine, associating seafood with meat (calves' sweetbreads with oysters, capers and lemon) as well as sweet and savoury flavours (*joie gras* with plum and pear chutney).

➕ **201 F2** ✉ **13 boulevard du Temple, 75003** ☎ **01 42 71 20 00; www.muranoresort.com** 🚇 **Daily noon–midnight** Ⓜ **Fillets du Calvaire**

L'Osteria €€

A lively, popular and often noisy Italian restaurant in the heart of the Marais. Venetian Toni Vianello offers a choice of immensely enjoyable dishes from his native region, including potato gnocchi with sage, delicious Venetian-style calves' liver cooked a melting pink, and a very moreish *osso buco*. The menu changes daily. Good choice of wines.

➕ **196 B5** ✉ **10 rue de Sévigné, 75004** ☎ **01 42 71 37 08**

🚇 **Tue–Fri noon–2.30, 8–10.30, Mon 8–10.30** Ⓜ **St-Paul**

Au Pied de Cochon €€

Parisians use this convivial, eternally open brasserie as a convenient and satisfying pit-stop following lengthy shopping expeditions or after a night out on the town. Established in 1946, it originally served Les Halles market traders and continues to offer classic fare, including the eponymous pigs' trotters, grilled or stuffed. The cheese-crusted French onion soup is wonderful, and for those who dislike offal the seafood and grilled steaks are excellent. The house wine is from the owner's own vineyard.

➕ **200 B2** ✉ **6 rue Coquillère, 75001** ☎ **01 40 13 77 00** 🚇 **24 hours** Ⓜ **Les Halles**

San €

Close to place de la Républic, this attractive modern Italian restaurant is run by a young team of enthusiasts. Carefully prepared tasty classic

Italian dishes are served in two dining rooms against a background of traditional Italian music and films (a different film is screened every day). The menu lists no fewer than 20 different pizzas! Excellent value for money.

➕ **201 F2** ✉ **27 boulevard du Temple, 75003** ☎ **01 44 61 73 45; www.sanristorante.com** 🚇 **Tue–Sat noon–2.30, 7.30–10.30** Ⓜ **Filles du Calvaire**

Au Trou Gascon €€€

If Alain Dutournier's prestigious restaurant in the 1st *arrondissement* (Carré des Feuillants, ▶ 113) is booked or too expensive, try this more accessible but equally memorable establishment, though this meat-oriented eatery is not for vegetarians. Many courses include regional specialities such as *cassoulet* and duck confit, but extend to flavoursome beef and chicken dishes. For the perfect conclusion, choose between Gascon cheese, one of the gorgeous desserts

(a moist chocolate cake is the crowning glory), or indulge in a vintage Armagnac.

➕ **196 off C1** ✉ **40 rue Taine, 75012** ☎ **01 43 44 34 26** 🚇 **Mon–Fri noon–2, 7.30–10** Ⓜ **Daumesnil**

À Deux Pas du Dos €€

Like its nearby sister restaurant, Le Dos de la Baleine (10 rue des Blancs-Manteaux, tel: 01 42 72 38 98), which shares the same quality of food and price range, this welcoming establishment focuses on flavour and fresh produce. The fantastic views of the Hôtel Salé (▶ 129), the mellow candlelit ambience and discreet service complete the picture. The gay-dominated clientele savour gastronomic delights such as oyster soup with saffron, and *filet mignon* of pork with spiced pears. The set lunch is incredibly good value.

➕ **201 E1** ✉ **101 rue Vielle du Temple, 75003** ☎ **01 42 77 10 52** 🚇 **Tue–Fri noon–2.30, 8–11, Mon 8–11** Ⓜ **St-Paul**

Where to... Shop

This part of the 2nd *arrondissement* was once the site of Les Halles, Paris's famous food market, which in 1969 was relocated to Rungis, in the suburbs south of Porte d'Italie. The rag trade is also based here.

The **market** on rue Montorgueil (Métro: Châtelet-Les-Halles) is about all that remains of the original Les Halles, and is a good place to go for cheese.

BHV, or the Bazar de l'Hôtel-de-Ville, which stands almost opposite the Hotel de Ville (Paris's town hall), is a wonderful store for DIY enthusiasts (in the basement), and for its odd bargain, though its fashions, accessories and home furnishings are somewhat down market.

Agnès B, just northwest of the Forum des Halles, is an international chain of high repute offering sharply-cut clothes with original details with separate boutiques for men, women, children and even babies! There are other boutiques nearby selling smart clothes from trendy designer labels, such as **Kabuki** (21 and 25 rue Etienne-Marcel) for men and women and **Notsobig** (38 rue Tiquetonne) for children.

Azzedine Alaya, in the Marais, is the place to go for very flattering figure-hugging dresses. Head for 18 rue de la Verrerie for last season's designs at bargain prices.

The Marais is also worth exploring for its numerous antiques shops and contemporary art galleries secreted down narrow lanes. **Red Wheelbarrow** is an English-language bookshop with, among other treasures, a good selection of books on the history of Paris.

To the north of the 3rd *arrondissement*, at 2–8 rue Perrée

(Métro: Temple), is the **Carreau du Temple**, a covered clothes market that opens every morning from 9am till noon, except Monday. Branches of **FNAC** (the Fédération Nationale des Achats de Cadres) offer a huge selection of CDs (not cheap in France), DVDs, software, books (some in English) and electronics. The Forum des Halles branch has excellent music books and a box office for theatre and concert tickets.

Mélodies Graphiques stocks a fantastic selection of stationery, including superb writing paper, numerous coloured inks, and old-fashioned items such as sealing wax and stamps. On the same street is **Papier+**, well worth seeking out for its excellent range of unusual stationery supplies.

Azzedine Alaya
✉ 7 rue de Moussy, 75004 ☎ 01 42 72 19 19 Ⓜ Hôtel de Ville

BHV
✉ 52 rue de Rivoli, 75004 ☎ 01 42 74 90 00 Ⓜ Hôtel de Ville

FNAC
✉ Level 3, Forum des Halles, 1 rue Pierre Lescot, 75001 ☎ 01 40 41 40 00 Ⓞ Closed Sun Ⓜ Les Halles; RER: Châtelet-Les Halles

Mélodies Graphiques
✉ 10 rue du Pont-Louis-Philippe, 75004 ☎ 01 42 74 57 68 Ⓞ Closed Sun Ⓜ Pont Marie/St-Paul

Papier+
✉ 9 rue du Pont-Louis-Philippe, 75004 ☎ 01 42 77 70 49 Ⓞ Closed Sun Ⓜ Pont Marie/St-Paul

Agnès B
✉ 2 (Enfant), 3 (Homme), 6 (Femme) and 19 (Bébé) rue de Jour, 75001 ☎ 01 40 39 96 88; www.agnesb.fr Ⓜ Les Halles

Red Wheelbarrow
✉ 22 rue St-Paul, 75004 ☎ 01 48 04 75 08 Ⓜ St-Paul

Where to...
Be Entertained

Rejuvenated by Beaubourg and other daring projects, Châtelet-Les Halles offers a contrasting array of evening entertainments, from classical and avant-garde contemporary music to raucous night-clubs. Due east, the Marais is the hub of the Paris gay scene; rainbow flags flutter over shop fronts, restaurants and bars, especially along the rue Ste-Croix-de-la-Bretonnerie, the lively main street. Further east still, partly egged on by the presence of Paris's new opera house, the Bastille area throbs with a vibrant night-life second to none. Tiny theatres, jazz bars and salsa joints burst at the seams most weekends.

CINEMAS

Le Latina cinema specialises in the films of Latin America, Spain, Portugal and Italy. The **Forum des Images** is an image bank of over 5,000 films, from adverts to documentaries, all featuring Paris.

MUSIC

IRCAM, next to the Centre Pompidou, is for devotees of avant-garde music. The **Opéra National de Paris Bastille** has its home in the controversial edifice at the southern end of place de la Bastille: operas and symphony orchestras benefit from the exceptional acoustics. At the **Théâtre du Châtelet-Théâtre Musical de Paris**, a grand neo-classical building, prices are often lower than elsewhere, and the repertoire includes ballet and the classics. With its extravagantly gilded interior, it's a perfect venue for baroque opera. The **Théâtre de la Ville** is a showcase for contemporary dance and music.

NIGHT-LIFE

Young European talent frequently heats up **Sunset** during memorable jam sessions for real jazz lovers. **Le Dépôt** is a huge dance factory and a cult venue for the gay community in the heart of the gay district. Expect techno, house, disco and cabaret theme nights. Naked torsos, frenzied dancing and a sweaty atmosphere are guaranteed.

Le Latina
20 rue du Temple, 75004 ☎ 01 42 78 47 86 Ⓜ Hôtel de Ville

Forum des Images
2 Grand Galerie, Porte St-Eustache, Forum des Halles, 75001 ☎ 01 44 76 62 00 Ⓜ Les Halles

IRCAM
1 place Igor Stravinsky, 75004 ☎ 01 44 78 48 43; www.ircam.fr Ⓒ Closed Jul–Aug Ⓜ Rambuteau/Hôtel de Ville

Opéra National de Paris Bastille
place de la Bastille, 75012 ☎ 08 92 89 90 90; www.opera-de-paris.fr Ⓒ Closed Aug Ⓜ Bastille

Théâtre du Châtelet-Théâtre Musical de Paris
1 place du Châtelet, 75001 ☎ 01 40 28 28 40; www.chatelet-theatre.com Ⓒ Closed Jul, Aug Ⓜ Châtelet

Théâtre de la Ville
2 place du Châtelet, 75004 ☎ 01 42 74 22 77 Ⓒ Closed Jul–Aug Ⓜ Châtelet

Sunset
60 rue des Lombards, 75001 ☎ 01 40 26 46 60 Ⓒ Concerts Mon–Sat 9pm, 10pm Ⓜ Châtelet

Le Dépôt
10 rue aux Ours, 75003 ☎ 01 44 54 96 96 Ⓒ Midnight–8am Ⓜ Etienne-Marcel

Montmartre

Getting Your Bearings

The hilltop settlement of Montmartre (often referred to by Parisians simply as La Butte or "the hill") remains first and foremost a village, overlooking the busy metropolis sprawled at its feet but far removed in character. For this is the Paris of poets and writers, of Toulouse-Lautrec, of cabarets and cancan girls, of windmills and vineyards, of Renoir, Utrillo, Van Gogh and all the other great artists who have made it their home.

Previous page: Montmartre – cradle of cabaret and the cancan

It's hard to beat the views from the steps of the Sacré-Coeur

After the broad boulevards of downtown Paris, the streets here feel pleasantly intimate. Some bustle with visitors (especially around such tourist honeypots as place du Tertre and the Sacré-Coeur), but others are so quiet that prowling cats are the only sign of life. And although many artists and writers have left the area and its fabled night-life no longer has the same charismatic charm, Montmartre still retains a nostalgic "village" atmosphere, thanks to its cobbled streets, its whitewashed cottages with tiny gardens tumbling down steep stairways lit by old-fashioned lamps, and its exquisite hidden squares that invite you to sit and watch the world go by or to admire street artists at work.

0   400 metres

0   400 yards

Lamarck-
Caulaincourt

Au Lapin Agile 12

**Moulin de la
Galette** 11 **Musée de
Montmartre**

1 6

**Cimetière
de Montmartre** 7 **Sacré-
Coeur**

Montmartre 8 9 10

5 **Place du Tertre**

**Bateau- Espace
Lavoir Montmartre
Salvador Dalí**

2 **Moulin
Rouge** Abbesses 4 **Place des
Abbesses**

3 **Musée de
l'Érotisme**

Blanche

BOULEVARD DE CLICHY

BOULEVARD DE ROCHECHOUART

Anvers

PLACE
PIGALLE

★ **Don't Miss**

7 **Montmartre** ➤ 148

10 **Basilique du Sacré-Coeur**
➤ 150

At Your Leisure

Further Afield

This one-day itinerary enables you to discover one of
the city's most enchanting districts, providing an evocative
glimpse of a quaint, bucolic past.

Montmartre in a Day

9am

Start at the **1** **Cimetière de Montmartre** (➤ 152), one of Paris's most romantic
graveyards, which contains the neatly ordered tombs of countless
musicians, artists, writers and poets who have been associated with la Butte
over the centuries.

10am

From the cemetery, climb the steep hill to the heart of **7** **Montmartre**
(➤ 148–149) or catch the **Montmartrobus** (➤ 153).
Stop off halfway to refuel yourself with a coffee and *pâtisserie* in one of the
tempting outdoor cafés.

11am

To get a taste of
**Montmartre's rustic
ambience**, take time
to explore its winding
streets and back
alleys, its long, steep
stairways, its wind-
mills, its famous vine-
yard (➤ 148, right)
and its tiny squares
and terraces, so
vividly portrayed in
the canvases of Van
Gogh, Renoir, Utrillo
and other artists.

12:30pm

Head to **9** **place du Tertre** (➤ 154) to watch the street artists at work in this
once prettiest of squares, now overrun by tourists.
If the fancy takes you, why not have your portrait sketched
(it only takes about 30 minutes)
or buy a painting to remind you of your stay?

1:30pm

Avoid place du Tertre for lunch: the restaurants are overpriced and overrated. Instead, choose from one of the many restaurants in the surrounding streets (➤ 158–159).

3pm

Visit the **Musée de Montmartre** (➤ 155, left), which, through paintings, documents, photographs and other artefacts, recounts the history of Montmartre from its earliest days.

5pm

No visit to Montmartre would be complete without a visit to the **Basilique du Sacré-Coeur** (➤ 150–151, interior pictured right). Dominating the hill, its unmistakable silhouette features a dazzling white dome and a massive bell tower, which contains one of the world's heaviest bells. The terrace of the basilica affords unforgettable views of the city, especially at sunset.

7pm

During your day in Montmartre, scan the menus of likely eateries you pass, targeting somewhere to return to in the evening. A. Beauvilliers (➤ 158) or Au Poulbot Gourmet (➤ 159) are good bets. Round off your evening in an intimate live-music bar, or if you fancy a glitzy Las Vegas-style night out with topless dancers, **Le Bal du Moulin Rouge** (➤ 152, left) is the place to go.

7 Montmartre

In the 19th century, Montmartre became a magnet for artists, writers, poets and musicians who gathered in this former hilltop village to enjoy the cabarets, dance halls and brothels that gave the *quartier* its thrillingly decadent reputation. Today's painters continue to thrive on the lively tourist trade, which has sprung up as hordes of eager visitors flood this picturesque district. However, in places it still manages to retain the relaxed, bohemian atmosphere of pre-war *gai Paris*.

Historically, however, la Butte was an important place of pilgrimage: Louis VI founded the Benedictine abbey of Montmartre here in 1133, of which only the church of St-Pierre now remains, forgotten in the shadow of Sacré-Coeur. Consecrated in 1147, it is one of the city's oldest churches. Like most medieval abbeys in France, Montmartre became involved in wine production, and soon the hilltop was covered in vineyards.

In the 16th century, 30 windmills (of which only two remain, ➤ 152) were built to press the grapes and grind the grain produced by the surrounding villages. Place Blanche ("White Square") at the foot of la Butte takes its name from the clouds of chalky dust churned up by carts carrying crushed wheat and flour from the nearby windmills.

By the end of the 17th century Montmartre was a thriving village, supplying the city with wheat, wine and so much gypsum ("plaster of Paris") that a popular saying emerged: "There's more of Montmartre in Paris, than there is of Paris in Montmartre." The gypsum quarries closed during the 18th century, and at the same time Montmartre was annexed as part of Paris. Wine production also ceased, owing to increasing competition from vineyards in the south of France – though one **small vineyard** still remains. The Clos de Montmartre on rue des Saules produces around 500 bottles of red wine annually (➤ 10). Look out for it on sale at the tourist office and, if you're fortunate enough to be in the area on the first Saturday of October, you can join in the harvest parade.

Above: The village of Montmartre – centre of nightlife

Left: Artists still thrive in Montmartre

Abbesses, Anvers, Blanche, Lamarck-Caulaincourt

TAKING A BREAK

Watch the world go by at tiny **Le Consulat** (18 rue Norvins, 75018, tel: 01 46 06 50 63, Métro: Abbesses). Once frequented by Picasso, Utrillo and fellow artists, it still serves simple, hearty fare on its sunny terrace.

MONTMARTRE: INSIDE INFO

Top tip Visit the Syndicat d'Initiative (tourist office) **for up-to-date information about what's on** (21 place du Tertre, 75018, tel: 08 92 68 30 00, open 10–7).

Hidden gems One of the quaintest corners of Montmartre is Villa Léandre, a tiny residential cul-de-sac of **creeper-smothered houses and tiny gardens** off avenue Junot, in a style so English that one house bears the sign "10 Downing Street".

One to miss The sleazy Pigalle red-light district at the foot of la Butte – its garish neon lights, prostitutes, peep shows and erotica shops are **best avoided by night**.

In more depth The movie Amelie (Le Fabuleux Destin d'Amelie Poulain), directed by Jean-Pierre Jeunet, is set in Montmartre.

10 Basilique du Sacré-Coeur

Dominating the skyline of la Butte, the gleaming white Basilica of the Sacred Heart is one of the most conspicuous buildings in Paris – a confection of neo-Byzantine domes, turrets and towers which, viewed from afar at dusk or sunrise, looks more like a mosque than a Catholic cathedral.

Opposite page: It's a long walk up to the Sacré-Coeur, but your efforts will be richly rewarded at the top

During the Franco-Prussian War of 1870–71, which led to the humiliating fall of the Empire, two laymen, Alexandre Legentil and Hubert Rohault de Fleury, vowed to build a church dedicated to the Sacred Heart of Christ should France be spared. Constructed as an act of penitence following the bloodshed of the war, the basilica took 40 years to construct and was financed mainly by Parisian Catholics fearful of an anti-clerical backlash under the new republican regime. Astonishingly, every hour, day and night since 1 August, 1885 (even in 1944 as bombs shattered the windows), someone has been "on duty" here, to atone for the sins of the 1870 war.

Before entering the gloomy, cavernous interior, note the three statues over the entrance depicting Christ flanked by Joan of Arc and St Louis, both on horseback. Inside, the mighty gold mosaic above the altar depicts Christ with the Virgin Mary, the Pope, the saints of France and even the project's initiators.

But the highlight of Sacré-Coeur is the climb to the top of the dome (the second-highest point in Paris after the Eiffel Tower), for its dizzying views over the city and down into the interior of the basilica.

TAKING A BREAK

Au Poulbot Gourmet is a delightful place to take lunch (➤ 159).

What's in a Name?

The Romans were the first to build a place of worship here – a temple dedicated to Mercury. The hill became known as Mons Mercurii, until early Christian times when it was renamed Mont des Martyrs, following the martyrdom of St Denis. Denis was the first bishop of Paris in the 3rd century AD. He was beheaded by Romans at the top of the hill, whereupon he reputedly picked up his head, carried it to a nearby fountain to wash the blood from his face, then walked to the spot where he is now commemorated by the Basilique St-Denis.

✚ 202 D3 ✉ 35 rue du Chevalier-de-la-Barre, 75018 ☎ 01 53 41 89 00; www.sacre-coeur-montmartre.com 🕐 Basilica: daily 6am–11pm; crypt and dome: daily 9–6 (7pm Apr–Nov) 🚇 Anvers, then walk to funicular 💷 Free; dome moderate

BASILIQUE DU SACRÉ-COEUR: INSIDE INFO

Top tips Try to **attend Mass** (Mon–Fri 11:15am, 6:30pm, 3pm (Fri only), 10pm; Sat 11:15am, 10pm; Sun 11am, 6pm, 10pm; also other services): you **cannot walk about during the service**, but it brings an otherwise gloomy interior to life.
• Rather than climb the steps to the church, take the **sleek funicular** from square Willette. It runs all day (6am–12:30am) and costs one Métro ticket each way.
• The basilica **is most photogenic** when viewed from the gardens below.

One to miss Don't bother with the crypt, unless you are interested in gloomy chapels, dusty relics from the Royal Abbey of Montmartre and a slide show on the construction of Sacré-Coeur.

At Your Leisure

❶ Cimetière de Montmartre

Montmartre's cemetery, established on the site of disused quarries was first used as a mass grave during the Revolution. Here are the graves of composers Berlioz, Delibes and Offenbach, writers Heine, Zola (whose remains are now in the Panthéon), Stendhal and Alexandre Dumas the younger, artists Degas and Creuze, film director François Truffaut, dancer Vaslav Nijinsky and other Montmartre celebrities. Pick up a plan of the graves at the main entrance.

➕ 202 B3 ✉ 20 avenue Rachel, 75018 ☎ 01 53 42 36 30
🕐 Mid-Mar to early Nov Mon–Fri 8–6, Sat 8:30–6, Sun 9–6; rest of year Mon–Fri 8–5:30, Sat 8:30–5:30, Sun 9–5:30 (last entry 15 mins before closing)
🚇 Place de Clichy/Blanche

❷ Moulin Rouge

The "Red Windmill" opened as a dance hall in 1889, when saucy, colourful dance shows were all the rage, as immortalised in the posters and paintings of the artist Toulouse-Lautrec. It soon gained a reputation for staging the hottest show in Paris and today it trades shamelessly on its worldwide reputation for scantily clad, cancan-dancing chorus girls.

➕ 202 B2 ✉ 82 boulevard de Clichy, 75018 ☎ 01 53 09 82 82; www.moulinrouge.fr
🕐 Spectacles nightly at 9 and 11. Combined dinner and show at 7pm
🚇 Blanche 🍽 Expensive

❸ Musée de l'Érotisme

The Erotic Museum, one of Paris's newest museums, and the only one which can be visited both day and night – is appropriately situated near Pigalle, a district long associated with the sex trade. Devoted to erotic art from different world cultures, it displays more than 2,000 items – paintings, models, statues and sex aids – from every continent spanning the 2nd century to the present day in an attempt to raise the smutty Zeitgeist of the area to a loftier plane.

➕ 202 B2 ✉ 72 boulevard de Clichy, 75018 ☎ 01 42 58 28 73; www.musee-erotisme.com 🕐 Daily 10am–2am 🚇 Blanche
🍽 Moderate

Place des Abbesses – one of only a few art nouveau Métro entrances in Paris

4 Place des Abbesses

This tranquil triangular square boasts one of the city's few remaining art nouveau Métro entrances (another is at Porte Dauphine), a delicate swirling mass of glass and iron designed by Hector Guimard at the turn of the 20th century. At 40m (130 feet) it is also the deepest Métro station, with a spiral staircase decorated with frescoes by local artists (there's also a lift).

Centuries ago, the square marked the entrance to the women's abbey of Montmartre, hence the name. Legend has it that in 1590, handsome Henri de Navarre (later Henri IV, the "Vert Galant") kept Paris under siege from his garrison on the hill of Montmartre, while at the same time seducing the abbess, Claude de Beauvilliers. His lieutenants and the other nuns soon followed their example, and before long Parisians were talking about the "army's whorehouse on the hill". The enamoured Claude followed Henri to Senlis, where she foolishly introduced him to her pretty cousin, with whom he is alleged to have run off, granting Claude another abbey in recompense.

Dominating the square is St-Jean-de Montmartre (1904), the first church to be built entirely of reinforced concrete and a surprisingly graceful edifice with slender pillars and art nouveau-inspired floral motifs. Its builders made the mistake of facing it in red brick, however, earning it the epithet St-Jean-des-Briques.

🚏 202 C2 ✉ place des Abbesses, 75018
Ⓜ Abbesses

Cimetière de Montmartre

RUE ETEX
RUE JOSEPH DE MAISTRE
RUE TOURLAQUE
RUE CAULAINCOURT
AVENUE RACHEL
RUE LEPIC
RUE THOLOZE
RUE DES ABBESSES
BOULEVARD DE CLICHY
RUE HOUDON
RUE DES MARTYRS

1 Cimetière de Montmartre
2 Moulin Rouge
3 Musée de l'Érotisme
4 Place des Abbesses
5 Bateau-Lavoir
Abbesses

5 Bateau-Lavoir

An old timber piano factory here once housed – in fairly primitive conditions – a colony of up-and-coming painters whose numbers included Picasso, Modigliani, Van Dongen and Juan Gris. Local poet Max Jacob coined the name meaning "Boat Washhouse", claiming the studios resembled a paint-spattered boat, perpetually in need of a good hosing down. It was here at the turn of the century that Picasso and Braque made their first bold attempts toward the revolutionary concept of Cubism. The original Bateau-Lavoir burned down in 1970, to be replaced by a small and ugly concrete building (closed to the general public) that still contains artisans' studios.

🚏 202 C2 ✉ 13 place Emile-Goudeau, 75018 Ⓜ Abbesses

Getting Around

• Rather than puff your way up and down the hilly streets of Montmartre on foot, why not take the **Petit Train de Montmartre** – a mini train which chugs past most of the sights on a guided 40-minute tour? Huge fun for all the family (and a good option if you're pressed for time), it leaves place Blanche, passing the key sights and stopping outside place du Parvis du Sacré-Coeur (tel: 01 42 62 24 00, departs every 30 minutes 10–6 (midnight Jul and Aug); moderate. Single tickets (inexpensive) also available from place Blanche to Sacré-Coeur).

• Alternatively, take the **Montmartrobus** (tel: 08 92 68 77 14), run by the RATP, the main Paris bus company, which takes a circuitous route all over la Butte every 12 minutes (7:50–7:50). A map is posted at each bus stop. The bus uses the same ticket system as the Métro (one ticket per trip) and you can board at any stop.

6 Moulin de la Galette

One of just two remaining windmills in Montmartre, the "Biscuit Windmill", built in 1622, was once the venue for an open-air cabaret frequented by Van Gogh, Utrillo, Toulouse-Lautrec and Renoir, who portrayed it in his celebrated painting *Bal du Moulin de la Galette* (now in the Musée d'Orsay, ► 54–57). It is said that Debray, the original owner of the mill, was strung up on its sails and spun to death after attempting to defend Montmartre against invading Cossacks in 1814, and his widow had to collect his scattered remains in a flour sack in order to take them to the cemetery. His son transformed the mill into the celebrated dance hall in the 1860s, naming it the Moulin de la Galette after the delicious *galette* biscuits made here using the flour ground in the mill. Near by, on the corner of rue Lepic and rue Girardon, the other windmill, the Moulin Radet, sits on top of a restaurant named after the Moulin de la Galette.

🔢 202 C3 ✉ rue Tholozé, 75018
🕐 Privately owned 🚇 Abbesses

8 Espace Montmartre Salvador Dalí

More than 300 weird and wonderful works by the flamboyant Catalan

Tiny place du Tertre – a veritable tourist honeypot, crammed with cafés, bars and street artists

surrealist artist Salvador Dalí are displayed here, including some of his less familiar paintings, lithographs and sculptures, in a small museum with black walls and a distinctly surrealistic feel. The artist took up residence in Paris in the late 1920s.

🔢 202 C3 ✉ 11 rue Poulbot, 75018 ☎ 01 42 64 40 10
🕐 Daily 10–6 🚇 Abbesses
💶 Expensive

9 Place du Tertre

Bustling crowds and the colourful canvases of street artists crammed into the tree-shaded centre of the square, combined with the aroma of fresh coffee, lure you to the animated place du Tertre – a tiny café-bordered square where Montmartre's heart beats the loudest. During the winter, this delightful 18th-century hilltop square (*tertre* means hillock) retains its rural atmosphere, but for the rest of the year it is one of the most hectic tourist spots in Paris: a place to eat mediocre, overpriced food surrounded by artists all clamouring to sketch you. (If their attentions are unwelcome be firm, and remember that if they produce an

unsolicited portrait, you are not obliged to buy it.)

On one corner of the square (at No 6), the unassuming bistro La Mère Catherine (tel: 01 46 06 32 69) dates from the Napoleonic era and was a favourite with the Russian troops who occupied the city in 1814. Their habit of banging the table and shouting "bistro!" ("quick!") here gave rise to the name for any unpretentious eating place. Today, this is one of several spots where you can occasionally sample Montmartre's own wine.

➕ 202 C3 ✉ place du Tertre, 75018 🚇 Abbesses

🔟 Musée de Montmartre

This historic museum, set in picturesque grounds overlooking Montmartre's tiny vineyard (► 148), is housed in the oldest building (1650) on la Butte. In its turn-of-the-20th-century heyday, it was home to an illustrious group of cabaret artistes, writers and painters, including Dufy, Utrillo and Renoir. Its collections of models, lithographs, posters and paintings give a vivid insight into life during this bohemian period, and include a reconstruction of the Café de l'Abreuvoir and the composer Gustave Charpentier's study.

➕ 202 C3 ✉ 12 rue Cortot, 75018 ☎ 01 46 06 61 11 ⏰ Tue–Sun 10–6 🚇 Lamarck-Caulaincourt/Abbesses 💷 Inexpensive

🔟 Au Lapin Agile

This famous cabaret venue, situated bucolically beside the city's only vineyard, opened in 1860 as the Cabaret des Assassins, taking its name from a band of assassins who had allegedly broken in and murdered the owner's son! In 1880, artist André Gill painted a sign outside featuring a nimble rabbit (*lapin*) in a bowtie avoiding the cooking-pot – hence the play on his

name, the *lapin à Gill* or, as the cabaret thereafter became known, the *lapin agile*.

Bought in 1903 by the celebrated singer and cabaret entrepreneur, Aristide Bruant, it thrived as a popular cabaret club. Verlaine, Renoir and Clemenceau would come here for a jolly singsong, and Picasso paid for the occasional meal with paintings. Still atmospheric today, it is a popular venue for performers of traditional French *chansons*.

➕ 202 C3 ✉ 22 rue des Saules, 75018 ☎ 01 46 06 85 87; www.au-lapin-agile.com ⏰ Tue–Sun 9pm–2am 🚇 Lamarck-Caulaincourt 💷 Expensive

Au Lapin Agile – one of the best-known night-spots in Paris

Further Afield

La Villette

La Villette was for many years an abba-toir and livestock market for the whole of Paris. New refrigeration techniques developed in the 1960s rendered the area obsolete, and in 1984 its 55ha (136 acres) were turned into a vast and spectacular urban park and science city. Highlights in this astonishingly ambitious eclectic complex include La Cité des Sciences (a huge, dynamic science museum), Le Zénith (a pop-concert hall),La Géode (a spherical cinema) and La Cité de la Musique (which houses the Conservatoire

The mirror-like sphere of La Géode is 36m (118 feet) high and contains a cinema with a 180-degree screen

National Supérieur de Musique et de Danse, a concert hall and also a museum of musical instruments).

The main crowd-puller is undoubt-edly the Cité des Sciences et de l'Industrie – a cathedral-sized science and technology museum built on the site of the old Villette slaughterhouses. In the main part of the museum (on the first and second floors), called Explora, visitors can engage in a vari-ety of scientific activities: experienc-ing optical illusions, chatting to a robot, whispering to a friend 15m (50 feet) away through a special screen, flying a flight simulator, guessing certain smells in the Odorama and learning how special effects are created in films, to name only a few. On the ground floor, La Cité des Enfants introduces tinies to basic scientific principles through fun games and dazzling hands-on displays (sections for ages 3–5 and 5–12).

The park itself is also full of surprises, with maze-like playgrounds, a canal and a dozen red cube-shaped

The colourful Cité des Enfants at La Villette – hours of hands-on fun for children

One of the 13 individual *marchés* comprising the vast flea market at St-Ouen

buildings providing child care, cafés, information and other services. There's even a 1950s submarine to explore. But the park's *pièce de résistance* is La Géode (▶ 44). It looks like a giant, shiny steel marble, but inside you cannot help but be thrilled by the cinematographic special effects of the world's largest hemispherical movie screen.

➕ 201 off F5 ✉ Parc de la Villette, 75019 ☎ Musique: 01 44 84 44 84; www.cite-musique.fr Sciences: 01 40 05 70 00; www.cite-sciences.fr 🚇 Musique: Tue–Sat noon–6, Sun 10–6; Sciences: Tue–Sun 10–6 (Sun till 7). Closed Mon 🍴 Several cafés (€–€€) 🚇 Porte de la Villette 🎫 Moderate

Marché aux Puces de St-Ouen

The city's most famous flea market lies at St-Ouen, set up outside the city walls by rag merchants in the late-19th century in order to avoid paying tolls levied within the city. St-Ouen has the added advantage of attracting the inhabitants of la Butte, passing by on their way to and from the dance halls, and it was an instant success.

Today's flea market covers a total of 7ha (17 acres). The 2,000-plus stalls are grouped into 13 individual *marchés*, each with its own specialities. You name it, you'll find it here, from bric-à-brac, second-hand clothes and fake Chanel handbags to pricey antiques and glamorous lingerie. Keep a close watch on your bags and personal possessions, pay in cash and always haggle over the price.

➕ 202 off D3 ✉ Streets around rue des Rosiers, 93400 St-Ouen ☎ 01 58 61 22 90; www.parispuces.com 🚇 Sat–Mon 10–6 🚇 Porte de Clignancourt (not Porte de St-Ouen)

Open-air Gallery

Montmartre in the tourist season is one big open-air picture gallery, with **every square and railing hung with paintings,** and artists working at their easels while you watch. If you would like to have a go yourself, head for the Musée d'Art Naïf (Naive Art Museum) in the Halle Saint-Pierre, near the base of the Sacré-Coeur funicular, which has regular hands-on workshops, mainly for children.

Where to...
Eat and Drink

Prices
Expect to pay per person for a meal, excluding drinks:
€ up to €25   €€ €25–50   €€€ €50–100   €€€€ over €100

Au Pied du Sacré-Coeur €€

This restaurant, serving traditional French cuisine, is true to its name, being at the foot of the Montmartre landmark, Sacre-Coeur. Choose from dishes such as terrine of rabbit with raisins and cognac or the house speciality escalope of *foie gras* with balsamic vinegar. The décor is stylish and inviting, and in summer you can dine al fresco on the terrace.

🔒 202 D3 ⊠ 85 rue Lamarck, 75018 ☎ 01 46 06 15 26
🕐 Tue–Sun noon–3, 7–midnight
Ⓜ Lamarck-Caulaincourt

A. Beauvilliers €€–€€€

This flower-bedecked Montmartre institution must be one of the most romantic restaurants in Paris. Its cuisine has recently been rejuvenated by Yohan Marraccini's, with mouth-watering dishes such as *foie gras* with peppered hibiscus jelly, roast duck with a celery cream and hazelnut sauce, followed by *tarte tatin* with pears and ginger. The interior comprises several rooms, decorated in an elegant 19th-century fashion, featuring gilt-framed mirrors, oil paintings and crystal chandeliers, all creating an ideal place in which to celebrate that special occasion. For a truly memorable experience, dine on the leafy terrace in summer.

🔒 202 C3 ⊠ 52 rue Lamarck, 75018 ☎ 01 42 55 05 42 🕐 Tue–Sat 12:30–2, 7:30–10:30; Sun 12:30–2
Ⓜ Lamarck-Caulaincourt

Brasserie Wepler €€

Standing right on the busy place Clichy, Wepler combines the tradition and ambience of the late 19th century with a solidly classic and familiar menu that includes a splendid seafood platter. Shellfish (the oysters are particularly good) is not the only speciality, however. Try the substantial French onion soup, *bouillabaisse*, duck *foie gras*, *choucroute*, steak tartare and grilled sirloin. Nougat glacé, *crème brûlée* and chocolate profiteroles stand out among the desserts.

🔒 202 A2 ⊠ 14 place de Clichy, 75018 ☎ 01 45 22 53 24; www.wepler.com
🕐 Daily noon–1am
Ⓜ Place de Clichy

Chez Toinette €

The only downside of this gem is that it's not open for lunch, but the delicious candlelit dinners are well worth waiting for. Beef *carpaccio* seasoned with ground nutmeg is the speciality starter, while most of the main courses have a definite southern flavour, be they fish, meat or game. House wines are very reliable and amazingly good value, but probably the highlight is the choice of desserts, with an emphasis on fruit tarts. No credit cards and make sure you book, especially on Fridays and Saturdays.

🔒 202 C2 ⊠ 20 rue Germain-Pilon, 75018 ☎ 01 42 54 44 36
🕐 Tue–Sat 8pm–11pm. Closed Aug
Ⓜ Abbesses

La Famille €€

If you enjoy inventive cuisine, you will relish the fusion dishes of young Basque chef Inaki Aizpitarte, whose short, constantly changing menu combines French (and especially Basque) ingredients with more

maybe a wonderful iced chestnut charlotte for dessert.

**➕ 202 C3 ⊠ 39 rue Lamarck, 75018
☎ 01 46 06 88 00 ⊙ Mon–Sat
12:30–2, 7:30–10. Sun lunch only
Ⓜ Lamarck-Caulaincourt**

Au Rendezvous des Chauffeurs €

In a tiny street just north of the Métro and parallel to rue Ordener, this is a favourite rendezvous for local diners, who flock here for home-style cooking at reasonable prices and in simple, unpretentious surroundings. Juicy steaks come with fat *frites*, and kidneys, *andouilles* (chitterling sausage) and steak tartare are also popular, with a lovely, silky crème caramel to finish.

**➕ 202 off E3 ⊠ 11 rue des Portes-Blanches, 75018 ☎ 01 42 64 04 17
⊙ Thu–Tue noon–2:30, 7:30–10:30.
Closed Aug, Thu, in summer
Ⓜ Marcadet-Poissonniers**

Le Restaurant €

Yves Peladeau has established a loyal clientele for his imaginative,

contemporary cuisine. Herbs and spices play an important part in his creations, adapted from French, North African and Mediterranean recipes. Dishes are a well-balanced fusion of unusual flavours, as in goat's cheese with apple, cider and cream sauce, or honey-roast breast of duck with figs.

**➕ 202 C2 ⊠ 32 rue Véron, 75018
☎ 01 42 23 06 22 ⊙ Daily noon–3,
7:30–11:30 Ⓜ Blanche/Abbesses**

La Table d'Anvers €€

Located at the foot of Montmartre and overlooking the peaceful square d'Anvers, this restaurant offers traditional French cooking at affordable prices. Some of the tasty, carefully prepared dishes, such as the rabbit paté and the delicious *pot-au-feu* served in wintertime, are classics. Others denote a distinctive Mediterranean influence: for instance, mixed herb salad with Grano Padano (a cheese), as a starter, and roast sardines stuffed with feta cheese, served with

mashed potatoes seasoned with olive oil. Interesting wine list.

**➕ 202 D1 ⊠ 2 place d'Anvers,
75009 ☎ 01 48 78 35 21;
www.latabledanvers.com
⊙ Tue–Fri noon–2, 7:30pm–10:30pm;
Sat and Mon 7:30–10:30 Ⓜ Anvers**

Le Virage Lepic €

This cosy bistro along one of lower Montmartre's most atmospheric streets has a few outdoor tables, perfect for summer evenings, and the food is reliable and utterly delicious. The wine list includes an excellent house champagne and is strong on clarets, the perfect accompaniment for the meaty main courses. Puddings include a gratin of pears and other variations on familiar themes. These combined attractions, plus the laid-back ambience and friendly service mean you must book ahead. The *prix fixe* is low but they do accept credit cards.

**➕ 202 B3 ⊠ 61 rue Lepic, 75018
☎ 01 42 52 46 79 ⊙ Wed–Mon
7pm–11pm Ⓜ Blanche/Abbesses**

---

exotic flavours, resulting in dishes such as peach gaspacho, oyster ceviche, pan-fried *foie gras* with miso sauce and chocolate pot with Espelette chilli pepper. Away from Montmartre's tourist throng, the modern, simple interior and hip music add to the atmosphere, and the restaurant is especially popular for its help-yourself Sunday brunch of egg dishes and pastries.

**➕ 202 C2 ⊠ 41 rue des Trois-Frères, 75018 ☎ 01 42 52 11 12
⊙ Tue–Sat dinner, Sun brunch
Ⓜ Abbesses**

Le Poulbot Gourmet €€

Scenes of old Montmartre are depicted on the walls of this charming little restaurant. Chef-proprietor Jean-Paul Langevin's sophisticated menus have a mouthwatering appeal, matched by beautiful presentation. The *carte* changes two or three times a year, and might include game terrine, Barbary duck with baby turnips, lamb noisettes with thyme *jus*, and

Where to…
Shop

Montmartre is a tourist trap for shopping near place du Tertre. Further afield, there are some excellent finds. If you are planning a picnic, the bakery **Le Grenier à Pain** (38 rue Abbesses, 75018, Métro: Abbesses), and the traditional **Charcuterie** at No 30 should provide all the ingredients you need to enjoy a delicious snack in the square Jean Rictus nearby or in the Parc de la Turlure further uphill. For gifts, try **La Boutique des Anges** (2 rue Yvonne Le Tac, tel: 01 42 57 74 38, Métro: Abbesses) and if you want to by cheap clothing try **Tati** (4 boulevard de Rochechouart, 75018, tel: 01 55 29 50 00, closed Sun, Métro: Barbès-Rochechouart) known for its cut-price fashions. At the northern boundary is the **Marché aux Puces de St-Ouen** (▶ 157).

Where to…
Be Entertained

For those with a good working knowledge of French, *Chansonniers* (singing cabarets) make a great night out with their mix of popular music and sharp-edged repartee. **Au Lapin Agile** (▶ 155) is one of the best.

Montmartre is best known for the **Moulin Rouge** (▶ 152), which, along with the likes of the Eiffel Tower, is one of the city's landmarks, albeit a rather risqué one. Established in 1889, the venue is enjoying a revival since the eponymous Nicole Kidman Hollywood movie. Today, productions are very much geared towards the tourist market – but are lavish and visually spectacular. The entertainment is memorable, though very expensive. **Cabaret Michou** is a popular, if expensive, dinner/cabaret hosted by the irrepressible Michou. Book in advance, especially for dinner.

Folies Pigalle is a night-club emblematic of Paris's red-light district. The mid-20s crowd grooves to the sound of house in a highly charged atmosphere. For a great atmosphere and reasonably priced drinks, try **Le Divan du Monde**. This small and inviting concert venue runs theme nights, with an emphasis on world music. Ze Party on Fridays (11pm–6am) features live performances in a lively circus atmosphere.

Au Lapin Agile
✉ 22 rue des Saules, 75018
☎ 01 46 06 85 87; www.au-lapin-agile.com ⏰ Tue–Sun 9pm–2am
Ⓜ Lamarck-Caulaincourt

Moulin Rouge
✉ 82 boulevard de Clichy, 75018
☎ 01 53 09 82 82;
www.moulinrouge.fr
⏰ Daily 9pm and 11pm Ⓜ Blanche

Cabaret Michou
✉ 80 rue des Martyrs, 75018
☎ 01 46 06 16 04
⏰ Daily dinner/show 8:30pm
Ⓜ Pigalle

Folies Pigalle
✉ 11 place Pigalle, 75009
☎ 01 48 78 55 25 ⏰ Daily
11pm–4am Ⓜ Pigalle

Le Divan du Monde
✉ 75 rue des Martyrs, 75018
☎ 01 42 52 02 46
⏰ Daily 7pm–6am Ⓜ Pigalle

Excursions

On those rare occasions when the delights of Paris are overcome by the hustle, bustle and heat of urban life, the surrounding tranquil countryside of the Île-de-France provides a perfect escape, offering several excellent and varied excursions all within easy reach, thanks to the city's comprehensive public transport.

Swap sophisticated French culture for a day at the American fantasy world of Disneyland® Resort Paris at Marne-la-Vallée – an absolute must for the kids! Or, if time is limited, spend just half a day at Versailles, on the southwestern outskirts of Paris. Hard to believe when it was built, this massive palace was not large enough for the Sun King's entourage of 20,000 nobles and servants.

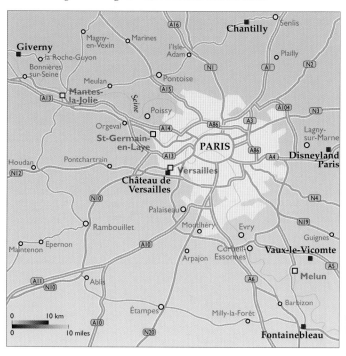

If time permits, visit the romantic fairytale château at Chantilly, or the historic château of Fontainebleau, nestling in a former royal hunting forest, and the majestic château of Vaux-le-Vicomte near by, the inspiration for Versailles. Giverny, home of painter Claude Monet, along the Seine to the west of Paris, is a place of pilgrimage for both garden fans and art-lovers, to see the celebrated gardens that so inspired the artist.

Previous page: Pomp and circumstance – the Queen's bedroom at Versailles

Giverny

This delightful little riverside village, 80km (50 miles) northwest of Paris, is the most visited attraction in Normandy. Crowds of art- and garden-lovers flock to see the home of Claude Monet and the world's most famous lily pond, immortalised in some of the best-known paintings of Impressionist art.

Right: Claude Monet at home in Giverny

Below: The gardens here provided constant inspiration for Monet during the final years of his life

Monet moved from the nearby Paris suburb of Argenteuil to this little pastel-pink house with grass-green shutters in 1883, having spotted the village out of a train window one day and decided it was where he wanted to live. Initially he rented the house, but once he became more widely known and his canvases had begun to sell well, he was able to buy it for the sum of 22,000 francs. He then laid out his famous gardens, considered by many of his contemporaries to be his greatest masterpiece.

Monet also purchased a further plot of land at the bottom of the

📧 84 rue Claude Monet, 27620 Giverny ☎ 02 32 51 28 21; www.fondation-monet.com 🕐 House and gardens: Tue–Sun 9:30–6, Apr–Oct; also open Easter Mon, Whitsun Mon 💷 Moderate

Monet's Japanese garden

main garden on the banks of the River Epte, where he created his celebrated **water garden**, with its water lilies and its Japanese bridge entwined with wisteria. No matter how many visitors are crowded into the gardens, they manage to retain a magical quality. You can almost feel the presence of the grand old master of Impressionism working on his huge, flower-filled canvases: as he used to say, "I am good for nothing except painting and gardening."

The main garden, the **Clos Normand**, now tended by 12 resident gardeners, still follows Monet's original design, with its dazzling palette of colours, changing from season to season. Each month is dominated by a particular colour, as is each room in his immaculately preserved house, with its bright yellow dining-room and its cool blue kitchen, decorated from wall to wall with his collection of Japanese prints. Just a stone's throw from the house is Monet's huge **atelier** where, with failing eyesight, he painted his famous water-lily series, *Décoration des Nymphéas*. The studio has been restored and is hung with gigantic reproductions of the artist's finest works. There is also a shop. The great "garden painter" remained in his beloved pink house in Giverny until his death in 1926.

GIVERNY: INSIDE INFO

Top tips Arrive at least **half an hour before the gardens open** to beat the jostling crowds of camera-happy tourists, all attempting to capture their own impression of Monet's water-lilies.
• The gardens are at their **peak of perfection in May or June** when the rhododendrons and the wisteria on the famous Japanese bridge are in bloom.

Hidden gem If time permits, **visit Giverny's modern Musée Americain** (99 rue Claude Monet, tel: 02 32 51 94 65, open Apr–Oct Tue–Sun 10–6, moderate, free 1st Sun of month) which reveals the huge influence of French Impressionism on American painting. Artists such as Cassat, Whistler, Robinson and Sargent sought inspiration here until the outbreak of World War I, when they returned home, marking the end of an era.

Getting there Trains leave **Gare St-Lazare** for the 50-minute ride to Vernon (train information tel: 08 36 35 35 35). From here, take a taxi or bus to Giverny or rent a bike at the train station for the 6km (4-mile) ride to Monet's garden.

Versailles

The monumental palace of Versailles, 23km (14 miles) southwest of Paris, is on every visitor's must-see list. And it's all thanks to one person – Louis XIV, the Sun King – whose extravagant taste, passion for self-glorification and determination to project both at home and abroad the absolute power of the French monarchy (then at the height of its glory) created one of France's great treasures.

Two decades into his 72-year reign (1643–1715), he decided to adapt his father's modest hunting lodge and weekend retreat into a palace large enough to house some 20,000 courtiers and ministers. He commissioned the greatest artists and craftsmen of the day: architects Louis Le Vau and Jules Hardouin-Mansart planned the buildings; Charles Le Brun designed the interior and the great landscaper André Le Nôtre set to work on the gardens, flattening hills, draining marshes and relocating forests to lay out the fine gardens. Some 30,000 workers toiled on the 580m (1,900-foot) long structure for more than 50 years. No expense was spared, but it wrought havoc on the kingdom's finances.

The Château de Versailles, the largest palace in Europe

The palace became the centre of political power in France and the seat of the royal court from 1682 until 1789 when

✉ 78008 Versailles ☎ 01 30 83 78 00; www.chateauversailles.fr
🕒 Grands Appartements: Tue–Sun 9–5:30 (Apr–Oct until 6:30). Grand Trianon: Apr–Oct daily noon–6:30; noon–5:30, rest of year. Petit Trianon: Apr–Oct daily noon–6:30, gardens only rest of year. Gardens: 8–dusk (open 7am in summer). Closed some public holidays 💶 Palace: expensive; Grand Trianon and Petit Trianon (combined ticket): moderate (entrance to Versailles is free Nov–Mar on the first Sun of every month); Gardens: moderate Apr–Oct, free rest of year

Formidable Fountains

The vast grounds, covering 100ha (247 acres), are as over-whelmingly ornate and rigidly planned as the palace interior, with marble-paved courtyards, colonnades, urns, sculptures, an orangery, a canal and lakes and ponds in a variety of shapes and sizes dissecting the velvety lawns and orderly flowerbeds. But they are most famous for their many fountains, which spring to life on Sunday after-noons (and on Saturday nights in summer, for special displays with music and fireworks). Be sure to see the Bassin de Neptune (Fountain of Neptune) with its sea god, dragons and cherubs, and the Bassin d'Apollo (Fountain of Apollo) depicting the sun god emerging from the water in his chariot surrounded by sea monsters.

Above: The Bacchus fountain

Impressive statue of Frederick the Great

Revolutionary mobs massacred the palace guard and seized the despised King Louis XVI and Marie-Antoinette, dragging them to Paris and eventually to the guillotine.

The vast palace complex is divided into **four main parts** – the palace itself with its innumerable wings, great halls and chambers (only certain parts are open to the public), the extensive gardens and two smaller châteaux in the grounds, used as royal guesthouses – the Grand Trianon and the Petit Trianon.

The sumptuous interior of the palace has undergone surpris-ingly few alterations since it was constructed, although the majority of the furnishings disappeared during the Revolution. Most visited are the **Grands Appartements** (State Apartments) on the first floor of the vast complex, containing the royal bedchambers and the great Galerie des Glaces (Hall of Mirrors; reopened in 2007 after restoration). This grandiose gallery with 17 giant mirrors facing tall arched windows was used for state

Galerie des Glaces – Hall of Mirrors occasions, and in 1919 was the scene of the ratification of the Treaty of Versailles, which ended World War I. In the north wing is Mansart's beautiful two-storey **Chapelle Royale** and the **Opéra**, a late addition completed in 1770, in time for the marriage of Louis XVI and Marie-Antoinette, and built entirely of wood for financial reasons, then painted to resemble marble.

VERSAILLES: INSIDE INFO

Top tips Avoid the crowds by arriving early in the morning or around 3:30–4. If you have a **Paris Museum Pass** (▶ 36), you can go straight to Entrée B2. Avoid visiting on weekends or Tuesdays. The museum offers a **One Day Pass** (expensive) which enables you to bypass the queues.
• **Pick up a plan** of the palace grounds at the main entrance.
• It's impossible to see everything in one visit. If this is your first time, **concentrate on the Grands Appartements**, either at your own pace with an audioguide or with one of the frequent guided tours (in various languages).
• If you can't face the huge queues, **you can still have a great day** in the grounds alone, enjoying the fountains and architecture. Why not bring a picnic with you?

One to miss If you have visited the main palace, **forget the smaller châteaux** – the Grand Trianon and the Petit Trianon – in the northwest corner of the gardens.

Hidden gem The **Hameau de la Reine** (Queen's Hamlet), Marie-Antoinette's refuge, makes a delightful contrast after the grandeur of the palace. To reach it, catch a tram from the north side of the main complex.

Getting there Catch either the **RER (Line C)** to Versailles-Rive Gauche (around 35 minutes, requiring a Zone 1–5 ticket) or a **main-line train** (about every 15 minutes) from Gare Montparnasse to Versailles-Chantiers (around 20 minutes). Alternatively, trains from Gare St-Lazare head via La Défense to the Versailles-Rive Droite (about 35 minutes). All three stations are within walking distance.

Chantilly

Chantilly, 48km (30 miles) north of Paris, has always enjoyed a reputation for fine cuisine (even though its most famous chef, Vatel, committed suicide in the château because the fish he had ordered for Louis XIV arrived late), and the name of the town is indelibly associated with fresh whipped and sweetened cream, ordered in the best restaurants worldwide as *crème chantilly*.

Inside the
Living Horse
Museum

Visitors to Chantilly today come not for the cream but for the impressive (albeit heavily restored) Renaissance château, with its exceptional art collection (including works by Corot, Delacroix, Ingres and Raphael), and its palatial 17th-century stables which contain the Musée Vivant du Cheval (Living Horse Museum), known for its skilful dressage demonstrations. Chantilly is now as famous for its thoroughbred horses as for its cream.

☎ Château: 03 44 62 62 62; www.chateaudechantilly.com Musée Vivant du Cheval: 03 44 57 40 40, www.museevivantducheval.fr ⏰ Château: mid-Mar to Oct Wed–Mon 10–6; rest of year Wed–Mon 10:30–5. Musée Vivant du Cheval: Apr–Oct Wed–Mon 10:30–5:30 (and some Tue); rest of year Wed–Fri, Mon 2–5, Sat, Sun 10:30–5:30 💰 Château: moderate; Horse Museum: expensive 🚊 Numerous trains from Gare du Nord to Chantilly-Gouvieux. The journey takes around 30 mins and the château is a 35-minute walk from the station, or you can take a taxi or (infrequent) bus

Disneyland® Resort Paris

Despite shaky finances since its opening in 1992, these theme parks are now Europe's most popular family tourist destinations. Disneyland® Park offers such thrilling rides as Big Thunder Mountain, Indiana Jones and the Temple of Peril (including 360-degree loops backwards) and, scariest of all, Space Mountain Mission 2. Peter Pan's Flight, "it's a small world" and the Mad Hatter's Tea Cups are geared to toddlers, and a whole host of American-style eateries, shops and parades ensure non-stop entertainment. There is also the thrilling Walt Disney Studios® Park. It's not an inexpensive option, but for most children it has to be the ultimate treat. Avoid weekends and mornings, when the inevitable queues are at their worst.

✉ 77777 Marne-la-Vallée ☎ 01 60 30 60 30; www.disneylandparis.com ⏰ Times vary according to season; phone for the latest information 💰 Expensive (the 2- or 3-day "Park Hopper" is good value) 🚊 The RER (line A) takes around 35 mins to reach Marne-la-Vallée/Chessy; the entrance to Disneyland® is 100m (110 yards) from the station exit

Fontainebleau

If you can't face the crowds at Versailles, come to this château instead. It's equally grand and surprisingly overlooked. This splendid royal residence, 65km (40 miles) southeast of Paris,

Opposite page:
Chantilly –
famous for its
château,
its horses and
its cream

The Château de Fontainebleau – once a royal residence started out as a hunting pavilion and ornamental fountain (hence the name) at the heart of a dense forest – the Forêt de Fontainebleau – a hunting ground for the long line of French kings who resided here. François I converted the lodge into the beautiful Renaissance château it is today: one of France's largest erstwhile royal residences (1,900 rooms), celebrated in particular for its splendid interior furnishings and immaculate grounds.

☎ 01 60 71 50 70; www.musee-chateau-fontainebleau.fr
🕐 Château: Jun–Sep Wed–Mon 9:30–6; rest of year Wed–Mon 9:30–5. Gardens: May–Sep daily 9–7; Mar, Apr, Oct 9–6; rest of year 9–5. Closed 1 Jan, 1 May, 25 Dec 💶 Moderate 🚆 Trains leave Paris's Gare de Lyon approx every hour for Fontainebleau-Avon. Regular buses run from the train station to the château. Total journey time: about 1 hour

Vaux-le-Vicomte

This magnificent château in the classical style, 50km (31 miles) southeast of Paris, was the inspiration for Versailles. It was constructed in 1656 by Louis XIV's ambitious finance minister, Nicolas Fouquet, who employed France's most talented craftsmen to carry out his grandiose plans. It was completed in five years. His extravagance, however, proved to be his downfall. After the lavish party thrown by Fouquet, Louis XIV was so enraged at being upstaged by his minister that he had him arrested for embezzlement and thrown into prison until his death in 1680.

Today the interior has been beautifully restored. The gardens, with their ornamental terraces, manicured lawns, canal, fountains and statues, are a delight. You can even rent mini electric-cars to visit the extensive grounds.

☎ 01 64 14 41 90; www.vaux-le-vicomte.com 🕐 Château and gardens: mid-Mar to early Nov daily 10–6 (elaborate fountain displays from 3 to 6 on the second and last Sun). Candlelit tours on Sat (and some Fri) evenings, in summer 💶 Expensive 🚆 Train from Paris's Gare de Lyon to Melun, then taxi

Walks & Tours

1 RIVER TRIP

Tour

Paris is one of the few capital cities that may be visited by river. Hour-long cruises run both day and night along the main sightseeing reaches of the Seine, presenting a new and magical perspective on many of the city's most famous monuments and bridges. This trip follows the route of the Vedettes du Pont Neuf.

Photogenic Paris – the Eiffel Tower is best viewed from the river

TIME 1 hour
START AND END POINT square du Vert-Galant, Pont Neuf ➕ 195 D5

1–2

Set sail from the square du Vert-Galant below the Pont Neuf on the Île de la Cité. Initially, the boat heads westwards under the Pont des Arts (the city's first cast-iron bridge, constructed in 1804 and rebuilt in 1984), which occasionally provides an unusual setting for sculpture exhibitions. As you pass the **Louvre** (▶ 96–101) on your right, Paris's largest museum and for centuries the home of kings and queens, the boat glides under the Pont du Carrousel. This bridge, begun as World War II broke out, boasts

special telescopic lights; designer Raymond Subes continued his work in secret, completing the lamps in 1941.

2–3

After the Pont Royal (a gift from Louis XIV to the people of Paris), on the left you will see the **Musée d'Orsay** (▶ 54–57), the city's most important collection of Impressionist art housed in a spectacular, converted railway station.

3–4

Two bridges later is the Pont de la Concorde, built in 1791, the year of the French Revolution. To the right is the immense place de la Concorde (where the guillotine was erected), one of the finest examples of sophisticated 18th-century Parisian town-planning. The 3,200-year-old obelisk at its centre is the city's most ancient monument. To the left is the

5–6

Two bridges after Pont Alexandre III, look for the statue of a soldier on the central pier of the Pont de l'Alma, used to measure the level of the Seine when it is in flood.

6–7

Have your camera ready before you round the next curve of the Seine, because the **Eiffel Tower** (▲ 50–53) now looms large, offering breathtaking photographic opportunities. Remarkably, this extraordinary edifice manages to remain in harmony with the perfect symmetry and the beautiful vista of the **Champ-de-Mars** (▲ 61) beyond, and of the fountain-filled Jardins du Trocadéro which roll down towards it on the Right Bank – another stroke of French town-planning genius.

alliance in 1893 and named after Tsar Alexander III. The ornate candelabra are copies of the lamps on Trinity Bridge in St Petersburg. It is flanked by the Grand Palais and Petit Palais (▲ 109), both equally lavish in their architectural style, in stark contrast with the more sober **Invalides** complex (▲ 60–61) on the Left Bank opposite.

18th-century neo-classical Palais Bourbon, home of the Assemblée Nationale (the lower house of the French Parliament).

4–5

The most decorative bridge comes next: Pont Alexandre III, built to commemorate the Franco-Russian

7-8

The boat will turn here and head eastwards, returning to the Île de la Cité. Notice the many boats and barges moored alongside the wharfs, some converted into bars and restaurants, others now used as houseboats. When you reach the island, the boat will bear right, passing under several bridges including the Petit Pont, the smallest in the city spanning just 33m (108 feet), and passing **Notre-Dame** (▶ 80–83), one of the high spots of the cruise, on your left.

8-9

Continuing onwards, the boat now encircles the tranquil **Île St-Louis** (▶ 84), where graceful willows bow to meet the waters of the river: it is hard to believe that this island, where elegant residences now line the waterfronts, was once a swampy wasteland. As the dramatist Pierre Corneille wrote: "An entire city, built here with pomp, seems miraculously to have sprung out of an old ditch" (*Le Menteur*, 1643).

9-10

The boat returns past the northern side of île de la Cité, lined with the imposing façades of the Hôtel Dieu, Paris's oldest hospital and the site of a major battle between the Paris police and German forces in 1944. It also passes the splendid **Palais de Justice** (▶ 76), the city's first public clock (still working six centuries on), and the medieval, turreted **Conciergerie** (▶ 76) – former royal palace-cum-prison, where Queen Marie-Antoinette spent two months before losing her head in 1793.

10-start

The final bridge on the cruise is the majestic **Pont Neuf**. Despite its name (meaning "new

bridge"), it is the oldest bridge in Paris, dating from the 17th century, and was the first to be built with no houses on it. The many grimacing heads that decorate it are supposed to represent the friends and ministers of Henri IV who built it – a somewhat dour-looking bunch. The cruise ends just beyond the bridge, at its start point beside the beautiful **square du Vert-Galant** (▶ 28).

Taking a Break

There is a small snack bar on board.

When?

Small **Vedettes du Pont-Neuf** boats run Mar–Oct daily at 10, 11:15, noon and every half-hour from 1:30 to 7pm, and at 8, 9, 9:30, 10, 10:30pm; rest of year Mon–Thu at 10:30, 11:15, noon, 2, 2:45, 3:30, 4:15, 5, 5:45, 6:30, 8 and 10; Fri–Sun at 10:30, 11:15, noon, then every 45 minutes from 2 to 6:30 and at 8, 9, 9:45 and 10:30pm. For further information tel: 01 46 33 98 38; www.vedettesdupontneuf.com
The big *bateaux-mouches* (▶ 118) depart from Pont de l'Alma.

Pont Neuf ("New Bridge") is the oldest in Paris

2 LE MARAIS
Walk

DISTANCE 3.5km (2 miles) **TIME** 3 hours **START POINT** place de l'Hôtel de Ville ✛ 195 F5
END POINT place St-Gervais ✛ 195 F5

From after the Revolution until the 1950s, this district, which had once been favoured by kings and courtiers, was one of the city's poorest areas. Now rediscovered and with its gracious aristocratic mansions restored, the chic and sophisticated Marais *quartier* has uniquely preserved most of its pre-Revolutionary architecture. A stroll through its streets is rather like walking around a giant open-air museum.

Statues standing to attention atop the 17th-century Hôtel de Ville

1–2

Start in place de l'Hôtel de Ville. From the northeastern corner, head one block eastwards (past the BHV department store) along rue de Rivoli then turn left into rue des Archives. At No 24 (on your right) you will find the tiny sand-coloured **Cloître des Billettes**, the only surviving medieval cloister in Paris, built in the

2–3

Continue along rue des Archives to reach the newly restored, early 18th-century **Hôtel de Soubise**, home to the Archives Nationales, on the corner of rue des Francs-Bourgeois. The **Musée de l'Histoire de France**, housed in its rococo salons, makes an unbeatable introduction (in French) to the history of France (tel: 01 40 27 60 96, open Mon–Sat 9–6).

3–4

Turn right along rue des Francs-Bourgeois, a street lined with private homes that derives its name from the almshouses for the tax-exempt poor that stood here in the 14th century. On your right is the church of **Notre-Dame-des-Blancs-Manteaux**, named after the white habits worn by the Augustinian friars who founded a convent here in 1258. Further on, at the intersection with rue Vielle du Temple, stands the **Hôtel Hérouet**, an unusually ornate Gothic-style building, adorned with turrets and stone carvings, built originally by Jean Hérouet

Flamboyant Gothic style and dating from 1427. Further on at No 40 is **Maison Coeur**, one of the oldest houses in Paris, built by the granddaughter of Jacques Coeur, Charles VII's celebrated minister of finance in the 15th century.

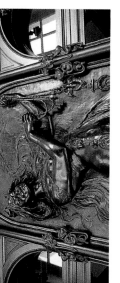

treasurer to Louis XII in 1510, and cleverly reconstructed in the 19th century.

4–5

Turn right here down rue Vieille-du-Temple, then left into rue des Rosiers. This area, known as the **Pletzl**, is one of the city's liveliest Jewish neighbourhoods, and the street is lined with tempting kosher delicatessens, restaurants and falafel vendors.

5–6

Just before the end of rue des Rosiers, turn left into rue Pavée, so-named because it was the first "paved street" in the capital. On the corner of rue Pavée and rue des Francs-Bourgeois stands the **Hôtel de Lamoignon**, built in 1585 for Diane de France (illegitimate daughter of Henri II), and now home to the **Bibliothèque Historique de la Ville de Paris**. Step inside the courtyard to appreciate the mansion's grandeur.

6–7

Turn left along rue des Francs-Bourgeois past countless alluring fashion boutiques and designer shops – but don't be too distracted by the window displays, or you will miss the architecture of the splendid mansions that house them. The first turning to the right takes you up

Reconstructed art nouveau shop-front in the Musée Carnavalet

rue Elzévir, past the **Musée Cognacq-Jay** (tel: 01 40 27 07 21, open Tue–Sun 10–6), a little-known treasure trove of 18th-century French *objets d'art*, lovingly assembled by Ernest Cognacq and his wife Louise Jay, founders of La Samaritaine, once Paris's largest department store.

7–8

Turn right into rue du Parc Royal, lined with grand pastel-coloured mansions, past a small park (square l'Achille), and right again down rue de Sévigné, past the main entrance to the **Musée Carnavalet**, an impressive homage to Parisian history (▲ 134). The church looming large at the end of the street is **St-Paul-St-Louis** (▲ 177)

8–9

Turn left into rue des Francs-Bourgeois to reach **place des Vosges**, a stunning arcaded square of

red-brick town houses, with manicured lawns and elegant fountains (▲ 131). Leave place des Vosges by the southwestern corner, passing through the ivy-hung courtyard of the **Hôtel de Sully**, a stylish mansion built in 1624 by a notorious gambler known as Petit Thomas, who lost his entire fortune in one night. It is now the headquarters of the **Centre des Monuments Nationaux (Monum)** (the organisation responsible for preserving many of France's historic monuments).

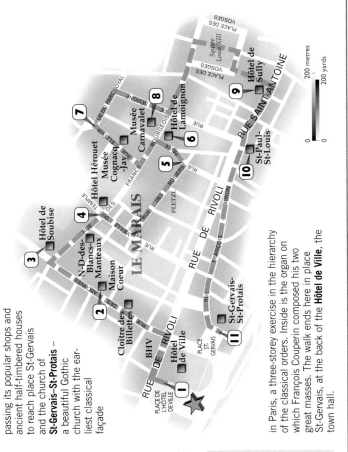

9-10

Turn right on to one of the city's oldest streets, rue St-Antoine, in medieval times a favourite place for jousting and for ceremonial entries into the city. Henri II was fatally wounded here in 1559 when he took part in a tournament to celebrate his daughter's wedding. Today it is a main thoroughfare linking rue de Rivoli with place de la Bastille. Cross over and continue westwards past the imposing façade of **St-Paul-St-Louis**, a 17th-century Jesuit foundation whose numerous art treasures include Delacroix's *Christ in the Garden of Olives*.

passing its popular shops and ancient half-timbered houses to reach place St-Gervais and the church of **St-Gervais–St-Protais** – a beautiful Gothic church with the earliest classical façade

10–11

Fork left into rue François-Miron, one of the first roads to cross the marshy area of the *marais*,

in Paris, a three-storey exercise in the hierarchy of the classical orders. Inside is the organ on which François Couperin composed his two great masses. The walk ends here in place St-Gervais, at the back of the **Hôtel de Ville**, the town hall.

Taking a break

You'll be spoiled for choice of cafés, bars and restaurants here, especially in rue des Francs-Bourgeois, rue des Rosiers and place des Vosges.

When?

Avoid Saturday (the Sabbath), when the Jewish area is deserted.

3 ST-GERMAIN

Walk

This relaxing walk leads you through the artists' quarter of the Left Bank, down into the Odéon district and the Jardin du Luxembourg, capturing the frequently changing character of St-Germain-des-Prés en route.

DISTANCE 3km (2 miles) **TIME** 4 hours
START POINT/END POINT St-Germain-des-Prés ⊞ 194 B5

1–2

Start at the ancient church of **St-Germain-des-Prés** (▶ 58–59). Walk eastwards along boulevard St-Germain and turn left up **rue de Buci**, venue of one of the city's liveliest food markets, then left again along rue de Bourbon-le-Château.

2–3

Cross rue de l'Echaudé and rue Cardinale, with their charming small boutiques and continue up rue de l'Abbaye, taking the first right into rue de Furstemberg, named after Cardinal von Furstemberg, a 17th-century abbot of the monastery of St-Germain. This leads to **place Furstemberg**, a charming, tiny stage-set of a

square, complete with a tree, iron lamppost and park bench. Tucked into the left-hand corner is the former home and studio of romantic artist Delacroix, today a small **museum** (▶ 62).

3–4

Continue to the end of rue de Furstemberg. Turn left into rue Jacob, then right into rue Bonaparte past the famous **École des Beaux-Arts**, which numbers Degas, Matisse, Monet and Renoir among its former students.

4–5

Continue up rue Bonaparte to the river. Turn right along the embankment past **les bouquinistes** (▶ 24). These quaint green bookstalls lining the Seine date back three centuries to the time when second-hand booksellers piled up their wares on the riverbank. On your right, note two imposing buildings: the **Institut de France**, home to the illustrious Académie Française, which since 1635 has been the watchful guardian of the French language, and the **Musée de la Monnaie,** formerly the Paris mint and now a coin museum (tel: 01 40 46 55 35, open: Tue–Fri 11–5:30, Sat, Sun noon–5:30, moderate).

5–6

At the Pont Neuf, turn right and head south down rue Dauphine to the carrefour de Buci. Turn left into rue St-André-des-Arts, and immediately right into **Cour du Commerce-St-André,** a narrow cobbled passageway that was once a hive of Revolutionary activity. Megalomaniac residents Marat and Danton (Nos 8 and 20 respectively) used to meet at **Le Procope** (▶ 15), with anatomy professor Dr Guillotin (who proposed the use of his later notorious "philanthropic beheading machine" to prevent unnecessary pain). He lived at No 9.

6–7

The exit from the passage is on boulevard St-Germain. Go straight over the road, across the Carrefour de l'Odéon and into rue de l'Odéon, passing the neo-classical **national theatre** to your left at the top of the hill.

7–8

Cross rue de Médicis to enter the idyllic **Jardin du Luxembourg** (right, ▶ 63) – an old favourite

with Parisians, especially the student community, and an ideal location in which to relax.

8–9

Leave via the park's rue de Vaugirard exit. Turn right then immediately left down rue Férou to place St-Sulpice with its splashy, flamboyant fountain. The austere neo-classical **church of St-Sulpice,** dominating the square, boasts France's largest organ, and some spectacular frescoes by Delacroix.

9–10

From the church's main portal, cross the square (past the fountain) and turn right up rue Bonaparte. This popular shopping street leads back to the **church of St-Germain-des-Prés** and the end of the walk.

Taking a Break
One of Paris's most famous cafés, **Les Deux Magots** (▶ 15) is conveniently situated at the start/end of the walk.

When?
Mornings are best, before the rue de Buci market closes.

MONTMARTRE
4 Walk

Explore the back streets of Paris's historic hilltop "village", with its leafy cobbled streets and steep stairways lined with iron lamps, its quaint whitewashed cottages and country gardens, its picturesque café-lined squares and its sweeping panoramas, and you will soon understand why so many generations of artists, writers and poets have fallen in love with this atmospheric neighbourhood.

DISTANCE 3km (2 miles) **TIME** 4 hours
START POINT place Blanche ⊞ 202 B2
END POINT place des Abbesses ⊞ 202 C2

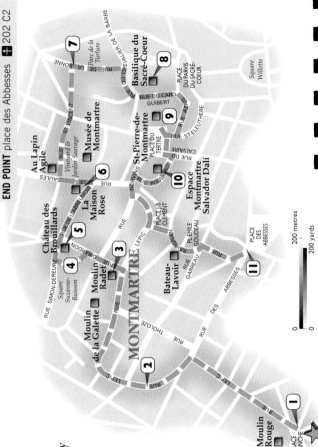

1–2

From place Blanche climb up rue Lepic past tempting delicatessens and cafés. Turn left at the top and branch right, still on rue Lepic. Van Gogh lived in an apartment at No 54 from 1886–88, taking his inspiration from the wind-mills and gardens of Montmartre.

on your right was once used as a shelter for homeless artists. Pierre-Auguste Renoir lived and worked in one of the houses on the left from 1890 to 1897.

5–6

At the end of allée des Brouillards, carry straight on up the cobbled rue de l'Abreuvoir, once a country lane used by horses and cattle *en route* to the watering trough (*abreuvoir*) which stood on the site of No 15. Number 14 was formerly the Café de l'Abreuvoir, frequented by many great artists in Montmartre's heyday. Continuing up the hill, Impressionist painter Camille Pissarro rented No 12 between 1888 and 1892. Note the charming sundial on the wall of No 4, with a picture of a rooster promising *Quant IV sonnera, je chanterai* ("When four strikes, I'll crow"). The restaurant at No 2, **La Maison Rose** (The Pink House, ▶ 182), made famous in an early Utrillo canvas, makes a pleasant lunch stop.

2–3

Continue to climb rue Lepic, following the road round to the right. Note the steep flights of steps on your left leading up to countrified private villas, and high above you (opposite the intersection with rue Tholoze), the **Moulin de la Galette** (▶ 154), once the venue for a notorious open-air cabaret. A few steps beyond (on the corner with rue Girardon), Montmartre's only other remaining windmill – **Moulin Radet** – is now part of a restaurant.

3–4

Turn left here, and cross avenue Junot, where artists Utrillo and Poulbot once lived at Nos 11 and 13. Soon after, turn left into **square Suzanne-Buisson**, a lovely secluded park where St Denis allegedly washed his decapitated head in a fountain (▶ 150). Today a statue of the saint marks the spot, overlooking a *boules* pitch.

4–5

Turn right at the statue, descend into place Casadesus, in rue Simon-Dereure and turn right up several steps into allée des Brouillards. Here, the 18th-century **Château des Brouillards**

Left: Picturesque rue de l'Abreuvoir
Right: La Maison Rose – ideal for lunch

There's always a bustling atmosphere in place du Tertre

6–7

Turn left immediately after La Maison Rose and head down steep rue des Saules, past the city's last remaining **vineyard** (▲ 148) to the legendary **Au Lapin Agile** (▲ 155). Turn right along rue St-Vincent, skirting the vineyard and a tiny **Jardin Sauvage** ("wild garden"; open Apr–Sep Sat only 10:30–1:30, 2–6:30; Oct 10:30–1:30, 2–6), designed to preserve the natural flora and fauna of Montmartre. Cross rue du Mont Cenis, where composer Hector Berlioz once lived at No 22, and continue uphill to rue de la Bonne and the entrance to neat and shady **Parc de la Turlure** with magnificent city vistas.

7–8

Stroll through the park, leaving it by rue du Chevalier de la Barre round the back of the **Sacré-Coeur** (▲ 150–151), and carrying on into rue du Cardinal Guibert, which runs alongside the basilica to its entrance on place du Parvis du Sacré-Coeur. (Note that the entrance to the crypt and the dome is in rue du Cardinal Guibert.)

8–9

On leaving the Sacré-Coeur, head right along rue Azaïs, admiring the distant views of Paris as you go. A right turn up rue St-Eleuthere will lead you to the church of **St-Pierre-de-Montmartre** (▲ 149), consecrated in 1147 and one of Paris's oldest churches.

9–10

As you leave the church, continue straight ahead into place du Tertre (▲ 154), once a delightful 18th-century village square, now a veritable tourist honeypot. Leave the square via rue du Calvaire. A right turn just before a descending flight of steps will lead you across cobbled place du Calvaire to rue Poulbot and the **Espace Montmartre Salvador Dalí** (▲ 154), which houses a permanent display of more than 300 works by the eccentric Spanish artist.

10–11

Follow rue Poulbot round to rue Norvins. Turn left, then almost immediately left again, and head downhill, passing the grassy square of place Jean-Baptiste Clément on your left. Turn right at the intersection into rue Ravignan, and follow the road round to the left into place Émile Goudeau, past the **Bateau-Lavoir** (▲ 153) on your right. Leave the square down a small flight of steps. Cross over rue Garreau and continue downhill on rue Ravignan. A left turn at the next intersection will take you straight to the art nouveau Métro stop at **place des Abbesses** (▲ 153) and the end of the walk.

Taking a Break

Avoid the pricey, tourist cafés in place du Tertre. Try **La Maison Rose** (tel: 01 42 57 66 75; open Apr–Oct daily; closed Wed lunch and Tue, Thu dinner, rest of year) on rue de l'Abreuvoir instead, or enjoy a picnic in the Parc de la Turlure.

When?

Avoid Sundays, when the district is always crowded.

GETTING ADVANCE INFORMATION

Websites

- Paris Tourist Office: www.parisinfo.com (this site also has information for visitors with disabilities)
- Paris Tourisme: www.paris-tourism.com
- French Tourist Office: www.franceguide.com

In the UK
French Government Tourist Office
178 Piccadilly
London W1J 9AW
☎ 09068 244123

BEFORE YOU GO

WHAT YOU NEED

	UK	Germany	USA	Canada	Australia	Ireland	Netherlands	Spain
Passport (or National Identity Card where applicable)	●	●	●	●	●	●	●	●
Visa (regulations can change – check before you travel)	▲	▲	▲	▲	▲	▲	▲	▲
Onward or Return Ticket	▲	▲	▲	▲	▲	▲	▲	▲
Health Inoculations (tetanus and polio)	▲	▲	▲	▲	▲	▲	▲	▲
Health Documentation (► 188, Health)	●	●	●	●	●	●	●	●
Travel Insurance	○	○	○	○	○	○	○	○
Driving Licence (national)	●	●	●	●	●	●	●	●
Car Insurance Certificate	○	○	n/a	n/a	n/a	○	○	○
Car Registration Document	●	●	n/a	n/a	n/a	●	●	●

● Required   ○ Suggested   ▲ Not required

Some countries require a passport to remain valid for a minimum period (usually at least six months) beyond the date of entry – check before you travel.

WHEN TO GO

☐ High season   ☐ Low season

JAN	FEB	MAR	APR	MAY	JUN	JUL	AUG	SEP	OCT	NOV	DEC
7°C	7°C	10°C	16°C	17°C	23°C	25°C	26°C	21°C	16°C	12°C	8°C
45°F	45°F	50°F	61°F	63°F	73°F	77°F	79°F	70°F	61°F	54°F	46°F

🌧 Wet   ☁ Cloud   ☀ Sun   🌦 Sun/Showers

Temperatures are the **average daily maximum** for each month.
The best time to visit Paris is June, a glorious month when the days are longest, with the most sunshine and average daytime temperatures a comfortable 23°C (73°F). The city reaches peak tourist capacity in hot, sunny July. August sees the Parisian exodus to the countryside leaving the city emptier than usual. It is the hottest, most humid month and the city is prone to sudden storms.
September and October have a high percentage of crisp days and clear skies, but rooms can be difficult to find as this is the peak trade-fair period.
Winter temperatures rarely drop below freezing, but it rains frequently, sometimes with hail, from November to January.

In the USA	In Australia	In Canada
French Tourist Office	French Tourist Office	French Tourist Office
444 Madison Avenue	Level 13	1800 avenue McGill College
16th Floor	25 Bligh Street	Suite 1010
New York, NY10022	Sydney, NSW 2000	Montreal H3A 3J6
☎ 514/288 1904	☎ (02) 9231 5244	☎ 514-288 2026

GETTING THERE

By Air Paris has two main **airports** – Roissy Charles de Gaulle and Orly. Numerous carriers operate **direct flights** from the US and Canada, including American Airlines, Delta and Air Canada. From the UK, British Airways, British Midland and easyJet operate a regular service; from Australia, Qantas and Continental are the major carriers. France's national airline, Air France (tel: 0820 820 820 in France; 0870 142 4343 in the UK; www.airfrance.com) has scheduled flights from Britain, mainland Europe and beyond, to both main airports. Approximate **flying times** to Paris: London (1 hour), Dublin (1.5 hours), New York (8 hours), West Coast USA (12 hours), Vancouver (10 hours), Montréal (7.5 hours), Sydney (23 hours), Auckland (21 hours).
Ticket prices tend to be highest in spring and summer (Easter to September). City Break packages may offer even more savings if a Saturday night is included. Check with the airlines, travel agents and the internet for current best deals and offers.

By Rail There are six major railway stations, each handling traffic to different parts of France and Europe. French Railways operates high-speed trains (**TGV**) to Paris from main stations throughout France. The **Eurostar** passenger train service (tel: 08705 186186 in Britain; www.eurostar.com) from London's St Pancras International via the Channel Tunnel to Paris Gare du Nord takes 2 hours 15 minutes.

By Sea Ferry companies operate regular services from England and Ireland to France, with rail links to Paris. Crossing time: 35 minutes to 6 hours (England); 14–18 hours (Ireland).

TIME

France is on Central European Time, one hour ahead of Greenwich Mean Time (GMT +1). From late March, when clocks are put forward one hour, until late October, French summer time (GMT +2) operates.

CURRENCY AND FOREIGN EXCHANGE

Currency The French unit of currency is the **Euro (€)**. Coins are issued in denominations of 1, 2, 5, 10, 20 and 50 Euro cents and €1 and €2. There are 100 cents in €1. Notes (bills) are issued in denominations of €5, €10, €20, €50, €100, €200 and €500.

Exchange You can exchange **travellers' cheques** at some banks and at bureaux de change at airports, main railway stations or in some department stores, and exchange booths. All transactions are subject to a hefty commission charge, so you may prefer to rely on cash and credit cards. Travellers' cheques issued by American Express and VISA can also be changed at many post offices.

Credit cards are widely accepted in shops, restaurants and hotels. VISA, MasterCard and Diners Club cards with four-digit PINs can be used in most ATM cash dispensers.

TIME DIFFERENCES

GMT 12 noon	France → 1 PM	Spain → 1 PM	USA (NY) ← 7 AM	USA (West Coast) ← 4 AM	Sydney → 10 PM

WHEN YOU ARE THERE

CLOTHING SIZES

UK	France	USA	
36	46	36	
38	48	38	
40	50	40	
42	52	42	
44	54	44	
46	56	46	Suits
7	41	8	
7.5	42	8.5	
8.5	43	9.5	
9.5	44	10.5	
10.5	45	11.5	
11	46	12	Shoes
14.5	37	14.5	
15	38	15	
15.5	39/40	15.5	
16	41	16	
16.5	42	16.5	
17	43	17	Shirts
8	34	6	
10	36	8	
12	38	10	
14	40	12	
16	42	14	
18	44	16	Dresses
4.5	38	6	
5	38	6.5	
5.5	39	7	
6	39	7.5	
6.5	40	8	
7	41	8.5	Shoes

NATIONAL HOLIDAYS

1 Jan	New Year's Day
Mar/Apr	Easter Sunday and Monday
1 May	May Day
8 May	VE (Victory in Europe) Day
6th Thu after Easter	Ascension Day
May/Jun	Whit Sunday and Monday
14 Jul	Bastille Day
15 Aug	Assumption Day
1 Nov	All Saints' Day
11 Nov	Remembrance Day
25 Dec	Christmas Day

Banks, businesses, museums and most shops (except *boulangeries*) are closed on all or some of these days.

OPENING HOURS

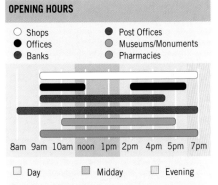

○ Shops   ● Post Offices
● Offices   ● Museums/Monuments
● Banks   ○ Pharmacies

8am 9am 10am noon 1pm 2pm 4pm 5pm 7pm

☐ Day   ☐ Midday   ☐ Evening

Shops In addition to the times shown above, some shops close noon–2pm, and all day Sunday and Monday. Large department stores open until 9pm or 10pm one day a week. Food shops open 7am–1:30pm and 4:30–8pm, and may open Sunday until noon.
Banks Some open extended hours including Saturday morning.
Museums City museums usually close Monday. Most national museums close Tuesday, except Versailles and Musée d'Orsay, which close Monday.

POLICE 17

FIRE 18

AMBULANCE 15

DOCTOR (24-hour call out) 01 47 07 77 77

PERSONAL SAFETY

Petty crime, particularly theft of wallets and handbags, is fairly common in Paris. Be aware of scruffy, innocent-looking children: they may be working the streets in gangs, fleecing unwary tourists. Report any loss or theft to the *Police Municipale* (blue uniforms). To be safe:

- Watch your bag on the Métro, in busy tourist areas like Beaubourg and the Champs-Elysées and in museum queues.
- Cars should be well secured.
- Keep valuables in your hotel safe.
- Avoid walking alone in dark streets at night.

Police assistance:
 17 from any phone

TELEPHONES

In addition to coin-operated models, an increasing number of public phones can take a phonecard (*télécarte*). These are sold in units of 50 and 120 and can be bought from France Telecom shops, post offices, tobacconists and railway stations. Cheap rates generally apply Mon–Fri 7pm–8am, Sat–Sun all day.

All telephone numbers in France comprise ten digits. Paris and Île de France numbers all begin with 01. There are no area codes; simply dial the number.

International Dialling Codes
Dial 00 followed by

UK:	44
Ireland:	353
USA/Canada:	1
Australia:	61
Germany:	49
Spain:	34

POST

Post offices are identified by a yellow or brown "La Poste" sign. The main office at 52 rue du Louvre is open 24 hours. The branch at 71 avenue des Champs-Elysées is open Mon–Fri 9am–7:30pm, Sat 10am–7pm.

ELECTRICITY

The power supply in Paris is 220 volts. Sockets accept two-round-pin (or increasingly three-round-pin) plugs, so an adaptor is needed for most non-Continental appliances. A transformer is needed for appliances operating on 110–120 volts.

TIPS/GRATUITIES

Restaurant, café and hotel bills must by law include a service charge so a tip is not expected, although many people do leave a few coins in restaurants.

Yes ✓   No ✗

Taxis	✓	€0.50–1.50
Tour guides	✓	€0.50–1.50
Porters	✓	€0.50–1.50
Usherettes	✓	small change
Hairdressers	✓	€0.50–1.50
Lavatory attendants	✓	small change

EMBASSIES AND CONSULATES

UK
01 44 51 31 00

USA
01 43 12 22 22

Australia
01 40 59 33 00

Canada
01 44 43 29 00

New Zealand
01 45 01 43 43

HEALTH

Insurance
Citizens of EU countries receive free or reduced-cost emergency medical treatment with relevant documentation (European Health Insurance Card), but private medical insurance is still advised and essential for all other visitors.

Dental Services
As for general medical treatment (see above, **Insurance**), nationals of EU countries can obtain dental treatment at reduced cost. Around 70 per cent of standard dentists' fees are refunded, but private medical insurance is still advised for all.

Weather
July and August are sunny and hot. When sightseeing, cover up, apply a good sunscreen, wear sunglasses and drink plenty of fluids.

Drugs
Pharmacies – recognised by their green cross sign – possess highly qualified staff able to offer medical advice, provide first-aid and prescribe a wide range of drugs, although some are available by prescription (*ordonnance*) only.

Safe Water
Tap water is safe to drink, but never drink from a tap marked *eau non potable* (not drinking water). Mineral water is widely available.

CONCESSIONS

Students/Youths Holders of an International Student Identity Card (ISIC) are entitled to discounted admission to museums and sights, air and ferry tickets and meals in some student cafeterias. Holders of the International Youth Travel Card (or GO 25 Card) qualify for similar discounts as ISIC holders.

Senior Citizens If you are over 60 you can get discounts (up to 50 per cent) in museums, on public transport and in places of entertainment. You will need a *Carte Vermeil* which can be purchased from the *Abonnement* office of any main railway station. You may get a discount simply by showing your passport.

TRAVELLING WITH A DISABILITY

Many older public facilities and attractions lack amenities for people with disabilities, although most hotels with two or more stars have lifts. Few Métro stations have lifts, but RATP and SNCF run an Accompaniment Service to assist people with reduced mobility (tel: 01 53 11 11 12). The service is not free, however, and you will need to book in advance of your journey.

CHILDREN

Children are welcomed in most hotels and restaurants. Many sights and attractions offer reductions; entrance to museums for under 18s is free. Baby-changing facilities are excellent in newer museums and attractions, but limited elsewhere.

LAVATORIES

Some older establishments have a squat lavatory, but there are modern pay lavatories throughout the city. Café lavatories are for customers only.

WILDLIFE SOUVENIRS

Importing wildlife souvenirs sourced from rare or endangered species may be illegal or require a special permit. Check your country's customs regulations.

SURVIVAL PHRASES

Yes/no **Oui/non**
Hello **Bonjour/bonsoir**
Goodbye **Au revoir**
How are you? **Comment allez-vous?**
Please **S'il vous plaît**
Thank you **Merci**
Excuse me **Excusez-moi**
I'm sorry **Pardon**
You're welcome **De rien/avec plaisir**
Do you have...? **Avez-vous...?**
How much is this? **C'est combien?**
I'd like... **Je voudrais...**

DIRECTIONS

Is there a phone box around here?
Y a-t-il une cabine téléphonique dans le coin?
Where is...? **Où se trouve...?**
...the nearest Métro
le Métro le plus proche
...the telephone **le téléphone**
...the bank **la banque**
...the lavatory **les toilettes**
Turn left/right **tournez à gauche/droite**
Go straight on **allez tout droit**
The first/second (on the right)
le premier/le deuxième (à droite)
At the crossroads **au carrefour**

IF YOU NEED HELP

Could you help me, please?
Pouvez-vous m'aider?
Do you speak English?
Parlez-vous anglais?
I don't understand
Je ne comprends pas
Could you call a doctor quickly,
please? **Voulez-vous appeler un médecin d'urgence, s'il vous plaît?**

RESTAURANT

I'd like to book a table **Puis-je réserver une table?**
A table for two please **Une table pour deux personnes, s'il vous plaît**
Do you have a fixed price menu?
Vous avez un menu?
Could we see the menu please?
Nous pouvons voir la carte?
Could I have the bill please?
L'addition, s'il vous plaît
A bottle/glass of... **Une bouteille/un verre de...**

MENU READER

The menu

apéritifs appetisers
boissons alcoolisées alcoholic beverages
boissons chaudes hot beverages
boissons froides cold beverages
carte des vins wine list
coquillages shellfish
fromage cheese
gibier game
hors d'oeuvres starters
légumes vegetables
plats chauds hot dishes
plats froids cold dishes
plat du jour dish of the day
pâtisserie pastry
plat principal main course
potages soups
service compris service included
service non compris service not included
spécialités régionales regional specialities
viandes meat courses
volaille poultry

NUMBERS

0	**zéro**	12	**douze**	30	**trente**	110	**cent dix**
1	**un**	13	**treize**	31	**trente et un**	120	**cent vingt**
2	**deux**	14	**quatorze**	32	**trente-deux**	200	**deux cents**
3	**trois**	15	**quinze**			300	**trois cents**
4	**quatre**	16	**seize**	40	**quarante**	400	**quatre cents**
5	**cinq**	17	**dix-sept**	50	**cinquante**	500	**cinq cents**
6	**six**	18	**dix-huit**	60	**soixante**	600	**six cents**
7	**sept**	19	**dix-neuf**	70	**soixante-dix**	700	**sept cents**
8	**huit**	20	**vingt**	80	**quatre-vingts**	800	**huit cents**
9	**neuf**			90	**quatre-vingt-dix**	900	**neuf cents**
10	**dix**	21	**vingt et un**	100	**cent**		
11	**onze**	22	**vingt-deux**	101	**cent un**	1,000	**mille**

agneau lamb
ail garlic
ananas pineapple
anguille eel
banane banana
beurre butter
bifteck steak
bière (bière pression) beer (draught beer)
boeuf beef
boudin noir/blanc black/white pudding
brochet pike
cabillaud cod
calmar squid
canard duck
champignons mushrooms
chou cabbage
choucroute sauerkraut
chou-fleur cauliflower
choux de Bruxelles Brussels sprouts
citron lemon
civet de lièvre jugged hare
concombre cucumber
confiture jam
coquilles Saint-Jacques scallops
cornichon gherkin
côte/côtelette chop
côtelettes dans l'échine spare ribs
couvert cutlery
crevettes grises shrimps
crevettes roses prawns
croque monsieur toasted ham and cheese sandwich
cru raw
crustacés seafood
cuisses de grenouilles frogs' legs
cuit (à l'eau) boiled
eau minerale

gazeuse/non gazeuse sparkling/still mineral water
ecrevisse crayfish
entrecôte sirloin steak
entrées first course
épices spices
épinards spinach
épis de maïs corn (on the cob)
escargots snails
farine flour
fenouil fennel
fèves broad beans
figues figs
filet de boeuf fillet
filet mignon fillet steak
filet de porc tenderloin
fines herbes herbs
foie gras goose/duck liver
fraises strawberries
framboises raspberries
frit fried
friture deep-fried
fruit de la passion passion fruit
fruits de saison seasonal fruits
gaufres waffles
gigot d'agneau leg of lamb
glace ice-cream
glaçons ice cubes
grillé grilled
groseilles redcurrants
hareng herring
haricots blancs haricot beans
haricots verts french beans
homard lobster
huîtres oysters
jambon blanc/cru/fumé ham (cooked/Parma style/smoked)
jus de citron lemon juice
jus de fruits fruit juice

jus d'orange orange juice
lait demi-écrémé/entier milk semi-skimmed/full-cream
langouste crayfish
langoustine scampi
langue tongue
lapin rabbit
lentilles lentils
lotte monkfish
loup de mer sea bass
macaron macaroon
maïs sweetcorn
marron chestnut
menu du jour/à la carte menu of the day/à la carte
morilles morels
moules mussels
mousse au chocolat chocolate mousse
moutarde mustard
myrtilles bilberries
noisette hazelnut
noix walnut
noix de veau fillet of veal
oeuf à la coque/dur/au plat egg soft/hard-boiled/fried
oignon onion
origan oregano
pain au chocolat croissant with chocolate centre
part portion
pêche peach
petite friture fried fish (whitebait or similar)
petits (biscuits) salés savoury biscuits
petit pain roll
petits pois green peas

pintade guinea fowl
poire pear
pois chiches chick peas
poisson fish
poivre pepper
poivron green/red pepper
pomme apple
pommes de terre potatoes
pommes frites chips
poulet (blanc) chicken (breast)
prune plum
pruneaux prunes
queue de boeuf oxtail
ragoût stew
ris de veau sweetbread
riz rice
rôti de boeuf (rosbif) roast beef
rouget red mullet
saignant rare
salade verte lettuce
salé/sucré salted/sweet
saumon salmon
saucisses sausages
sel salt
soupe à l'oignon onion soup
sucre sugar
thon tuna
thym thyme
tripes tripe
truffes truffles
truite trout
truite saumonée salmon trout
vapeur (à la) steamed
venaison venison
viande hachée minced meat/mince
vin blanc white wine
vin rosé rosé wine
vin rouge red wine
vinaigre vinegar
xérès sherry

Streetplan

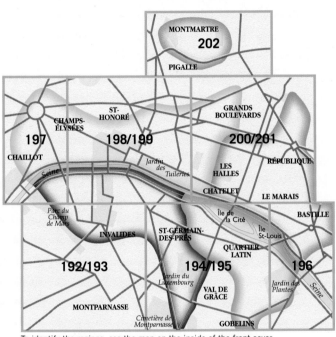

MONTMARTRE
202

PIGALLE

ST-HONORÉ

CHAMPS-ÉLYSÉES

GRANDS BOULEVARDS

197

198/199

200/201

CHAILLOT

RÉPUBLIQUE

Seine

Jardin des Tuileries

LES HALLES

CHÂTELET

LE MARAIS

Parc du Champ de Mars

Île de la Cité

BASTILLE

Île St-Louis

INVALIDES

ST-GERMAIN-DES-PRÉS

QUARTIER LATIN

192/193

194/195

196

Jardin du Luxembourg

VAL DE GRÂCE

Jardin des Plantes

Seine

MONTPARNASSE

Cimetière de Montparnasse

GOBELINS

To identify the regions, see the map on the inside of the front cover

Key to Streetplan

Main road	Important building
Other road	Featured place of interest
Pedestrian street	Métro station
Rail line	RER station

0   100   200   300   400   500 metres

0   100   200   300   400   500 yards

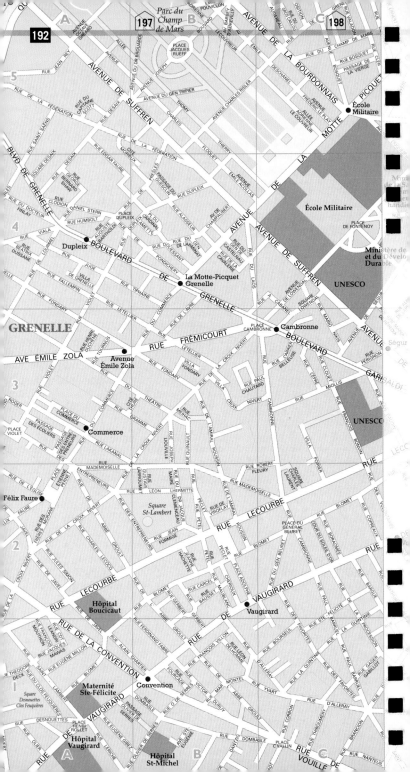

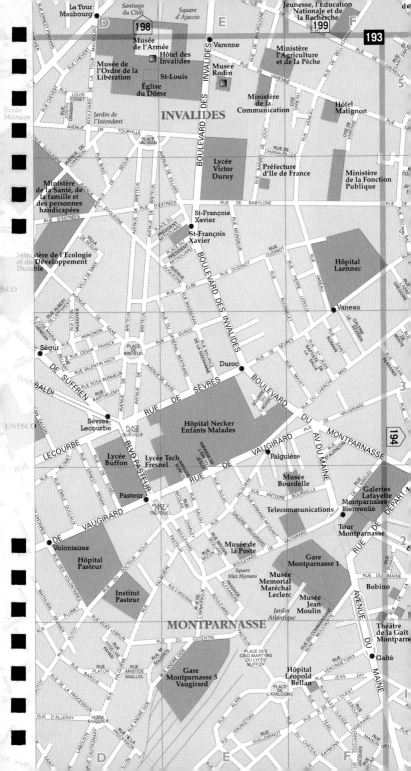

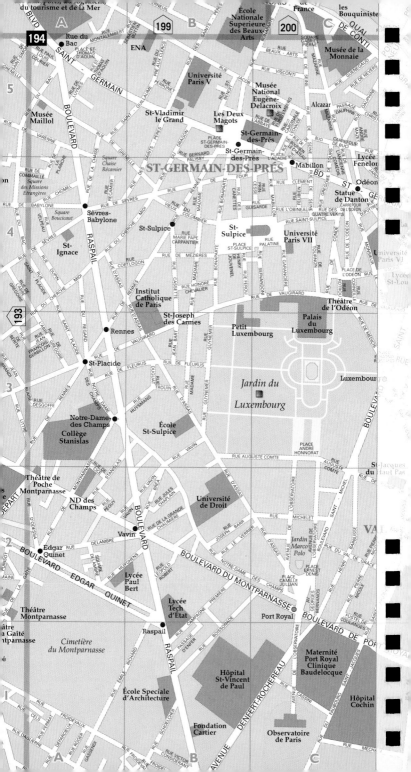

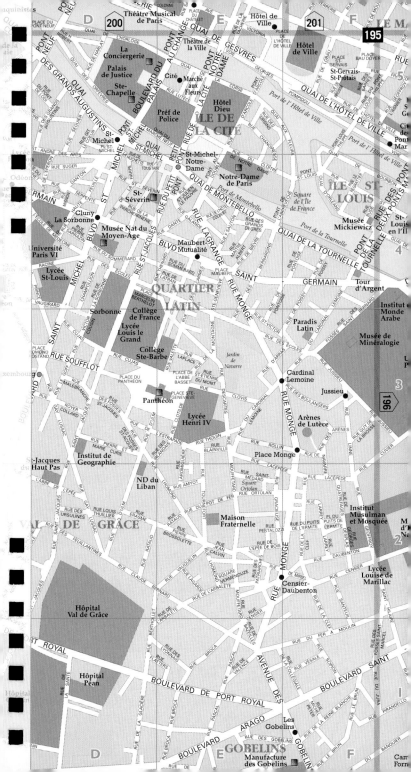

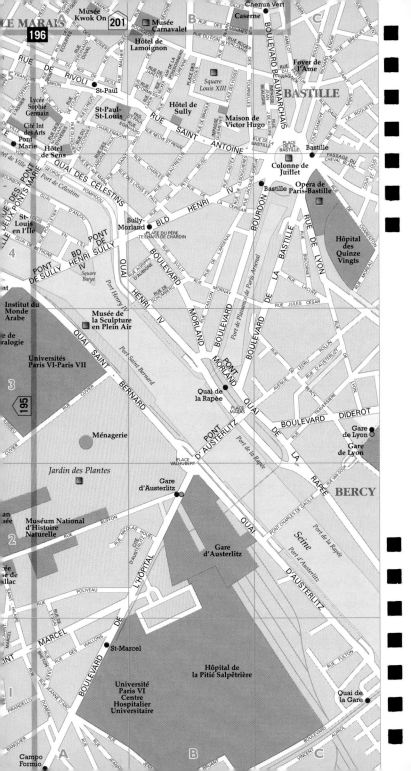

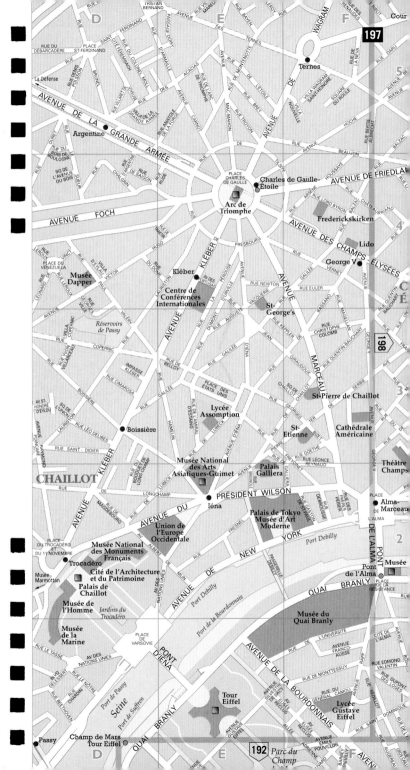

Cour

Ternes

Argentine

AVENUE DE LA GRANDE ARMÉE

La Défense

RUE DU DÉBARCADÈRE

PLACE ST-FERDINAND

PLACE CHARLES DE GAULLE

Charles de Gaulle-Étoile

Arc de Triomphe

AVENUE FOCH

AVENUE DE FRIEDLAN

AVENUE DES CHAMPS-ELYSÉES

Frederickskirken

Lido

George V

KLÉBER

Musée Dapper

Kléber

Centre de Conférences Internationales

Réservoirs de Passy

St-George's

St-Pierre de Chaillot

Lycée Assomption

Boissière

St-Etienne

Cathédrale Américaine

Théâtre Champs

Musée National des Arts Asiatiques-Guimet

Palais Galliera

CHAILLOT

PRÉSIDENT WILSON

Iéna

Alma-Marceau

Palais de Tokyo Musée d'Art Moderne

PLACE DU TROCADÉRO ET DU 11 NOVEMBRE

Union de l'Europe Occidentale

AVENUE DU

Musée Marmottan

Trocadéro

Musée National des Monuments Français

Cité de l'Architecture et du Patrimoine

Palais de Chaillot

Musée de l'Homme

Jardins du Trocadéro

NEW YORK

Port Debilly

Pont de l'Alma

PLACE DE LA RÉSISTANCE

Musée

Musée de la Marine

PLACE DE VARSOVIE

PONT D'IÉNA

Musée du Quai Branly

QUAI BRANLY

AVENUE DE LA BOURDONNAIS

Seine

Port de Passy

Port de Suffren

Lycée Gustave Eiffel

Passy

Champ de Mars Tour Eiffel

Tour Eiffel

QUAI BRANLY

192 Parc du Champ

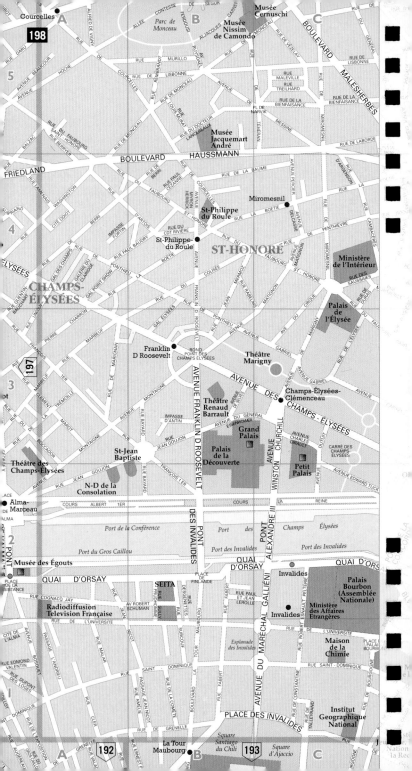

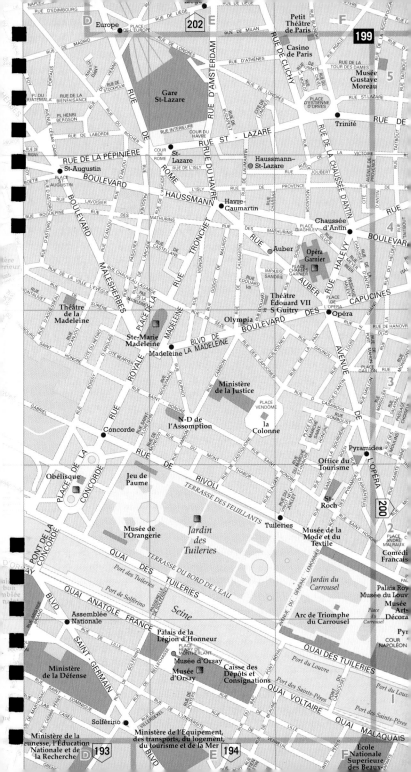

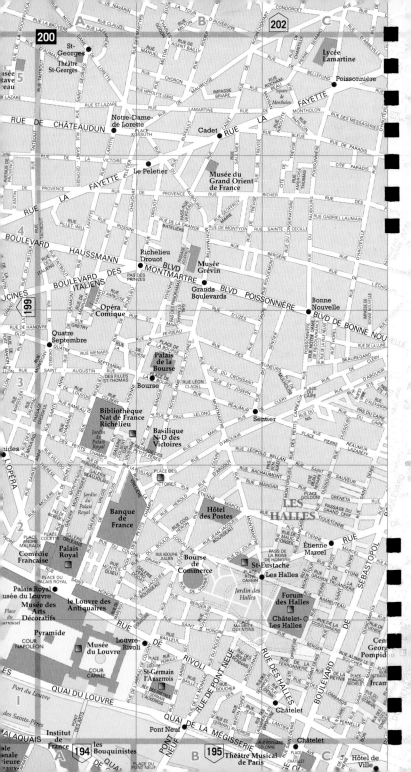

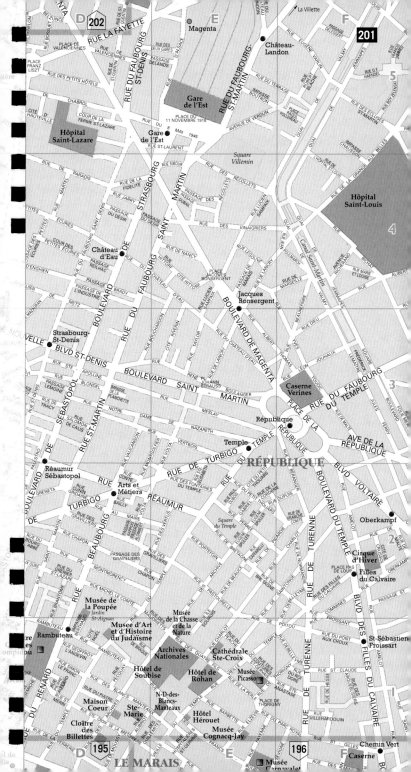

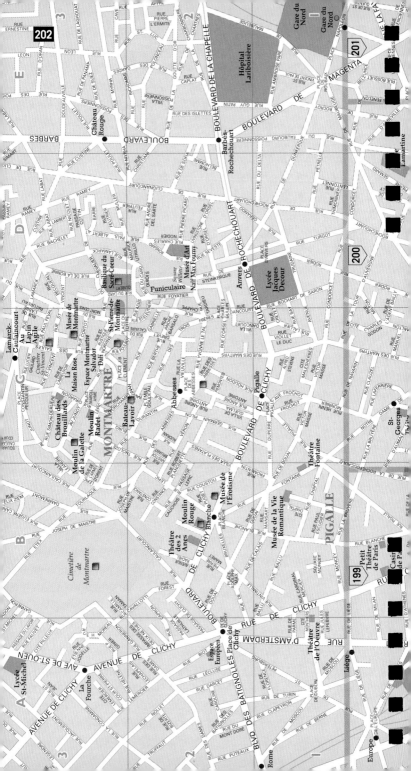

STREETPLAN INDEX

blvd	boulevard
av	avenue
pl	place
pass	passage
carr	carrefour
imp	impasse
gal	galerie(s)
sq	square

Isly, rue de l' **199 E4**
Italiens, blvd des **200 A4**
Italiens, rue des **200 A4**

Jacob, rue **194 B5**
Jacquemont, rue **202 A3**
Jacques Bonsergent, pl
 201 E4
Jacques Coeur, rue
 196 B4
Jacques et Thérèse
Trefouel, pl **193 D2**
Jacques Garner, allée
 198 B5
Jacques Mawas, rue
 192 A1
Jacques Rueff, pl **192 B5**
Jardinet, rue du **194 C4**
Jardins St-Paul, rue des
 196 A4
Jarente, rue de **196 B5**
Jarry, rue **201 D4**
Javel, rue de **192 A2**
Jean-Baptiste Clément, pl
 202 C3
Jean Bart, rue **194 B3**
Jean Beausire, imp
 196 C5
Jean Beausire, rue
 196 C5
Jean Calvin, rue **195 E2**
Jean Daudin, rue **192 C3**
Jean Ferrandi, rue **193 F3**
Jean Formigé, rue **192 B2**
Jean François Gerbillon,
 rue **194 A3**
Jean Giraudoux, rue
 197 E3
Jean Goujon, rue **198 A2**
Jean Jacques Rousseau,
 rue **200 B2**
Jean Lantier, rue **200 B1**
Jean Mermoz, rue
 198 B4
Jean Nicot, pass **198 B1**
Jean Nicot, rue **198 A2**
Jean Poulmarch, rue
 201 F4
Jean Rey, rue **192 A5**
Jean Zay, rue **193 F1**
Jeanne d'Arc, rue **196 A1**
Jeanne Hachette, rue
 192 B2
Jemmapes, quai de
 201 F5
Jenner, rue **196 B1**
Jeuneurs, rue des **200 C3**
Johann Strauss, pl
 201 E3
José-Maria de Hérédia,
 rue **193 D3**
Joseph Barr, rue **194 B2**
Joseph Bouvard, av
 192 B5
Joseph Granier, rue
 193 D5
Joseph Liouville, rue
 192 B3
Joseph de Maistre, rue
 202 B2
Joubert, rue **199 F4**
Jouffroy, pass **200 B4**
Jour, rue du **200 B2**
Jouy, rue de **196 A5**

Juge, rue **192 A4**
Juges Consuls, rue des
 200 C1
Jules Breton, rue **196 A1**
Jules César, rue **196 C4**
Jules Chaplain, rue
 194 B2
Jules Ferry, blvd **201 F3**
Jules Guesde, rue **193 F1**
Jules Lefebvre, rue
 202 A1
Jules Simon, rue **192 A2**
Julienne, rue de **195 E1**
Junot, av **202 C3**
Jura, rue du **195 F1**
Jussieu, rue **195 F3**

Keppler, rue **197 F3**
Kléber, av **197 E4**
Kléber, imp **197 D3**
Kossuth, pl **200 B5**

Labat, rue **202 D3**
Laborde, rue de **198 C5**
Labouste, rue **193 D1**
Lacépède, rue **195 F2**
Lacuée, rue **196 C4**
Laferrière, rue **200 A5**
Laffitte, rue **200 A4**
Lagarde, rue **195 E2**
Laghouat, rue de **202 E3**
Lagrange, rue **195 E4**
Lakanal, rue **192 A3**
Lallier, rue **202 C1**
Lamarck, rue **202 D3**
Lamartine, rue **200 B5**
Lambert, rue **202 D3**
Lamenais, rue **198 A4**
Lancry, rue de **201 E4**
Laos, rue du **192 B4**
Laplace, rue **195 E3**
Laromiguière, rue **195 E2**
Larrey, rue **195 F2**
Las Cases, rue **199 D1**
Lathuille, pass **202 A2**
Latran, rue de **195 E4**
Laumartin, rue de **199 E4**
Lauriston, rue **197 D3**
Lavandières
 Ste-Opportune, rue des
 200 B1
Lavoir, pass du **202 A3**
Lavoisier, rue **199 D4**
Léandre, villa **202 B3**
Lebouis, rue **193 F1**
Lechapelais, rue **202 A2**
Lécluse, rue **202 A2**
Lecourbe, rue **192 A2**
Ledru Rollin, av **196 C3**
Legendre, rue **202 A3**
Legouvé, rue **201 E4**
Lemercier, cité **202 A3**
Lemercier, rue **202 A2**
Lemoine, pass **201 F3**
Lentonnet, rue **202 D1**
Léo Delibes, rue **197 D3**
Léon Cladel, rue **200 B3**
Léon Delhomme, rue
 192 B1
Léon Jouhaux, rue
 201 F3
Léon Lhermitte, rue
 192 B2
Léon Vaudoyer, rue

 193 D3
Léon, rue **202 E3**
Léonard de Vinci, rue
 197 D4
Léonce Reynaud, rue
 197 F3
Léopold Bellan, rue
 200 B3
Léopold Robert, rue
 194 B2
Lepic, pass **202 B2**
Lepic, rue **202 C3**
Leriche, rue **192 A1**
Leroux, rue **197 D4**
Lesdiguieres, rue de
 196 B4
Letellier, rue **192 B3**
Lhomond, rue **195 E2**
Liège, rue de **202 A1**
Lille, rue de **199 D1**
Lincoln, rue **198 A3**
Linne, rue **195 F3**
Lions St-Paul, rue des
 196 B4
Lisbonne, rue de **198 B5**
Littré, rue **193 F3**
Livingstone, rue **202 D2**
Lobau, rue de **195 F5**
Lombards, rue des
 200 C1
Londres, cité de **199 E5**
Londres, rue de **199 E5**
Longchamp, rue de
 197 D2
Lord Byron, rue **197 F4**
Louis Codet, rue **193 D5**
Louis le Grand, rue
 199 F3
Louis Murat, rue **198 B5**
Louis Philippe, pont
 195 F5
Louis Thuillier, rue
 195 D2
Lourmel, rue de **192 A4**
Louvois, rue de **200 A3**
Louvre, pass du **200 B1**
Louvre, quai du **200 A1**
Louvre, rue du **200 B2**
Lowendal, av de **192 C4**
Lowendal, sq **192 C4**
Lubeck, rue de **197 E3**
Lucien Gaulard, rue
 202 C3
Lucien Sampaix, rue,
 201 E4
Lune, rue de la **200 C3**
Lutèce, rue **195 E5**
Luynes, rue de **194 A5**
Lyon, rue de **196 C4**
Lyonnais, rue des **195 E1**

Mabillon, rue **194 C4**
Mac-Mahon, av **197 E5**
Madame, rue **194 B4**
Madeleine, blvd de la
 199 E3
Madeleine, pass de la
 199 D4
Madeleine, pl de la
 199 E3
Mademoiselle, rue
 192 B2
Madrid, rue de **199 D5**
Magdebourg, rue de

 197 D2
Magellan, rue **197 F3**
Magenta, blvd de
 201 E3
Mail, rue du **200 B3**
Maine, av du **193 F1**
Maine, rue du **193 F2**
Maison Dieu, rue **193 F1**
Maître Albert, rue **195 E4**
Malaquais, quai **199 F1**
Malar, rue **198 A1**
Malebranche, rue **195 D3**
Malesherbes, blvd
 198 C5
Malesherbes, cité **202 C1**
Maleville, rue **198 C5**
Malher, rue **196 A5**
Malté, rue de **201 F3**
Mandar, rue **200 C2**
Mansart, rue **202 B1**
Manuel, rue **200 B5**
Mar Montel, rue **192 B1**
Marais, pass de **201 E4**
Marbeuf, rue **198 A3**
Marceau, av **197 F3**
Marcel Aymé, pl **202 C3**
Marcelin Berthelot, pl
 195 D4
Marché Neuf, quai du
 195 D5
Marché St-Honoré, pl du
 199 F3
Marché St-Honoré, rue du
 199 F3
Maréchal Galliéni, av du
 198 C1
Marengo, rue de **200 A2**
Marie, pont **196 A4**
Marie et Louise, rue
 201 F4
Marie Pape Carpantier,
 rue **194 B4**
Marignan, rue de **198 A3**
Marigny, av de **198 C3**
Mario Nikis, rue **192 C3**
Marivaux, rue de **200 A4**
Marseille, rue de **201 F4**
Marsollier, rue **199 F3**
Martel, rue **201 D4**
Martignac, rue de
 199 D1
Martyrs, rue des **200 B5**
Masseran, rue **193 E4**
Mathurin Régnier, rue
 193 D2
Mathurins, rue des
 199 E4
Matignon, av **198 C4**
Maubert, pl **195 E4**
Maubeuge, rue de
 200 B5
Maublanc, rue **192 B2**
Mauc-Onseil, rue de
 200 C2
Maudrietts, rue des
 201 E1
Maurice Maignen, rue
 193 D1
Maurice Quentins, pl
 200 B1
Maurice de la Sizeranne,
 rue **193 E3**
Maurice Utrillo, rue
 202 D2

Picture Credits

Abbreviations for terms appearing below: (t) top; (b) bottom; (l) left; (r) right; (c) centre.

Cover Acknowledgements

Front & back covers: (t) AA Photo Library/Max Jordan; (ct) AA Photo Library/Tony Stone; (cb) AA Photo Library/Ken Paterson; (b) AA Photo Library/Tony Souter; (spine) AA Photo Library/David Noble

The Automobile Association wishes to thank the following photographers and libraries for their assistance in the preparation of this book:

Bridgeman Art Library 7 The Taking of the Bastille, 14th July, 1789 by Jean-Pierre Houel (1735–1813) (Musee Carnavalet, Paris, France), 94 (b) Venus de Milo, Greek Hellenistic period, c100 BC (marble) (Peter Willi/Louvre, Paris, France), 98 The Lacemaker, 1669–70 (oil on canvas) by Jan Vermeer (1632–75) (Louvre, Paris, France), 101 Mona Lisa, c1503–6 (panel) by Leonardo da Vinci (1452–1519) (Louvre, Paris, France); Corbis 2 (ct) (Ric Ergenbright), 2 (b) (Charles & Josette Lenars), 12 (t), 18 (l) (Bettmann), 18 (r) (Neal Preston), 19 (l), 21 (Owen Franken), 29 (Nathan Benn), 33 (Ric Ergenbright), 69 (Charles & Josette Lenars), 137 (b) (Bettmann), 148/9 (Bob Krist), 171 (Rob Holmes);
DACS, London 2000 126 "The Sadness of the King, 1952" by Henri Matisse (© Sucession H Matisse), 129 (b) "Femme Assise aux Bras Croises" by Pablo Picasso (© Sucession Picasso);
DIAF 3 (b) (Rosine Mazin), 11 (b), 14 (b), 20 (t), 24 (Jean-Daniel Sudres), 49 (t) (Arnaud Fevrier), 74, 145, 161 (Rosine Mazin), 164 (Arnaud Fevrier), 165 (Rosine Mazin), 166 (t), 166 (b) (D Thierry), 167 (Rosine Mazin), 168 (Jacques Kerebel), 169, 179, 181 (l), 181 (r) (D Thierry);
Mary Evans Picture Library 76;
T Fisher 8, 9 (t), 136, 147 (t);
Robert Harding Picture Library 2 (t), 5;
Magnum Photos 2 (cb) (Robert Capa), 14 (t) (Sergio Larrain), 16 (t), 45 (Robert Capa), 80 (t) (Rai Raghu);
Rex Features 12 (b), 13 (Steve Wood), 19 (r); Roger-Viollet 25 (t), 50, 51 (t), 128, 163 (t);
Tony Stone Images 3 (t), 10 (b), 11 (t), 20 (b), 22/3, 91, 99, 104/5, 183.

All remaining pictures are held in the Association's own library (AA Photo Library) with contributions from the following photographers:
72 (b), 81, 96, 97, 172 (Philip Enticknap); 125 (b) (Max Jourdan); 26/7, 123 (b), 129 (t), 131, 135, 175 (Paul Kenward); 163 (b) (Rob Moore); 170 (David Noble); 9 (b), 25 (b), 26, 31, 49 (c), 49 (b), 59, 61 (t), 63, 70, 72 (t), 73 (b), 77, 80, 95 (c), 108, 109, 110, 123 (t), 125 (t), 130, 132, 133, 144/5, 148, 176 (Ken Paterson); 15, 16 (b), 28 (t), 85, 103, 137 (b), 152, 174 (B Rieger); 3 (ct), 51 (b), 52/3, 54, 55, 58, 73 (t), 73 (c), 82, 83, 100 (b), 102, 119, 154, 157, 182 (Clive Sawyer); 3 (cb), 10 (t), 57, 95 (t), 120, 122, 129 (b), 143, 147(b), 151, 155 (Tony Souter); 6, 30, 48 (t), 48 (c), 48 (b), 56 (t), 56 (b), 62, 75, 78, 79, 84, 86, 94(t), 95 (b) (James Tims); 61(b) (Wyn Voysey).

Acknowledgements

Teresa Fisher wishes to thank the Millennium Hôtel Paris-Opéra, Anna MacLellan of ANA Communications, Victoria Riela of Room Service and Hôtel Plessis, the Maison de la France in London and the Paris Tourist Office for their assistance during the research of this book.

Questionnaire

Dear Traveler

Your comments, opinions and recommendations are very important to us. So please help us to improve our travel guides by taking a few minutes to complete this simple questionnaire.

Send to: Spiral Guides, MailStop 66, 1000 AAA Drive, Heathrow, FL 32746–5063

Your recommendations...

We always encourage readers' recommendations for restaurants, nightlife or shopping – if your recommendation is added to the next edition of the guide, we will send you a FREE AAA Spiral Guide of your choice. Please state below the establishment name, location and your reasons for recommending it.

_____

_____

_____

_____

_____

Please send me AAA Spiral _____

(see list of titles inside the back cover)

About this guide...

Which title did you buy?

_____ **AAA Spiral**

Where did you buy it? _____

When? m m / y y

Why did you choose a AAA Spiral Guide? _____

_____

_____

_____

Did this guide meet your expectations?

Exceeded ☐   Met all ☐   Met most ☐   Fell below ☐

Please give your reasons _____

_____

_____

_____

continued on next page...

Were there any aspects of this guide that you particularly liked?

_____

_____

_____

_____

_____

Is there anything we could have done better?

_____

_____

_____

_____

_____

About you...

Name (Mr/Mrs/Ms) _____

Address _____

_____

_____ **Zip** _____

Daytime tel nos. _____

Which age group are you in?

Under 25 ☐   25–34 ☐   35–44 ☐   45–54 ☐   55–64 ☐   65+ ☐

How many trips do you make a year?

Less than one ☐   One ☐   Two ☐   Three or more ☐

Are you a AAA member? Yes ☐   No ☐

Name of AAA club _____

About your trip...

When did you book? m m/ y y   **When did you travel?** m m/ y y

How long did you stay? _____

Was it for business or leisure? _____

Did you buy any other travel guides for your trip? ☐ Yes   ☐ No

If yes, which ones? _____

_____

Thank you for taking the time to complete this questionnaire.